Judaism and the Interpretation of Scripture

Judaism and the Interpretation of Scripture

Introduction to the Rabbinic Midrash

Jacob Neusner

© 2004 by Jacob Neusner

Hendrickson Publishers, LLC
P. O. Box 3473
Peabody, Massachusetts 01961-3473

ISBN 1-56563-706-2

All rights reserved. No part of this book may be reproduced or transmitted in any form or by any means, electronic or mechanical, including photocopying, recording, or by any information storage and retrieval system, without permission in writing from the publisher.

Printed in the United States of America

First Printing — November 2004

Cover Art: Stylized elements from a Torah shield. Berlin, 1788–1802. Original Photo Credit: Erich Lessing / Art Resource, NY.

Library of Congress Cataloging-in-Publication Data

Neusner, Jacob, 1932–
    Judaism and the interpretation of scripture : introduction to the rabbinic midrash / Jacob Neusner.
        p. cm.
    Includes index.
    ISBN 1-56563-706-2 (alk. paper)
    1. Midrash—History and criticism. 2. Rabbinical literature—History and criticism. 3. Bible. O.T. Pentateuch—Criticism, interpretation, etc., Jewish. I. Title.
    BM514.N473 2004
    296.1'4061—dc22
                                          2004020517

Table of Contents

Preface   vii

1. How Does Judaism Read Scripture?   1

2. An Overview of the Rabbinic Midrash-Compilations   15

3. Genesis in *Genesis Rabbah:* Recasting the Patriarchs into the Models for Israelite Conduct   30

4. Exodus in *Mekhilta attributed to R. Ishmael:* Reorganizing the Facts of Scripture into Coherent Expositions on Important Topics   46

5. Leviticus in *Sifra:* Mediating between the Two Torahs, Oral and Written   60

6. Leviticus in *Leviticus Rabbah:* Turning Scripture's Laws into the Design of Holy Israel's Social Order   74

7. Numbers in *Sifré to Numbers:* Systematically Reading and Expounding Scripture's Narratives in Accord with the Rabbinic Model   88

8. Deuteronomy in *Sifré to Deuteronomy:* Turning Scripture's Cases into Laws, and Laws into an Entire Social System   102

9. Esther in *Esther Rabbah I:* A Woman Saves Israel   116

10. Ruth in *Ruth Rabbah:* A Gentile Woman Saves Israel through the Torah   131

11. Song of Songs in *Song of Songs Rabbah:* Reading Holy Israel's Relationship to God within the Symbols of a Love-Song   145

12. Lamentations in *Lamentations Rabbah:* Updating Scripture's   159
    Response to the First Temple's Destruction by Showing How
    an Event Defines a Pattern

13. The Calendar of Judaism in *Pesiqta deRab Kahana:* Telling Time   174
    by Judaism's Clock

14. The Sages in *The Fathers according to Rabbi Nathan*   192

15. The Theology of Rabbinic Midrash   207

Index of Scripture and Ancient Sources   225

Preface

Midrash defines the way that Judaism interprets Scripture. Its initial statement is contained in the *Rabbinic* Midrash, which is set forth by the canonical documents of the Rabbinic sages of the first six centuries of the common era. That classification of Midrash, particularly Rabbinic Midrash, as canoncial is important because it mediates Scripture to those who by faith meet God in the whole Torah of Sinai, oral and written. This book introduces the Rabbinic Midrash compilations and their theology. It both stands on its own and also serves as prologue to *The Rabbinic Midrash.*[1]

What is Midrash?

The root of the word Midrash is *darash,* which is used at Gen. 25:22. There Rebecca goes "to seek counsel of" *(liderosh)* the Lord.[2] In line with that generic usage, Midrash represents the effort to seek truth in Scripture: to address this morning's question to ancient, enduring revelation.

In more general terms: *Midrash* is the Hebrew word for interpretation, amplification, exegesis of a holy, revealed text: the written Torah. But the word, Midrash, bears several meanings. In current usage the word Midrash has three levels of meaning, as follows:

(1) the process, that is, a particular way of reading and interpreting a verse of the Hebrew Scriptures;

(2) the result of that process, thus a given verse and its interpretation;

---

[1] Peabody, Mass.: Hendrickson Publishers, forthcoming. Second printing, in twelve volumes, of *The Components of the Rabbinic Documents: From the Whole to the Parts.* I. *Sifra.* II. *Esther Rabbah I.* III. *Ruth Rabbah.* IV. *Lamentations Rabbati.* V. *Song of Songs Rabbah.* VI. *The Fathers according to Rabbi Nathan.* VII. *Sifré to Deuteronomy.* VIII. *Mekhilta attributed to R. Ishmael.* IX. *Genesis Rabbah.* X. *Leviticus Rabbah.* XI. *Pesiqta deRab Kahana.* XII. *Sifré to Numbers.* Atlanta, 1997–1998: Scholars Press for USF Academic Commentary Series.

[2] I learned this fact from Professor Ithamar Gruenwald, Tel Aviv University.

(3) the collection of the results of such a process, that is, the compilation of such interpretations, e.g., concerning a particular book of the Hebrew Scriptures or a particular theological theme, as we see in the pages of this book.

Thus we may say: (1) with respect to process, "the ancient rabbis executed Midrash for Genesis 1:1"; (2) with respect to results, "the Midrash on Genesis 1:1 says that . . ."; (3) with respect to collection, "*Genesis Rabbah* is a compilation of Midrash exegeses of the book of Genesis."

People tend to use the word in any of these three senses. But this leads to confusion. For clarity's sake, then, when I mean "a book of Midrash interpretations," I say, "Midrash compilation." When I mean "Midrash on this verse," I say, "Midrash interpretation." When I refer to a process of exegesis that embodies the Rabbinic hermeneutics in particular, I speak of Midrash process.

Is Midrash—as a process of interpretation—unique to the sages and writings of Rabbinic Judaism?

It is not possible to define a particular way of interpreting verses of Scripture singular to the sages of Rabbinic Judaism, that is, a mode of interpretation simply not known outside of Rabbinic-Judaic circles. Rabbinic Judaism employs common methods of interpretation (or exegesis) to realize a hermeneutics that embodies a theology unique to itself, as I explain in Chapter Fifteen. The different methods of interpretation that we find in the Rabbinic literature can be shown comparable to methods we find in the Dead Sea Scrolls, which derive from a Judaic group different from the ancient Rabbinic sages, to the methods of Greek writers who interpret Homer, and to those of the Christian writers who interpret, in light of the advent of Jesus and the end of days, what they call "the Old Testament." So if there are Midrash ways of reading Scripture that are uniquely Rabbinic, I do not know what they are. The methods that produce Midrash are common, the messages set forth by Rabbinic Judaism are particular. What makes Rabbinic Midrash unique is its theology, embodied in its hermeneutics but not in its methods of exegesis.

Is Midrash unique to Judaism?

Yes and no. No, because all religions that appeal to a governing canon of written books develop a literature of interpretation, analysis, articulation, extension, and amplification. So if by "Midrash" we refer to that kind of writing, then we mean midrash, with a small m, which forms a standard element of canonical religions. But midrash with a small m is simply a fancy way of saying, "exegesis," or "interpretation." Yes, because Midrash with a capital M, meaning the interpretation of the written Torah set forth by the Rabbinic sages, belongs to normative Judaism alone. Midrash of legal texts (Midrash

Halakhah) and of narrative, exhortative, and theological texts (Midrash Aggadah) of Scripture comprise *its* native categories, and designate *its* emblematic and definitive writing.

In these nuanced senses Midrash is unique to Rabbinic Judaism, while midrash is common to all religions that privilege particular scriptures.

Is Midrash done today?

If when people say "modern Midrash," they mean "classical Rabbinic ways of reading a text carried on by contemporary readers," then the answer is "yes." It is a commonplace of the synagogue pulpit to interpret Scripture with the guidance of the great masters of ancient, medieval, and modern Torah-learning. If, however, people mean—as is usually the case—just "what I personally, creatively, have to say about this, which is midrash, and since I am modern, it is Modern Midrash," then this is self-indulgence. Most of what people call "modern midrash" has nothing to do with the modes of exegesis that guided the rabbis of the Midrash compilations of Judaism in the formative age. It has, moreover, very little to do even with the Rabbinic sages' goal, which is to read Scripture as a letter posted that very morning from God to them. It is using midrash with a small m. But Midrash with a capital M, referring to the Rabbinic Midrash, has meaning and use as a word only when it bears specific points of reference as defined here.

In this book I begin in Chapter One with an account of how, through Midrash, Judaism reads Scripture. I proceed, in Chapter Two, to an overview of Rabbinic Midrash and conclude, in Chapter Fifteen, with a account of the systematic-theological traits that characterize all of the Rabbinic Midrash compilations, their processes and their outcomes. In the core of the book, Chapters Three through Fourteen, I introduce each of the principal documents, with emphasis on their theological foci: the point that each set of compilers wishes to make about the book of Scripture they propose to mediate to the community of the faithful. The volumes of translation and outline, to which this book serves as an introduction, present the details of the construction and exposition of each of the Midrash compilations.

My overall argument is that the Rabbinic sages could have found no more perfect medium for their message than that embodied in the Midrash exegesis of those selected books of Scripture.

A word of explanation of the reference-system is required. It is customary to assign to verses of Scripture numbers indicating the chapter and the verse, e.g., Gen. 1:1 refers to the first verse of the first chapter of Genesis. I have supplied to the Rabbinic documents of the formative age, from the Mishnah through the Bavli, including all the contemporary Midrash-compilations, a reference-system as well. That system involves the name of the document, a capital Roman numeral indicating the chapter (or parashah) of the document that is under discussion, a lowercase Roman numeral indicating a subsection of the chapter, an Arabic numeral indicating the paragraph of that subsection, and, sentence by sentence, a capital letter for easy location of the sentences. Thus *Genesis Rabbah* I:i.1A refers to *Genesis Rabbah* chapter one, section one, paragraph one, the first sentence.

Jacob Neusner

1

How Does Judaism Read Scripture?

In showing how, through the Rabbinic Midrash, Judaism reads Scripture, I explain the way in which, in the Midrash compilations, the Bible becomes the Torah: God's instruction. That is, I show in what manner a collection of writings is transformed into the definitive event in the life of holy Israel with God.[1] That took place when Judaism in its classical, normative canon of Midrash compilations turned the Hebrew Scriptures into a theological system and structure for Israel's social order. These dictate the issues that come to bear upon the interpretation of Scripture. They define the context in which Scripture is studied.

How Judaism in the Midrash compilations does not read Scripture

To understand the Rabbinic sages' approach to Scripture in the Midrash compilations, we have to begin with a negative question: how is Rabbinic Midrash unlike contemporary readings of Scripture? People nowadays want Scripture to yield historical facts, not religious truths, except as a byproduct of history. Rabbinic Midrash for its part uncovers the Torah's enduring truths.

The prevailing contemporary approach[2] treats Scripture as a history book to be checked against the facts of archaeology. In modern times Scripture has found itself portrayed as a one-time historical account of something that happened in secular time, once upon a time, long ago. It is defended as reliable by reason of its historical accuracy, and thus assessed in terms of its historicity. At issue in

---

[1] By "holy Israel" I mean the supernatural community assembled at Sinai to receive the Torah, embodied in the here and now by the sacred congregation *(qehillah qedoshah)* of the synagogue.

[2] Excluding certain sectors of the Torah-camp of Orthodox Judaism.

interpreting Scripture is what the original writer meant at the moment of his writing. And by "original writer" few mean God's instruction and Moses's writing.

But that is not how, for most of the history of Western civilization, the Hebrew Scriptures have been read by Judaism (or by Christianity). The idea of "history," with its rigid distinction between one time in the past and this moment in the present, and its careful sifting of connections from the one to the other, came quite late onto the scene of the Judaic—and the Christian—intellectual life. Both Judaism and Christianity for most of their histories have read the Hebrew Scriptures in an other-than-historical framework. While, to be sure, they took for granted the historical facticity of Scripture, that was not the main point they sought in Scripture. Rather, they found in Scripture's words paradigms of an enduring present, by which all things must take their measure. That is because they possessed no conception whatsoever of the pastness of the past or of a gap between present and past.

The presence of the past, the pastness of the present

Conceptually, we understand the Rabbinic-Judaic mode of receiving Scripture when we understand that, for the Rabbinic sages the past took place in the acutely present tense of today, and the present also found its locus in the presence of the ages. At issue were the eternal verities, the rules that govern, without distinction between past and present, context and circumstance. And that is something historical thinking, resting on particularization, cannot abide.

Rabbinic Midrash, the Torah is not history and it is not culture. The Torah is God's word: truth in the way in which logic and mathematics mark truth; true for all time and for every circumstance. By definition, the Torah is to be received as a design for the human condition, not as the record of one-time, one-dimensional events of a secular, historical character. That is why in the discussion of whether or not the Torah is God's revelation to Moses, historical and archaeological facts simply do not register.

Archaeological facts, accordingly, do not bear upon the issues of faith, because for Rabbinic Judaism the Torah—God's instruction—yields not one-time history, but eternal truth in the form of story. Thus for the synagogue, the Torah speaks in the present, not the past tense. Its acute contemporaneity is proclaimed every time the Torah-scrolls are displayed and the community of holy Israel proclaims, "This is the Torah that Moses set before the children of Israel at the command of God." In the context of the living faith of holy Israel declaimed in synagogue lection, the Torah is not the story of what happened only once. It is, as I just said, the presentation, through narrative, of eternal truth. In that context archaeology proves nothing worth knowing. It is not going to find Eden or Noah's ark, and history cannot evaluate the tangible evidence of the voice of silence that Elijah heard or uncover the cleft in the rock where God sheltered Moses.

If not history, then what?

The written Torah as mediated by the oral Torah contained in the Midrash compilations makes a coherent, systematic statement. The Rabbinic Midrash reads the Bible by transforming the genres of Scripture into patterns that apply to the acutely contemporary world as much as to times past and that interpret this morning's newspaper in the light of that ancient, enduring paradigm as well. For Judaism, the past is present, and the present is part of the past, so past, present, and future form a single plane of being.

Let me give a very simple example of this approach to the record of Scripture as a model, much as, in mathematics, we construct models of reality. The character of paradigmatic time is captured in the following, which incorporates the entirety of Israel's being (its "history" in conventional language) within the conversation that is portrayed between Boaz and Ruth:[3]

Ruth Rabbah XL:i.1–5

1. A. "And at mealtime Boaz said to her, 'Come here and eat some bread, and dip your morsel in the wine.' So she sat beside the reapers, and he passed to her parched grain; and she ate until she was satisfied, and she had some left over":
   B. R. Yohanan interpreted the phrase "come here" in six ways:
   C. "The first speaks of David.
   D. "'Come here:' means, to the throne: 'That you have brought me here' (2 Sam. 7:18).
   E. "'. . . and eat some bread:' the bread of the throne.
   F. "'. . . and dip your morsel in vinegar:' this speaks of his sufferings: 'O Lord, do not rebuke me in your anger' (Ps. 6:2).
   G. "'So she sat beside the reapers:' for the throne was taken from him for a time."
   I. [Resuming from G:] "'and he passed to her parched grain:' he was restored to the throne: 'Now I know that the Lord saves his anointed' (Ps. 20:7).
   J. "'. . . and she ate and was satisfied and left some over:' this indicates that he would eat in this world, in the days of the messiah, and in the age to come.
2. A. "The second interpretation refers to Solomon: 'Come here:' means, to the throne.
   B. "'. . . and eat some bread:' this is the bread of the throne: 'And Solomon's provision for one day was thirty measures of fine flour and three score measures of meal' (1 Kgs. 5:2).

---

[3] I abbreviate the passage to highlight only the critical components.

C. "'... and dip your morsel in vinegar:' this refers to the dirty of the deeds (that he did).

D. "'So she sat beside the reapers:' for the throne was taken from him for a time."

G. [Reverting to D:] "'and he passed to her parched grain:' for he was restored to the throne.

H. "'... and she ate and was satisfied and left some over:' this indicates that he would eat in this world, in the days of the messiah, and in the age to come.

3. A. "The third interpretation speaks of Hezekiah: 'Come here:' means, to the throne.

B. "'... and eat some bread:' this is the bread of the throne.

C. "'... and dip your morsel in vinegar:' this refers to sufferings (Is. 5:1): 'And Isaiah said, Let them take a cake of figs' (Is. 38:21).

D. "'So she sat beside the reapers:' for the throne was taken from him for a time: 'Thus says Hezekiah, This day is a day of trouble and rebuke' (Is. 37:3).

E. "'... and he passed to her parched grain:' for he was restored to the throne: 'So that he was exalted in the sight of all nations from then on' (2 Chr. 32:23).

F. "'... and she ate and was satisfied and left some over:' this indicates that he would eat in this world, in the days of the messiah, and in the age to come.

4. A. "The fourth interpretation refers to Manasseh: 'Come here:' means, to the throne.

B. "'... and eat some bread:' this is the bread of the throne.

C. "'... and dip your morsel in vinegar:' for his dirty deeds were like vinegar, on account of wicked actions.

D. "'So she sat beside the reapers:' for the throne was taken from him for a time: 'And the Lord spoke to Manasseh and to his people, but they did not listen. So the Lord brought them the captains of the host of the king of Assyria, who took Manasseh with hooks' (2 Chr. 33:10–11)."

K. (Reverting to D:) "'and he passed to her parched grain:' for he was restored to the throne: 'And brought him back to Jerusalem to his kingdom' (2 Chr. 33:13).

N. "'... and she ate and was satisfied and left some over:' this indicates that he would eat in this world, in the days of the messiah, and in the age to come.

5. A. "The fifth interpretation refers to the Messiah: 'Come here:' means, to the throne.

B. "'... and eat some bread:' this is the bread of the throne.

C. "'... and dip your morsel in vinegar:' this refers to suffering: 'But he was wounded because of our transgressions' (Is. 53:5).

D. "'So she sat beside the reapers:' for the throne is destined to be taken from him for a time: 'For I will gather all nations against Jerusalem to battle and the city shall be taken' (Zech. 14:2).
E. "'. . . and he passed to her parched grain:' for he will be restored to the throne: 'And he shall smite the land with the rod of his mouth' (Is. 11:4)."
I. "so the last redeemer will be revealed to them and then hidden from them."

The paradigm—the Messiah is enthroned, suffers, loses the throne, and is restored to the throne—here may be formed of these units: (1) David's monarchy; (2) Solomon's reign; (3) Hezekiah's reign; (4) Manasseh's reign; (5) the Messiah's reign. All form a single pattern. So paradigmatic time conforms scriptural events to the parameters of its model. The transaction of Ruth and Boaz contains the whole of Israel's future history of redemption through possession, loss, and restoration: the Messiah is like Israel in having, losing, and regaining the throne, as Israel lost but was restored to the Land—and will be once more by that same Messiah. All things happen on a single plane of time. Past, present, future are undifferentiated, and that is why a single action contains within itself an entire account of Israel's social order under the aspect of eternity.

The foundations of the paradigm rest on the fact that David, Solomon, Hezekiah, Manasseh, and therefore also, the Messiah, all descend from Ruth's and Boaz's union, and all gained, lost, and regained the throne. Then, within the framework of the paradigm, the event that is described here—"And at mealtime Boaz said to her, 'Come here and eat some bread, and dip your morsel in the wine.' So she sat beside the reapers, and he passed to her parched grain; and she ate until she was satisfied, and she had some left over"—forms not an event but a pattern, and the exegesis shows how the details of the pattern are realized in the successive Davidic monarchs, culminating with the Messiah. The pattern transcends time. More accurately, aggregates of time, the passage of time, the course of events are all simply irrelevant to what is in play in Scripture. Rather we have a tableau,[4] joining persons who lived at widely separated moments, linking them all as presences at this simple exchange between Boaz and Ruth; imputing to them all, whenever they came into existence, their parts in the shape and structure of that simple moment. Thus we see the presence of the past, for David, Solomon, Hezekiah, and so on, and also the pastness of the present in which David or Solomon—or the Messiah for that matter—lived or would live (it hardly matters: verb tenses prove hopelessly irrelevant to paradigmatic thinking).

---

[4] For the notion of the representation of Israel's existence as an ahistorical tableau, see my *Judaism: The Evidence of the Mishnah*. Chicago: University of Chicago Press, 1981.

Transforming historical narratives into exemplary patterns

That certainly was not the plan for those who compiled Genesis through Kings as a coherent narrative of a past broken off from the present but indicative of the future. The Hebrew Scriptures for their part had set forth Israel's life as history, with a beginning, middle, and end; a purpose and a coherence; a teleological system. All accounts agree that the Scriptures distinguished past from present, present from future and composed a sustained narrative, made up of one-time, irreversible events. All maintain that, in Scripture's historical portrait, Israel's present condition appealed for explanation to Israel's past, perceived as a coherent sequence of weighty events, each unique, all formed into a great chain of meaning. But, as our case has shown us, in the Midrash compilations the past takes place in the present. The present embodies the past. And there is no indeterminate future over the horizon, only a clear and present path to be chosen if people will it. With distinctions between past, present and future time found to make no difference, and in their stead, different categories of meaning and social order deemed self-evident, the Midrash transforms ancient Israel's history into the categorical structure of eternal Israel's society, so that past, present, and future meet in the here and now.

In that construction of thought, history finds no place, time, or change; the movement of events toward a purposive goal have no significance; and a different exegesis of happenings supplants the conception of history. Here we deal with a realm in which the past is ever present, the present a reformulation of the past. When people recapitulate the past in the present, and when they deem the present to be no different from a remote long ago, they organize and interpret experience in an other-than-historical framework. It is one that substitutes paradigms of enduring permanence for patterns of historical change. Instead of history, thought proceeds through the explanation of paradigms, the likenesses or un-likenesses of things to an original pattern. The familiar modes of classifying noteworthy events, the long ago and the here and now, lose currency. Memory as the medium of interpretation of the social order falls away, and historical thinking ceases to serve. Universal paradigms govern, against which all things, now, then, anytime, are compared; events lose all specificity and particularity.

In this reading of the Torah, time and change signify nothing. In its normative statements Rabbinic Judaism is ahistorical because it is paradigmatic in its structure and sensibility. So, with the loss of the experience of memory in favor of a different kind of encounter with time past, present, and future, time as a concept in the measurement of things ceased to serve. Time simply is not a factor in thinking about what happens and what counts. Instead, transcendent and permanent paradigms for the formation of the social order govern, so that what was now is, and what will be is what was and is. Paradigmatic thinking treats the case not as a one-time event but as an example; it seeks the rules that cases adumbrate; it asks about the patterns that narratives realize in concrete instances. It is like a mathematical model, which translates the real world into abstract principles, and like social science in that it seeks to generalize about particularities. Both disciplines are able to account for local variation by defining the norm.

Thinking in paradigms: mathematics as the metaphor for Midrash

Paradigmatic reasoning forms a counterpart to mathematical reasoning that produces models. Specifically, mathematicians compose models that, in the language and symbols of mathematics, set forth a structure of knowledge that forms a "surrogate for reality."[5] These models state in quantitative terms the results of controlled observations of data, and among them, the one that generates plausible analytical generalizations will serve. Seeking the regularities of the data in order to account for a variety of variables among a vast corpus of data, the framer of a model needs more than observations of fact, e.g., regularities or patterns. What is essential is a structure of thought, which mathematicians call "a philosophy":

> As a philosophy it has a center from which everything flows, and the center is a definition.... [6]

What is needed for a model is not data alone, however voluminous, but some idea of what you are trying to compose, a model of the model:

> Unless you have some good idea of what you are looking for and how to find it, you can approach infinity with nothing more than a mishmash of little things you know about a lot of little things.[7]

So, in order to frame a model of explanation, we start with a model in the computer, and then test data to assess the usefulness of the model. We may test several models, with the same outcome: the formation of a theory in the mathematical sense which I shall hereafter refer to as a philosophy. To understand the relevance of this brief glimpse at model-making in mathematics, let me cite the context in which the matter comes to me, the use of mathematics to give guidance on how to fight forest fires:

> If mathematics can be used to predict the intensity and rate of spread of wildfires of the future (either hypothetical fires or fires actually burning but whose outcome is not yet known), why can't the direction of the analysis be reversed in order to reconstruct the characteristics of important fires of the past? Or why can't the direction be reversed from prophecy to history?[8]

---

[5] Norman Maclean, *Young Men and Fire* (Chicago: University of Chicago Press, 1992), p. 257.
[6] Maclean, p. 261.
[7] Maclean, p. 262.
[8] Maclean, p. 267.

Here the reversibility of events, their paradigmatic character, their capacity to yield a model unlimited by context or considerations of scale, i.e., the principal traits of paradigmatic thinking, turn out to enjoy a compelling rationality of their own. Reading those words, we can immediately grasp what use models or patterns or paradigms served for the Rabbinic sages, even though the framing of mathematical models began long after the birth of this writer, and even though the Rabbinic sages lived many centuries before the creation of the model-yielding mathematics to which sages' paradigms correspond in kind and function. In Midrash we find a mode of thought that is entirely rational and the very opposite of insubstantial.

What is at stake in the appeal to "paradigm" or "model"? Such an appeal indicates that philosophy has now taken the place of history in the examination of the meaning of human events and experience. By applying a philosophical model to organize such relevant data, the Rabbinic sages found ready at hand the pattern of the destruction of the Temple, alongside explanations of the event and formulations of how the consequences were to be worked out.

Rabbinic Midrash in context: the origins of paradigmatic thinking in real, historical time

First, whence the source of the sense of separation of present from past? Second, how did the Rabbinic sages select the pattern that predominated?

We find the answer to the first question when we turn to the setting in which, in Israel, history first was set down in a sustained narrative. That is after 586 B.C.E., when the Torah came to fruition in the books of Genesis through Kings, which reached closure in the aftermath of the destruction of the First Temple and the return to Zion. That sustained narrative, entirely historical in its perspective, recognizes the pastness of the past and explains how the past has led to the present. Faced with decisive closure, looking backward from the perspective of a radically different present, the thinkers who put together the Primary History took up two complementary premises. The first was the definitive pastness of the past, its utter closure and separation from the present. The second was the power of the (now completed) past to explain the present and of its lessons, properly learned, to shape the future.

The historical thinking that produced the continuous, purposeful narrative of Genesis through Kings took place at a very specific time and responded to an acute and urgent question by taking account of the facts of the moment. An age had come to a conclusion; the present drastically differed from the now-closed past. Since all scholarship concurs that the continuous historical narrative represented by Genesis through Kings came to closure at just this time, the allegation that historical thinking in Israel in particular reaches literary expression in the aftermath of the catastrophe of 586 rests upon solid foundations. Here is when people wrote history-books; here is why they wrote them; here, therefore, is the circumstance in which, for Israel, historical thinking took place. The advent of historical thinking and writing became possible precisely when great events from the past, viewed as one-time and unique, receded over the last horizon, and those responsible for the books at hand recognized a separation from those events and so produced a history of how things had reached their present state.

That brings us to the second question: whence the mode of paradigmatic thinking, whence the particular paradigm itself? Why did the Rabbinic sages evince no sense of separation between now and then? Why did they think in a different manner about the same events? To them, the present and past formed a single unit of time, encompassing a single span of experience, because to them times past took place in the present too. On that account, the present not only encompassed the past (which historical thinking concedes) but took place in the same plane of time as the past (which, to repeat, historical thinking rejects). How come? It is because the Rabbinic sages experienced the past in the present. The significant events of their day had happened before. The destruction of the Temple took place a second time. The unthinkable question then pressed: will the restoration of Israel to Zion not take place as it had, once more? And the answer of paradigmatic thinking was, the pattern is established, and when the conditions of restoration are met—repentance, reconciliation, atonement for the sins that had led to the destruction once, then twice—the restoration will take place. By generalizing according to that paradigm of thought concerning the axial event of the age, the Midrash exegetes sought to identify the patterns that link Scripture's one-time events into a coherent system, just as the Rabbinic sages discovered the paradigm that imparted order and sense to the events of their day.

The result of seeing events in patterns

A sequence of discrete events then was transformed into a series. That meant events themselves defined and conformed to paradigms. They yielded rules. A simple formulation of this mode of thought is as follows:

Mishnah-tractate Ta'anit 4:6

A. Five events took place for our fathers on the seventeenth of Tammuz, and five on the ninth of Ab.
B. On the seventeenth of Tammuz
    (1) the tablets (of the Torah) were broken,
    (2) the daily whole offering was cancelled,
    (3) the city wall was breached,
    (4) Apostemos burned the Torah, and
    (5) he set up an idol in the Temple.
C. On the ninth of Ab
    (1) the decree was made against our forefathers that they should not enter the land,
    (2) the first Temple and

(3) the second (Temple) were destroyed,
(4) Betar was taken, and
(5) the city was ploughed up (after the war of Hadrian).
D. When Ab comes, rejoicing diminishes.

We mark time by appeal to the phases of the moon; these then may be characterized by traits shared in common—and so the paradigm, from marking time, moves outward to the formation of rules concerning the regularity and order of events.

In the formulation just now given, we see the movement from event to rule. The happenings adhere to a common pattern, are classified, hence no longer unique. What is important about events is not their singularity but their capacity to generate a pattern, a concrete rule for the here and now. That is the conclusion drawn from the very passage at hand:

Mishnah-tractate *Ta^canit* 4:7

A. In the week in which the ninth of Ab occurs it is prohibited to get a haircut and to wash one's clothes.
B. But on Thursday of that week these are permitted,
C. because of the honor owing to the Sabbath.
D. On the eve of the ninth of Ab a person should not eat two prepared dishes, nor should one eat meat or drink wine.

Events serve to establish paradigms and therefore, also, to yield rules governing the here and now: what we do to recapitulate the paradigm.

This brings us back to our question: how a sequence of events turned into a series, singular moments into a pattern—what happened once into something that recurs. The answer, of course, lies in the correspondence (real or imagined) of the two generative events sages found definitive: the first destruction of the Temple and the second destruction of the Temple. The singular event that framed their consciousness recapitulated what had already occurred. For they confronted a second Temple in ruins, and, in the defining event of the age just preceding the composition of most of the documents surveyed here, they found quite plausible the notion that the past was a formidable presence in the contemporary world. And having lived through events that they could plausibly discover in Scripture—in Lamentations or Jeremiah, for example—they also found entirely natural the notion that the past took place in the present as well.

The concrete experience of an ever-present past

When we speak of the presence of the past, therefore, we raise not generalities or possibilities but the concrete experience that generations actively mourning the Temple endured. When we speak of the pastness of the present, we describe the consciousness of people who could open Scripture and find themselves right there, in its record—not only in Lamentations, but also in prophecy, and, especially, in the books of the Torah. Here we deal with not the spiritualization of Scripture, but with the acutely contemporary and immediate realization of Scripture, once again, as then; Scripture in the present day, the present day in Scripture. That is why it was possible for sages to formulate out of Scripture a paradigm that imposed structure and order upon the world that they themselves encountered.

Since, then, sages did not see themselves as removed in time and space from the generative events that established the pattern for the experience of the here and now, they also had no need to make the past contemporary. The Rabbinic sages saw matters in a different way altogether. They neither relived nor transformed one-time historical events, for they found another way to overcome the barrier of chronological separation. For, it seems to me clear, the idea that time and space separated the Rabbinic sages from the great events of the past simply did not register. The opposite idea defined matters: barriers of space and time in no way separated sages from great events, because the great events of the past endured for all time. How then are we to account for this remarkably different way of encounter, experience, and, consequently, explanation? The answer has already been adumbrated.

The Rabbinic sages took for granted that the destruction of the second Temple was to be understood by reference to the pattern of the destruction of the first. The colloquy between Aqiba and the sages about the comfort to be derived from the ephemeral glory of Rome and the temporary ruin of Jerusalem makes that point in so many words. A single story embodies paradigmatic thinking such as generated the reading of Scripture as Torah:

Lamentations Rabbah CXL:i.1–2

1. A. "for Mount Zion which lies desolate; jackals prowl over it:"
   B. Rabban Gamaliel, R. Joshua, R. Eleazar b. Azariah, and R. Aqiba went to Rome. They heard the din of the city of Rome from a distance of a hundred and twenty miles.
   C. They all begin to cry, but R. Aqiba began to laugh.
   D. They said to him, "Aqiba, we are crying and you laugh?"
   E. He said to them, "Why are you crying?"
   F. They said to him, "Should we not cry, that idolators and those who sacrifice to idols and bow down to images live securely and prosperously, while the footstool of our God has been burned down by fire and become a dwelling place for the beasts of the field? So shouldn't we cry?"
   G. He said to them, "That is precisely the reason that I was laughing. For if those who outrage him he treats in such a way, those who do his will all the more so!"

2. A. There was the further case of when they were going up to Jerusalem. When they came to the Mount of Olives they tore their clothing. When they came to the Temple mount and a fox came out of the house of the Holy of Holies, they began to cry. But R. Aqiba began to laugh.
   B. "Aqiba, you are always surprising us. Now we are crying and you laugh?"
   C. He said to them, "Why are you crying?"
   D. They said to him, "Should we not cry, that from the place of which it is written, 'And the ordinary person that comes near shall be put to death' (Num. 1:51) a fox comes out? So the verse of Scripture is carried out: 'for Mount Zion which lies desolate; jackals prowl over it.'"
   E. He said to them, "That is precisely the reason that I was laughing. For Scripture says, 'And I will take for myself faithful witnesses to record, Uriah the priest and Zechariah the son of Jeberechiah' (Isa. 8:2).
   F. "Now what is the relationship between Uriah and Zechariah? Uriah lived in the time of the first temple, Zechariah in the time of the second!
   G. "But Uriah said, 'Thus says the Lord of hosts: Zion shall be plowed as a field, and Jerusalem shall become heaps' (Jer. 26:18).
   H. "And Zechariah said, 'There shall yet be old men and old women sitting in the piazzas of Jerusalem, every man with his staff in his hand for old age' (Zech. 8:4).
   I. "And further: 'And the piazzas of the city shall be full of boys and girls playing in the piazzas thereof' (Zech. 8:5).
   J. "Said the Holy One, blessed be He, 'Now lo, I have these two witnesses. So if the words of Uriah are carried out, the words of Zechariah will be carried out, while if the words of Uriah prove false, then the words of Zechariah will not be true either.'
   K. "I was laughing with pleasure because the words of Uriah have been carried out, and that means that the words of Zechariah in the future will be carried out."
   L. They said to him, "Aqiba, you have given us consolation. May you be comforted among those who are comforted."

Here is how event becomes example, and a series of events yields a pattern. It is the outcome of that mode of reading Scripture that sustained the Midrash exegesis of Scripture we review in the documents at hand.

Sages recognized the destruction of the Second Temple and all took for granted that that event was to be understood by reference to the model of the destruction of the first. It follows that for the Rabbinic sages, the destruction of the Temple in 70 C.E. did not mark a break with the past, such as it had for their predecessors some five hundred years earlier, but rather a recapitulation of the past. Paradigmatic thinking then began in that very event that had earlier precipitated historical thinking, the end of the old order. But paradigm replaced history because what had taken place the first time as unique and unprecedented took place the second time in precisely the same pattern. Paradigm replaced history when history as an account of one-time, irreversible, unique events, arranged in linear sequence and pointing toward a teleological conclusion, lost all plausibility. If the first time around, history provided the medium for making sense of matters, then the second time around, history lost all currency.

After history: paradigm versus cycle

The real choice facing the Rabbinic sages was not—despite my implications to the contrary—linear history as against paradigmatic thinking, but rather, *paradigm as against cycle*. This is because in light of the destruction of the second Temple, history, having yielded no explanation, could have yielded to a theory of the *cyclicality* of events. As nature yielded its spring, summer, fall and winter, so the events of humanity or of Israel in particular could have been asked to conform to a cyclical recurrence in line, for example, with Qohelet's view that what has been is what will be. But the Rabbinic sages obviously did not adopt that cyclical view at all.

They rejected cyclicality in favor of an altogether different ordering of events. They did not believe the Temple would be rebuilt and destroyed again, rebuilt and destroyed, and so on into endless time. They stated the very opposite: the Temple would be rebuilt but never again destroyed. And that represented a view of the second destruction that rejected cyclicality altogether. Sages instead opted for patterns because they developed that notion for the specific and concrete meaning of events that characterized Scripture's history, even while rejecting the historicism of Scripture. What they maintained, as we have seen, is that a pattern governed, and the pattern was not a cyclical one. Here, Scripture itself imposed its structures, its order, its system—its paradigm. And the history told from Genesis through Kings left no room for the conception of cyclicality. If matters do not repeat themselves endlessly but do conform to a pattern, then the pattern itself must be identified.

Midrash and paradigm

Viewed as a whole, the narrative from Genesis through Kings did not only tell a story. It also constituted the paradigm of Israel's existence, formed out of the selected components of Eden and the Land, Adam and Israel, Sinai; then given movement through Israel's responsibility to the covenant and Israel's adherence to, or violation of, God's will, which is fully exposed in the Torah that marked the covenant of Sinai. Scripture laid matters out, and the Rabbinic sages then drew conclusions from that layout that conformed to their experience. So the second destruction precipitated thinking about paradigms of Israel's life, such as came to full exposure in the thinking behind the Midrash compilations we survey in this book. Having incorporated the episode into a series, sages' paradigmatic thinking asked of Scripture questions different from the historical ones of 586 because the Rabbinic sages brought to Scripture different premises, drawing from Scripture different conclusions. But in point of fact, not a single paradigm set forth by sages can be distinguished in any important component from its counterpart in Scripture, not Eden and Adam in comparison to the land of Israel and Israel, and not the tale of Israel's experience in the spinning out of the tension between the word of God and the will of Israel.

Now we turn to the Midrash compilations that convey the system in its Scriptural context. After an overview of the canonical compilations of Midrash, the bulk of the book outlines the theology that animated the Rabbinic sages' reading of the several books of Scripture on which they produced systematic Midrash compilations. Then at the end we shall take up the theology of the Midrash viewed as a whole.

2

An Overview of the Rabbinic Midrash-Compilations

Writing with Scripture

Through (1) Midrash method, producing (2) Midrash exegeses, commonly collected in (3) Midrash compilations, the sages of Rabbinic Judaism *wrote with Scripture*.[1] They expressed what they wished to say by commenting on assembled verses or biblical cases (heroes, events). Through the juxtaposition of two or more disparate examples they would make a point or establish a proposition not contained within any one of them. When the examples were combined, an encompassing proposition emerged as implicit in them all.

How is that different from writing in a propositional manner? There we articulate a proposition, cite facts and evidence and expose the argumentation. The combination of proposition, evidence, and argument establishes the point we wish to make. When we write with Scripture, by contrast, we do not articulate the proposition but present it by implication. Thus we conduct our argumentation by asking the reader to perceive the commonalities among episodes that, all together, point to the conclusion we wish to reach. The hearer or reader becomes an active participant in the conversation precipitated by verses of Scripture.

There are three types, or modes, of Rabbinic Midrash exegesis, that is, of writing with Scripture.

(1) The first is verse-by-verse exegesis of a given scriptural book, with episodic compositions that set forth propositions;

---

[1] See *Writing with Scripture: The Authority and Uses of the Hebrew Bible in the Torah of Formative Judaism.* Philadelphia, 1989: Fortress Press. Second printing: Atlanta: Scholars Press for South Florida Studies in the History of Judaism, 1994. The idea encapsulated in the phrase, "writing with Scripture," not to mention the phrase itself, originates with Professor William Scott Green, University of Rochester.

(2) the second, propositional compositions formed from groups of diverse verses and their exegesis, *not* organized around the sequential verses of a single scriptural book;

(3) the third is the repetition of the same point, again and again, in sequential exegesis of a given book of Scripture.

These types surface in chronological order: exegesis, generalization, exegesis of sequences of details yielding generalization.

First, the earliest Rabbinic Midrash compilations (ca. 200–300 C.E.), exemplified below by a selection from *Sifré to Deuteronomy,* cover the verses of a biblical book in a sequential structure, occasionally forming a set of Midrash exegeses into a propositional composite. Among the canonical compilations of Midrash, *Mekhilta (attributed to R. Ishmael)* for Exodus (Chapter Three), *Sifra on Leviticus* (Chapter Four), *Sifré to Numbers* (Chapter Five) and *Sifré to Deuteronomy* (Chapter Seven) exemplify that type of Midrash compilation. The sages to whom exegeses are attributed in these compilations flourished in the period in which the Mishnah took shape and are called Tannaim, "repeaters," that is, bearers of traditions handed down since Sinai. The collections are called Tannaite Midrashim. They also are called Halakhic Midrashim because they work on legal passages of the Pentateuch as well as on theological ones.

Genesis Rabbah of a later period, ca. 450 C.E., (Chapter Three) mainly conforms to the pattern of verse-by-verse commentary as well, though it forms a bridge to what follows.

Second, the next set of Midrash compilations, exemplified below by *Leviticus Rabbah,* puts forth propositions that define the structure of large-scale compositions and composites. These do not take shape around the sequential exegesis of passages or chapters, let alone whole books, of Scripture. Besides *Leviticus Rabbah,* ca. 450 C.E., a fine example of this approach (Chapter Six), important components of *Genesis Rabbah* follow suit. *Pesiqta deRab Kahana,* ca. 500 C.E. (Chapter Thirteen), establishes propositions that pertain not to a particular book of Scripture but to singular events in the sacred calendar: the New Year, Hanukkah, Passover, the Ninth of Ab, and the like.

Third, the set of Midrash compilations produced at the end of the formative age, alongside the Talmud of Babylonia, ca. 500–600 C.E., exemplified below by *Song of Songs Rabbah* (Chapter Eleven), reverted to the organizing principle of the first mode of Midrash exegeses, that is, verse-by-verse sequential; but it adopted the argumentation of the second mode of the exegesis, namely, large-scale, propositional compositions. By repeating one thing about many things, the third mode of Midrash exegesis united the form of the first mode with the intellectual method of the second. *Song of Songs Rabbah* is the best example of this. Less exact examples are provided by *Lamentations Rabbah* (Chapter Twelve), *Ruth Rabbah* (Chapter Ten), and *Esther Rabbah I* (Chapter Nine).

In this Introduction we meet, also, ʾ*Abot deR. Natan, (The Fathers according to Rabbi Nathan),* ca. 500 C.E. (Chapter Fourteen), a biographical expansion of tractate *m. ʾAbot*, the Fathers, ca. 250 C.E. That is not, strictly speaking, a Midrash compilation at all, since it is made up of sayings and exemplary stories of sages. But the stories that are told about exemplary sages serve to amplify the moral sayings of tractate *ʾAbot* and so may be classified as a kind of writing with Scripture. It consists of biographical narratives that flesh out and illustrate wise sayings by sages of the Torah.

We conclude with a systematic theology: an account of the main ideas of the Midrash compilations viewed as a coherent statement.

The standing of Scripture in Midrash exegesis

Since we approach Rabbinic Midrash as a mode of writing with Scripture, we must ask, did Scripture serve only as a source of proof-texts and pretexts to certify propositions people formed on their own? Or is Midrash exegesis closely linked to Scripture's own deepest meanings? For the Midrash compilations, Israelite Scripture constituted not merely a source of validation but a powerful instrument of profound inquiry. The framers of the various Midrash compilations set forth propositions of their own, formed in constant dialogue with Scripture.

How so? For its part Scripture set forth facts for reflection, systematization, generalization, and testing. It raised questions, set forth premises of discourse and argument, constituted that faithful record of the rules and their implicit meanings. These facts of the supernatural order, revealed in the Torah and recording God's intervention into nature and society, required analysis. Their lessons were to be discovered. And that is where Midrash enters in: transforming facts into truth, learning into knowledge. So Scripture functioned in the Rabbinic sages' theological and legal venture as did nature for natural philosophy. Just as natural philosophy derived its rules of nature, subject to critical analysis, from the facts of physics or astronomy, so the Rabbinic sages read Scripture and sorted out its facts into laws. Midrash sets forth the results of analysis, the general rules for reconstruction. That forms one focus of the Rabbinic Midrash process in all three periods of its realization.

Not only so, but noteworthy traits inherent in a verse of Scripture itself can be shown on occasion to provoke the question answered by the Rabbinic exegete. These are often made explicit in the Midrash exegesis, e.g., a question is articulated and answered. But masters of Midrash exegesis in all periods, ancient, medieval, modern, have closely linked the Midrash exegesis to the verse that is expounded, sometimes through analysis of words and their meanings, sometimes through consideration of grammar, occasionally through the inquiry into theology, but always in dialogue with the present moment. Indeed, the debate goes forward: does the Midrash exegesis impose meaning on the verse that is cited, or does the cited verse yield the meaning articulated by the Midrash exegesis?

Proof-text or pretext?

The Midrash process treats Scripture as both and as neither. The power of the Rabbinic exegetes was in seeing the whole of Scripture contained in each one of its parts. They put the whole together systematically; they saw things complete and in proportion. Then they came to the parts and placed them into the context of that systematic reading of Scripture. Individual verses of Scripture then serve as proof-texts for conclusions reached in the reconstruction of the Scripture's own internal patterns and constructions. Individual verses of Scripture also provide the pretext for the recapitulation of that encompassing system.

Accordingly, the Midrash exegetes played the part of active partner in dialogue with Scripture. That is what writing with Scripture means: working from the whole to the parts. Whether or not their statement accorded with the position of Scripture on a given point, or merely stated the simple and obvious sense of Scripture, or found ample support in proof texts bears no material consequence. So the masters of Midrash made use of Scripture, but they did so by making selections, shaping a distinctive idiom of discourse in so doing.

True, verses of Scripture provided facts; they supplied proofs of propositions much as data of natural science proved propositions of natural philosophy. Writing with Scripture meant appealing to the facts that Scripture provided in order to prove propositions that the authorships at hand wished to prove, forming with Scripture the system that these writers proposed to construct to accommodate the whole of Scripture through its parts. (By "authorship" I mean those who brought the Pentateuch into being as redactor-authors. These individuals took older material and restructured and rearranged it, but also brought into that material some of their own work.) In fact, Midrash processes involve three relationships to Scripture.

Three relationships to Scripture

The first instructs us to look for evidence that a verse of the Israelite Scriptures illustrates a theme or provides information on a given subject. The Midrash masters organize Scripture's information by topics. In its scriptural context, that information is systemically inert. The second is comprised of Midrash compilations in which Scripture sets forth a problem. The Midrash masters identify and solve that problem. In the third type of Midrash compilations Scripture sustains a proposition that the Midrash masters formulate independently. They here ask Scripture to support that independently-attained proposition.

Midrash compilations in which Scripture supplies information

One way of forming a comprehensible statement is to draw together information on a single theme. The theme then imposes cogency on facts, which are deemed to illuminate aspects of that theme. Such an approach creates a topical "anthology." The materials in the anthology do not, all together, add up to a statement that transcends detail; they do not point toward a conclusion beyond themselves. Rather they comprise a series of facts, e.g., fact 1, fact 2, fact 3. Even when put together, these three facts do not yield yet another, nor do they point toward a proposition beyond themselves. They generate no generalization, prove no point, propose no proposition. *Mekhilta attributed to R. Ishmael* collects and arranges information by themes or topics, much like a scrapbook.

Midrash compilations in which Scripture sets forth a problem

A second mode of relationship will tell us that a verse of the Israelite Scriptures considered by itself presents a *problem*. Within the Midrash compilation, the problem will be identified and addressed because it is relevant to the system. That is not at all common in *Mekhilta attributed to R. Ishmael*, but *Sifra* takes a keen interest in verses and their meanings for large questions.

Midrash compilations in which Scripture sustains a proposition independently formulated

Yet a third mode points toward that utilization of Israelite Scriptures in the formation and expression of *an independent proposition,* one independent of the theme or even the facts contained within those verses of Scripture. *Sifra,* for instance, addresses and disposes of Scripture by rewriting it in ways of *Sifra's* authorship's design.

The logic of coherent discourse in Midrash compilations

How do the verse-by-verse exegeses of Scripture—citation and comment—hold together? What forms of the details a cogent construction?

Fixed association

A compilation may cohere formally, through the fixed association of the verses of the text of Scripture that is commented on, that is, only by following the sequences of the verses of Scripture to which they refer, but not by forming a proposition that all of them together sustain. In *Mekhilta attributed to R. Ishmael,* as well as in *Sifra* and *Sifré to Deuteronomy,* we have composites of materials that string together, upon the necklace of the words or phrases of a verse, diverse comments. The comments do not fit together or point to any broader conclusion; they do not address a single theme or form an anthology. Their association derives from the (external) verse that is cited. Intelligibility begins and ends in that verse and is accomplished by the amplification of the verse's contents. Without the verse before us, the words that follow form gibberish. But reading the words as amplifications of a sense contained within the cited verse, we can make good sense of them.

Proposition/syllogism

Other compilations, *Leviticus Rabbah* and *Pesiqta deRab Kahana,* for example, cohere because the proposition that is subject to demonstration links each of the components of a given exposition. In this case, the logic of coherent discourse is syllogistic and philosophical, nor merely formal and fabricated.

Lists of data that all together form a statement

A third manner of coherence involves the making of lists, e.g., of names, events, rites, mixed together. On their own, the items that are listed bear no hint as to the message attained through combining these items. Putting them together yields a proposition or evokes an emotion or expresses an attitude. *Song of Songs Rabbah* provides the best example of manipulating—combining and recombining—items into lists.

An example of verse-by-verse exegesis to demonstrate a proposition

Here is an example of a sustained composition, cogent beginning to end, which makes its points through the medium of writing with Scripture.

Sifré to Deuteronomy I:i.1–5

1. A. "These are the words that Moses spoke to all Israel in Transjordan, in the wilderness, that is to say in the Arabah, opposite Suph, between Paran on the one side and Tophel, Laban, Hazeroth, and Dizahab, on the other" (Dt. 1:1):
   B. ("These are the words that Moses spoke" [Dt. 1:1]) Did Moses prophesy only these alone? Did he not write the entire Torah?
   C. For it is said, "And Moses wrote this Torah" (Dt. 31:9).
   D. Why then does Scripture say, "These are the words that Moses spoke" (Dt. 1:1)?
   E. It teaches that (when Scripture speaks of the words that one spoke, it refers in particular to) the words of admonition.
   F. So it is said (by Moses), "But Jeshurun waxed fat and kicked" (Dt. 32:15).

The proposition, stated at E, is a philological one. "Speaking" in a specific sense implies a measure of rebuke or admonition. We are not offered the proposition as an introductory statement, e.g., a syllogism to be proved. The proposition occurs only in another way, at E–F. Let us proceed to follow the way in which the proposition is (1) stated, (2) illustrated and exemplified, and (3) proved—all through a barrage of cited verses of Scripture. The topic—the proposition—recurs at every paragraph, and the whole coalesces into a single, remarkably cogent statement.

2. A. So too you may point to the following:
   B. "The words of Amos, who was among the herdsmen of Tekoa, which he saw concerning Israel in the days of Uzziah, king of Judah, and in the days of Jeroboam, son of Joash, king of Israel, two years before the earthquake" (Amos 1:1):
   C. Did Amos prophesy only concerning these (kings) alone? Did he not prophesy concerning a greater number (of kings) than any other?
   D. Why then does Scripture say, "These are the words of Amos, (who was among the herdsmen of Tekoa, which he saw concerning Israel in the days of Uzziah, king of Judah, and in the days of Jeroboam, son of Joash, king of Israel, two years before the earthquake)" (Amos 1:1)?
   E. It teaches that (when Scripture speaks of the words that one spoke, it refers in particular to) the words of admonition.
   F. And how do we know that they were words of admonition?
   G. As it is said, "Hear this word, you cows of Bashan, who are in the mountain of Samaria, who oppress the poor, crush the needy, and say to their husbands, 'Bring, that we may feast'" (Amos 4:1).
   H. ("And say to their husbands, 'Bring, that we may feast'") speaks of their courts.
3. A. So too you may point to the following:
   B. "And these are the words that the Lord spoke concerning Israel and Judah" (Jer. 30:4).
   C. Did Jeremiah prophesy only these alone? Did he not write two (complete) scrolls?
   D. For it is said, "Thus far are the words of Jeremiah" (Jer. 51:64).
   E. Why then does Scripture say, "And these are the words (that the Lord spoke concerning Israel and Judah)" (Jer. 30:4)?
   F. It teaches that (when the verse says, "And these are the words that the Lord spoke concerning Israel and Judah" [Jer. 30:4]), it speaks in particular of the words of admonition.
   G. And how do we know that they were words of admonition?
   H. In accord with this verse: "For thus says the Lord, 'We have heard a voice of trembling, of fear and not of peace. Ask you now and see whether a man does labor with a child? Why do I see every man with his hands on his loins, as a woman in labor? and all faces turn pale? Alas, for the day is great, there is none like it, and it is a time of trouble for Jacob, but out of it he shall be saved'" (Jer. 30:5–7).
4. A. So too you may point to the following:
   B. "And these are the last words of David" (2 Sam. 23:1).

    C. And did David prophesy only these alone? And has it furthermore not been said, "The spirit of the Lord spoke through me, and his word was on my tongue" (2 Samuel 23:2)?

    D. Why then does it say, "And these are the last words of David" (2 Sam. 23:1)?

    E. It teaches that, (when the verse says, "And these are the last words of David" [2 Sam. 23:1]), it refers to words of admonition.

    F. And how do we know that they were words of admonition?

    G. In accord with this verse: "But the ungodly are as thorns thrust away, all of them, for they cannot be taken with the hand" (2 Sam. 23:6).

5. A. So too you may point to the following:

    B. "The words of Qohelet, son of David, king in Jerusalem" (Qoh. 1:1).

    C. Now did Solomon prophesy only these words? Did he not write three-and-a-half scrolls of his wisdom in proverbs?

    D. Why then does it say, "The words of Qohelet, son of David, king in Jerusalem" (Qoh. 1:1)?

    E. It teaches that (when the verse says, "The words of Qohelet, son of David, king in Jerusalem" [Qoh. 1:1]), it refers to words of admonition.

    F. And how do we know that they were words of admonition?

    G. In accord with this verse: "The sun also rises, and the sun goes down . . . the wind goes toward the south and turns around to the north, it turns round continually in its circuit, and the wind returns again—that is, east and west (to its circuits. All the rivers run into the sea" [Qoh. 1:5–7]).

    H. (Solomon) calls the wicked sun, moon, and sea, for (the wicked) have no reward (coming back to them).

Let us stand back and see the matter whole. The focus is upon the exegesis of the opening word of Deuteronomy, "(these are the) words. . . ." The problem is carefully stated. And yet, without the arrangement within what is going to be a commentary on Deuteronomy, we should have no reason to regard the composition as exegetical at all. In fact, it is a syllogism, aiming at proving a particular proposition concerning word-usages. Standing by itself, this syllogism makes a philological point, which is that the word "words of . . . ," bears the sense of "admonition" or "rebuke." Five proofs are offered. We know that we reach the end of the exposition when, at i.5H, there is a minor gloss, departing from the consistent form. That is a common mode of signaling the conclusion of discourse on a given point.

An example of philosophical discourse: from exegesis to proposition

When in the core of the book we come to *Leviticus Rabbah*, we shall see how statements become intelligible not contingently, that is, on the strength of an established text, but *a priori*, that is, on the basis of a deeper logic of meaning, an independent principle of rhetorical intelligibility. Logic is what joins one sentence to the next and forms the whole into paragraphs of meaning, intelligible propositions, each with its place and sense in a still larger, accessible system. Because of logic one mind connects to another, public discourse becomes possible, debate on issues of general intelligibility takes place, and an anthology of statements about a single subject becomes a composition of theorems about that subject.

Accordingly, with *Leviticus Rabbah* rabbis take up the problem of saying what they wish to say not in an exegetical, but in a syllogistic and freely discursive logic and rhetoric. The paramount exegetical construction is the base verse/intersecting-verse exegesis. In this construction, a verse of Leviticus is cited (hence: base verse), and another verse, from books such as Job, Proverbs, Qohelet, or Psalms, is then cited (hence: intersecting verse). The latter, not the former, is subjected to detailed and systematic exegesis. But the exegetical exercise ends up by leading the intersecting verse back to the base verse and reading the latter in terms of the former. The treatment of the festival of Tabernacles yields the proposition that Israel's history is explained by Israel's moral condition, therefore Israel itself commands its own destiny, by the will of God.

Leviticus Rabbah XXX:i.1–6

1. A. "(On the fifteenth day of the seventh month, when you have gathered in the produce of the land, you shall keep the feast of the Lord seven days. . . .) And you shall take on the first day (the fruit of goodly trees, branches of palm trees and boughs of leafy trees and willows of the brook, and you shall rejoice before the Lord your God for seven days)" (Lev. 23:39–40).
   B. R. Abba bar Kahana commenced (discourse by citing the following verse): "Take my instruction instead of silver, (and knowledge rather than choice gold)" (Prov. 8:10).
   C. Said R. Abba bar Kahana, "Take the instruction of the Torah instead of silver.
   D. "'Why do you weigh out money? Because there is no bread' (Is. 55:2).
   E. "'Why do you weigh out money to the sons of Esau' (Rome)? (It is because) "there is no bread," because you did not sate yourselves with the bread of the Torah.
   F. "'And (why) do you labor? Because there is no satisfaction' (Is. 55:2).
   G. "'Why do you labor while the nations of the world enjoy plenty? Because there is no satisfaction,' that is, because you have not sated yourselves with the wine of the Torah.
   H. "For it is written, 'Come, eat of my bread, and drink of the wine I have mixed'" (Prov. 9:5).
2. A. R. Berekhiah and R. Hiyya, his father, in the name of R. Yoséb. Nehori, said, "It is written, 'I shall punish all who oppress him' (Jer. 30:20) even those who collect funds for charity (and in doing so,

treat people badly), except (for those who collect) the wages to be paid to teachers and repeaters of Mishnah traditions.

B. "For they receive (as a salary) only compensation for the loss of their time, (which they devote to teaching and learning rather than to earning a living).

C. "But as to the wages (for carrying out) a single matter in the Torah, no creature can pay the (appropriate) fee in reward."

3. A. It has been taught: On the New Year, a person's sustenance is decreed (for the coming year),

B. except for what a person pays out (for food in celebration) of the Sabbath, festivals, the celebration of the New Month,

C. and for what children bring to the house of their master (as his tuition).

D. If he adds (to what is originally decreed), (in Heaven) they add to his (resources), but if he deducts (from what he should give), (in Heaven) they deduct (from his wealth).

4. A. R. Yohanan was going up from Tiberias to Sepphoris. R. Hiyya bar Abba was supporting him. They came to a field. He said, "This field once belonged to me, but I sold it in order to acquire merit in the Torah."

B. They came to a vineyard, and he said, "This vineyard once belonged to me, but I sold it in order to acquire merit in the Torah."

C. They came to an olive grove, and he said, "This olive grove once belonged to me, but I sold it in order to acquire merit in the Torah."

D. R. Hiyya began to cry.

E. Said R. Yohanan, "Why are you crying?"

F. He said to him, "It is because you left nothing over to support you in your old age."

G. He said to him, "Hiyya, my disciple, is what I did such a light thing in your view? I sold something which was given in a spell of six days (of creation) and in exchange I acquired something which was given in a spell of forty days (of revelation).

H. "The entire world and everything in it was created in only six days, as it is written, 'For in six days the Lord made heaven and earth' (Ex. 20:11).

I. "But the Torah was given over a period of forty days, as it was said, 'And he was there with the Lord for forty days and forty nights' (Ex. 34:28).

J. "And it is written, 'And I remained on the mountain for forty days and forty nights'" (Deut. 9:9).

5. A. When R. Yohanan died, his generation recited concerning him (the following verse of Scripture): "If a man should give all the wealth of his house for the love" (Song 8:7), with which R. Yohanan loved the Torah, "he would be utterly destitute" (Song 8:7).

6. A. Said R. Abba bar Kahana, "On the basis of the reward paid for one act of 'taking,' you may assess the reward for (taking) the palm branch (on the festival of Tabernacles).
   B. "There was an act of taking in Egypt: 'You will take a bunch of hyssop' (Ex. 12:22).
   C. "And how much was it worth? Four *manehs*.
   D. "Yet that act of taking is what made Israel inherit the spoil at the sea, the spoil of Sihon and Og, and the spoil of the thirty-one kings.
   E. "Now the palm-branch, which costs a person such a high price, and which involves so many religious duties—how much the more so (will a great reward be forthcoming on its account)!"
   F. Therefore Moses admonished Israel, saying to them, "And you shall take on the first day...." (Lev. 23:39).

Section i.1B seems to me to employ Is. 55:2 as an intersecting verse for the base verse of Prov. 8:10. That, at any rate, is the force of the exegesis of i.1C–G. Then the citation of Prov. 9:5 presents a secondary expansion of what has been said about Is. 55:2, that is, i.1F–G lead us directly to H. What has happened to Lev. 23:39? In fact, i.1B–H are inserted whole because of the use of the key word "take" at Lev. 23:39 and Prov. 8:10. From that point, Lev. 23:39 plays no role whatsoever. It is only at section i.6F that Lev. 23:39—with stress on the word "take"—recurs. The theme of the intervening passages is established at i.1B, namely, Torah and the value and importance of study of Torah. Sections i.2, i.3, i.4, and i.5, which I have slightly abbreviated, all present variations on amplifications of that theme. Since section i.6 ignores all that has gone before, and since section i.6 alone alludes to i.1A, we have to regard as remarkable the insertion of the rather sizable construction, i.1B through i.5E.

Theological discourse: saying one thing through many things

In the middle Midrash compilations, from *Genesis Rabbah* through *Leviticus Rabbah*, and routinely in all the late Midrash compilations, such as *Song of Songs Rabbah* and *Lamentations Rabbah*, we find a particular form that intends to conduct symbolic, as distinct from propositional and syllogistic discourse.[2] The form, "another matter," is based upon the repeated citation of a verse of Scripture, and the successive imputation of various meanings, entirely cogent with one another, to each component of that verse. A strikingly limited repertoire of persons, events, or actions comprises all of the lists of these "other matters." This is meant to provide a further illustration of the governing proposition, part of the

---

[2] On symbolic discourse in verbal form, see this writer's *Symbol and Theology in Early Judaism*. Minneapolis: Fortress Press, 1991. On "another matter" formations, see William Scott Green, "Writing with Scripture," which is Chapter Two of *Writing with Scripture*.

propositional exposition. "Another matter" means, "another example of the same proposition." It is, then, an exercise in propositional demonstration and part of an unfolding proof.

In the context of the "another-matter" composition, "Moses" or "David" or "Israel at the sea" serve no propositional purpose at all, but each is available for combination with other signs into aggregates meant to bear meaning, even to make points, solely in accord with the syntax and grammar of symbolic discourse. "David" or "Moses" in symbolic discourse bears no determinate meaning at all. Only in combination do "David" and "Moses" or "shofar" and "menorah" gain any signification at all. It emerges not from the words that are used, but from the combinations that are made; combinations of the (otherwise meaningless) parsed components of the verse at hand, along with the (otherwise senseless) symbolic signs that are used.

Let me give a single example of an "another-matter" composition.

Song of Songs Rabbah I:i.1, 3–9

1. A. "The song of songs:"
   B. This is in line with that which Scripture said through Solomon: "Do you see a man who is diligent in his business? He will stand before kings, he will not stand before mean men" (Prov. 22:29).
   C. "Do you see a man who is diligent in his business:"
   D. This refers to Joseph: "But one day, when he went into the house to do his work (and none of the men of the house was there in the house, she caught him by his garment, saying, 'Lie with me.' But he left his garment in her hand and fled and got out of the house)" (Gen. 39:10–13).

We skip an inserted gloss and yield directly to section i.3:

3. A. "He will stand before kings:"
   B. this refers to Pharaoh: "Then Pharaoh sent and called Joseph and they brought him hastily from the dungeon" (Gen. 41:14).
4. A. "he will not stand before mean men:"
   B. this refers to Potiphar, whose eyes the Holy One blessed be he darkened (the word for 'darkened' and 'mean men' share the same consonants), and whom he castrated.
5. A. Another interpretation of the verse, "Do you see a man who is diligent in his business" (Prov. 22:29):
   B. this refers to our lord, Moses, in the making of the work of the tabernacle.
   C. Therefore: "He will stand before kings."
   D. this refers to Pharaoh: "Rise up early in the morning and stand before Pharaoh" (Ex. 8:16).
   E. "he will not stand before mean men:"

      F. this refers to Jethro.
6.   A. Another interpretation of the verse, "Do you see a man who is diligent in his business" (Prov. 22:29):
      B. this refers to those righteous persons who are occupied with the work of the Holy One, blessed be he.
      C. Therefore: "He will stand before kings."
      D. this refers to "for they stand firm in the Torah:" "By me kings rule" (Prov. 8:15).
      E. "he will not stand before mean men:"
      F. this refers to the wicked: "And their works are in the dark" (Is. 29:15); "Let their way be dark and slippery" (Ps. 35:6).
7.   A. Another interpretation of the verse, "Do you see a man who is diligent in his business" (Prov. 22:29):
      B. this refers to R. Hanina.

The reference now receives the necessary gloss: what exactly made Hanina "diligent in his business?" I indent the gloss to highlight its function.

    8. A. They say:
        B. One time he saw people of his village bringing whole offerings and peace offerings up (on a pilgrimage to the Temple).
        C. He said, "All of them are bringing peace offerings to Jerusalem, but I am not bringing up a thing! What shall I do?"
        D. Forthwith he went out to the open fields of his town, the unoccupied area of his town, and there he found a stone. He went and plastered it and polished it and painted it and said, "Lo, I accept upon myself the vow to bring it up to Jerusalem."
        E. He sought to hire day-workers, saying to them, "Will you bring this stone up to Jerusalem for me?"
        F. They said to him, "Pay us our wage, a hundred gold pieces, and we'll be glad to carry your stone up to Jerusalem for you."
        G. He said to them, "Where in the world will I get a hundred gold pieces, or even fifty, to give you?"
        H. Since at the time he could not find the funds, they immediately went their way.
        I. Immediately the Holy One, blessed be he, arranged to have fifty angels in the form of men (meet him). They said to him, "My lord, give us five selas (a standard coin of daily use), and we shall bring your stone to Jerusalem, on condition that you help us with the work."
        J. So he put his hand to the work with them, and they found themselves standing in Jerusalem. He wanted to pay them their wage, but he could not find them.
        K. The case came to the Chamber of the Hewn Stone (where the high court was in session). They said to him, "It appears that in the case of our lord, ministering angels have brought the stone up to Jerusalem."

L. Immediately he gave sages that wage for which he had hired the angels.
9. A. Another interpretation of the verse, "Do you see a man who is diligent in his business" (Prov. 22:29):
B. this refers to Solomon son of David.
C. "He will stand before kings."
D. for he was diligent in building the house of the sanctuary: "So he spent seven years in building it" (1 Kgs. 6:38).

The basic outlines are not difficult to discern. We have an intersecting verse, Prov. 22:29, aimed at reaching the goal of Solomon, who is author of the Song of Songs, and presenting him in the context of Joseph, the righteous persons, and Moses, four in all. The reason in both cases is the same: each one of them "stood before kings, not before mean men." Our proposed fixed formula then involves examples of the righteous, who are judged by those worthy of judging them. The invocation of the figure of Joseph ought to carry in its wake the contrast between the impure lust of Potiphar's wife and the pure heart of Joseph, and, by extension, Solomon in the Song. But I do not see that motif present. Section i.2, which I have omitted, is then included as part of the Joseph-sequence, but it does not occur in the parallel. Section i.3 then resumes the broken form, and Section i.4 completes it. So the first statement of the formal program is not difficult to follow. The fact that the words for "mean" and "dark" share the same consonants accounts for the sequence of applications of the third clause to the theme of darkness. The second exercise, with Moses, is laid out with little blemish in Section i.5. Section i.6 goes on to the righteous, and here too the sages' passage is worked out with no interpolations. Section i.7, by contrast, provides an excuse to insert Section i.8. Without Section i.7, Section i.8 would prove incomprehensible in this context (though entirely clear standing on its own). Finally, at Section i.9, we come to Solomon.

Now to generalize on the case: In "another-matter" composites the figure of Moses, or the Exodus from Egypt, or Sennacherib, Nebuchadnezzar, and Belshazzar, occur over and over again, in one combination or another. In these combinations the restricted vocabulary of symbolic discourse makes possible a virtually limitless number of points. In this regard, therefore, these things occur not as denotative words, where sense is limited to particular circumstance. Nor do they appear bearing determinate sense, e.g., as solely connotative words, nor evoking a less-determinate sense, e.g., a particular emotion or an attitude that we can predict when a given word occurs. That explains why, as a matter of fact, the components of the "another-matter" compositions and composites, when seen in the aggregate, require classification not as words bearing determinate meaning (however broadly constructed) but as symbols in verbal, rather than iconic, representation. The reason for that claim requires emphasis: *whatever the words mean in particular has no bearing upon their utilization in symbolic discourse.*

The author of a given "another-matter" composition therefore accomplishes his goal through the combinations of things that he assembles to make his point.

It follows that, whether in iconic or verbal form, we deal with signs: words that are used as symbols as much as icons that are used as symbols.

Writing with Scripture: to what end?

So much for the classification of Midrash compilations: topical, propositional, symbolic. Through the classification and associated examples, we have seen how diverse and complex are the media that the Rabbinic sages devised for writing with Scripture: Midrash as exegetical method, Midrash as the result of that method, Midrash as the compilation of results. But however varied, all of their writings aim at a single reading of Scripture, to which we now turn, document by document.

3

Genesis in *Genesis Rabbah*

Recasting the Patriarchs into the Models for Israelite Conduct

What is the main point of *Genesis Rabbah*?

Classical Judaism reads the book of Genesis through the interpretative construction set forth in the Midrash compilation called *Genesis Rabbah*, a systematic, verse-by-verse analysis of the book of Genesis produced in the Land of Israel at ca. 450 C.E., about half a century after the Roman government legalized Christianity and adopted it as the religion of the state, a considerable crisis for the Rabbinic sages. They turned to Genesis to find in the stories of the beginnings the rules governing Israel, which would clarify the contemporary events and their meaning.

Genesis Rabbah transforms the book of Genesis from a genealogy and family history of Abraham, Isaac, Jacob, then Joseph, into a book of the laws of history and rules for the salvation of Israel. That is because the deeds of the founders become omens and signs for the final generations. The fundamental proposition, displayed throughout *Genesis Rabbah*, which yields the specific exegeses of many of the verses of the book of Genesis and even whole stories, is that the beginnings point toward the endings, and the meaning of Israel's past points toward the message that lies in Israel's future. The things that happened to the fathers and mothers of Israel, provide a sign for the things that will happen to the children later on.

In *Genesis Rabbah* the entire narrative of Genesis is so formed as to point toward the sacred history of Israel: its slavery and redemption; its restored Temple in Jerusalem; its exile and salvation at the end of time. The powerful message of Genesis in *Genesis Rabbah* proclaims that the world's creation commenced a single, straight line of events, leading in the end to the salvation of Israel and through Israel all humanity. Israel's history constitutes the counterpart of creation, and the laws of Israel's salvation form the foundation of creation. Therefore a given story out of Genesis, about creation, events from Adam to Noah and Noah to Abraham, the domestic affairs of the patriarchs, or Joseph, will bear a deeper message about what it means to be Israel, on the one side, and what in the end of days will happen to Israel, on the other.

So the persistent theological program requires sages to search in Scripture for meaning for their own circumstance and for the condition of their people. The single most important proposition of *Genesis Rabbah* is that, in the story of the beginnings of creation, humanity, and Israel, we find the message of the meaning and end of the life of the Jewish people. The deeds of the founders supply signals for the children about what is going to come in the future. So the biography of Abraham, Isaac, and Jacob also constitutes a protracted account of the history of Israel later on. If the sages could announce a single syllogism and argue it systematically, that is the proposition upon which they would insist.

As a corollary to the view that the biography of the fathers prefigures the history of the descendants, sages maintained that the deeds of the children—the holy way of life of Israel—follow the model established by the founders long ago. So they looked in Genesis for the basis for the things they held to be God's will for Israel. And they found ample proof. Sages invariably searched the stories of Genesis for evidence of the origins not only of creation and of Israel, but also of Israel's cosmic way of life, its understanding of how, in the passage of nature and the seasons, humanity worked out its relationship with God. The holy life that Israel lived through the seasons of nature therefore would make its mark upon the sages' understanding of the stories of the creation of the world and the beginning of Israel.

To what situation does *Genesis Rabbah* address itself?

Part of the reason sages pursued this interest derived from polemic: Christianity challenged Judaism on precisely these issues. From the first Christian century Christian theologians had maintained that salvation did not depend upon keeping the laws of the Torah. Abraham, after all, had been justified and he did not keep the Torah, which, in his day, had not yet been given. So sages time and again would maintain that Abraham indeed kept the entire Torah even before it had been revealed. For example, they attributed to Abraham, Isaac, and Jacob rules of the Torah enunciated only later on, as in the institution of prayer three times a day. But this Midrash interpretation also bears a different charge to Israel: to see how deeply embedded in the fabric of all reality were the patterns governing God's relationship to Israel. That relationship of human sin and atonement, divine punishment and forgiveness, expresses the most fundamental laws of human existence.

The world was created for Israel, and not for the nations. At the end of days everyone will see what only Israel now knows. Given that sages read Genesis as the history of the world with emphasis on Israel, then the lives portrayed, the domestic quarrels and petty conflicts with the neighbors, as much as the story of creation itself, all serve to yield insight into what was to be.

We now turn to a detailed examination of how sages spelled out the historical law at hand. The lives of the patriarchs prefigured the history of Israel. Every detail of the narrative therefore served to prefigure what was to be, and Israel found itself, time and again, in the revealed facts of the history of the creation of the world, the decline of humanity down to the time of Noah, and, finally, its ascent to Abraham, Isaac, and Israel. In order to illustrate the single approach to diverse stories, whether concerning Creation, Adam, and Noah, or concerning Abraham, Isaac, and Jacob, we focus on two cases: Abraham on the one side, and Rome on the other. In the former we see that Abraham serves, like Adam, to prove the point of it all. In the latter we observe how, in reading Genesis, the sages who compiled *Genesis Rabbah* discovered the meaning of the events of their own day.

Why the interest in the meaning of history?

Genesis Rabbah in its final form emerges from that momentous century in which the Roman Empire passed from pagan to Christian rule. In the aftermath of the Julian's abortive reversion to paganism, in ca. 360, which endangered the Christian character of the Roman empire, Christianity adopted a policy of repression of paganism that rapidly targeted Judaism as well. The issue confronting Israel in the Land of Israel therefore proved immediate: the meaning of the new and ominous turn of history, the implications of Christ's worldly triumph for the other-worldly and supernatural people, Israel, whom God chooses and loves. The message of the exegete-compositors addressed historical crisis and generated remarkable renewal, a rebirth of intellect in the encounter with Scripture, now in quest of the rules not of sanctification—these had already been found—but of salvation. So the book of Genesis, which portrays how all things had begun, would testify to the message and the method of the end: the coming salvation of patient, hopeful, enduring Israel.

In the view of the framers of the compilation, the entire narrative of Genesis is so formed as to point toward the sacred history of Israel, the Jewish people: its slavery and redemption; its coming Temple in Jerusalem; its exile and salvation at the end of time. In the reading of the authors at hand, therefore, the powerful message of Genesis proclaims that the world's creation commenced a single, straight line of events, leading in the end to the salvation of Israel and through Israel of all humanity. That message—that history's goal is Israel's salvation—the sages derived from the book of Genesis and was relevant to their own day. Therefore in their reading of Scripture a given story will bear a deeper truth about what it means to be Israel, on the one side, and what in the end of days will happen to Israel, on the other.

Why Rome in particular?

In the century prior to the closure of *Genesis Rabbah*, Rome had adopted Christianity as the state religion. This matter of deep concern focused sages' attention on the sequence of world-empires to which, among other nations, Israel was subjugated: Babylonia, Media, and Greece but Rome above all. What will follow? Sages maintained that beyond the rule of Rome lay the salvation of Israel:

Genesis Rabbah XLII:iv.4

A. Another matter: "And it came to pass in the days of Amraphael, king of Shinar" (Gen. 14:1) refers to Babylonia.
B. "Arioch, king of Ellasar" (Gen. 14:1) refers to Greece.
C. "Chedorlaomer, king of Elam" (Gen. 14:1) refers to Media.
D. "And Tidal, king of Goiim (nations)" (Gen. 14:1) refers to the wicked government (Rome), which conscripts troops from all the nations of the world.
E. Said R. Eleazar bar Abina, "If you see that the nations contend with one another, look for the footsteps of the king-messiah. You may know that that is the case, for lo, in the time of Abraham, because the kings struggled with one another, a position of greatness came to Abraham."

Obviously, Section iv.4 presents the most important reading of Gen 14:1, since it links the events of the life of Abraham to the history of Israel and even ties the whole to the messianic expectation. I suppose that any list of four kings will provoke inquiry into the relationship of the entries of that list to the four kingdoms among which history, in Israel's experience, is divided. The process of history flows in both directions. Just as what Abraham did prefigured the future history of Israel, so what the Israelites later on were to do imposed limitations on Abraham. Time and again events in the lives of the patriarchs prefigure the four monarchies, among which the fourth, last, and most intolerable was Rome.

Genesis is read as if it portrayed the history of Israel and Rome. That is the single obsession binding sages of *Genesis Rabbah* to common discourse with the text before them. Why Rome in the particular form it takes in *Genesis Rabbah*? And how come the obsessive character of the sages' disposition of the theme of Rome? Were their picture merely of Rome as tyrant and destroyer of the Temple three centuries earlier, we should have no reason to link the text to the problems of the age of Midrashic redaction and closure. But now it is Rome as Israel's brother, counterpart, and nemesis; Rome as the one thing standing in the way of Israel's, and the world's, ultimate salvation. So the stakes are different, and much higher. It is not a political Rome but a Christian and messianic Rome that is at issue: Rome as surrogate for Israel, Rome as obstacle to Israel. Why? The reason is that the religions, Judaism and Christianity, competed over shared Scripture, and Christians in the fourth century found in events the validation of their claim and the refutation of Judaism's claim. The confrontation with Rome came about because Rome in the reign of Constantine had first legalized Christianity, then adopted it as religion of the state. Christians claimed that their undreamt-of triumph validated their claim in behalf of Jesus Christ that he was King and royal Messiah. The Rabbinic sages looked to beginnings, just as the Church fathers from Eusebius in the time of Constantine to Augustine nearly a century later looked to beginnings, to explain contemporary events. And in Genesis the Rabbinic sages found the key to those events: Rome was Israel's competition and counterpart—and when Rome fell, Israel, God's people, would succeed at the end of days and all humanity would worship the one true God made known in the Torah of Sinai.

So Rome in its Christian form confronted Israel with a crisis that pagan Rome did not. The program of *Genesis Rabbah* constitutes a response to that crisis. With Christian Rome claiming that history had validated its reading of Scripture, the Rabbinic sages responded by facing that fact quite squarely and saying, "Indeed, it is as you say, a kind of Israel, an heir of Abraham as your texts explicitly claim. But we remain the sole legitimate Israel, the bearer of the birthright—we and not you. So you are our brother: Esau, Ishmael, Edom." And the rest follows.

By rereading the story of the beginnings, sages discovered the answer and the secret of the end. Rome claimed to be Israel, and, indeed, sages conceded, Rome shared the patrimony of Israel. That claim took the form of the Christians' appropriation of the Torah as "the Old Testament," so sages acknowledged a simple fact in acceding to the notion that, in some way, Rome too formed part of Israel. But it was the rejected part, the Ishmael, the Esau, not the Isaac, not the Jacob. The advent of Christian Rome precipitated the sustained, polemical, and, I think, rigorous and well-argued rereading of beginnings in light of the end. Rome then marked the conclusion of human history as Israel had known it. Beyond lie the coming of the true Messiah, the redemption of Israel, the salvation of the world, the end of time. So the issues were considerable, and when the sages spoke of Esau/Rome, as they often did, they confronted the life-or-death decision of the day.

What are the traits of the document?

Genesis Rabbah is made up of one hundred *parashiyyot,* and each *parashah,* or chapter, is comprised of as few as five and as many as fifteen subdivisions—probably five times larger than the book of Genesis itself. The hundred chapters' subdivisions each form cogent statements. That is to say, words join together to form autonomous statements, which then coalesce into cogent propositions in paragraph form. The smallest whole units of *Genesis Rabbah* contain cogent thought. We can discern the ideas presented in this composition. The use of the word "composition" is justified: there is thought, in logical sequence, in proportion, in order, with a beginning, a middle, and an end.

The coherence of the document derives from the program of the document as a whole, rather than from the joining of the smaller into the larger units of discourse and thought. The compilation does have its share of passages that hold together only through the logic of fixed association. But, overall, the document holds together through what we may call the governing purpose of the entire construction, not simply the sewing together of its components. What accomplishes the ultimate unification of *Genesis Rabbah* is two goals of its framers:

First, they wanted to read the book of Genesis in light of other books of the Hebrew Scriptures, so emphasizing the unity of the Scriptures. Second, they wanted to read the book of Genesis phrase by phrase, so emphasizing the historical progression of the tale at hand, from verse to verse, from event to event. So the book of Genesis now presents more than a single dimension. It tells the story of things that happened. The exegetes explain the meaning of these events, adding details and making explicit the implicit, unfolding the message. Read from beginning to end, time in the beginning moved in an orderly progression.

That brings us back to our starting point: in *Genesis Rabbah* the book of Genesis tells the laws that govern Israel's history. These laws apply at all times and under all circumstances. Facts of history, emerging at diverse times and under various circumstances, attest to uniform and simple laws of society and of history. That is why verses of Scripture originating here, there, everywhere, all serve equally well to demonstrate the underlying rules that govern. Out of the historical progression of Genesis is read a set of exemplifications of recurrent laws, and therein timeless rules take over. The book of Genesis is made greater than its first reading would suggest. Hence, *Genesis Rabbah* vastly expands the dimensions of the story of the creation of the world, humanity, and Israel.

A systematic exposition

Let us now turn to a systematic exposition of the principal theme of *Genesis Rabbah*: the convergence of past and future in Israel's immediate present and acutely contemporary presence. An important approach to the interpretation of Scripture that this document's framers pioneered is the imputation, to a single verse, of a wide variety of coherent, alternative readings. Later on this exegetical mode would be given its own form, introduced in Chapter 2 as "another matter," and a long sequence of "other matters" would be strung together. In fact, all of the "other matters" turn out to say the same thing, only in different ways, or to convey a single, coherent attitude, emotion, sentiment, or conception. But in the following, we find the substance of the hermeneutics, but not the form it would ultimately be given.

The point that the sequence of cases makes is, when Jacob saw the well in the field (Gen. 29:1) he perceived a tableau of the entirety of what we should call "Judaism," that is, the salvific moments of Israel's life, whether events or persons or celebrations or locations or activities.

Genesis Rabbah LXX:viii.2–7
(to Genesis 28:20–29:30)

2. A. "As he looked, he saw a well in the field [and lo, three flocks of sheep lying beside it, for out of that well the flocks were watered. The stone on the well's mouth was large, and when all the flocks were gathered

there, the shepherds would roll the stone from the mouth of the well and water the sheep, and put the stone back in its place upon the mouth of the well" (Gen. 29:1)]:

B. R. Hama bar Hanina interpreted the verse in six ways (that is, he divides the verse into six clauses and systematically reads each of the clauses in light of the others and in line with an overriding theme):

C. "'As he looked, he saw a well in the field:' this refers to the well (of water in the wilderness, Num. 21:17).

D. "'. . . and lo, three flocks of sheep lying beside it:' specifically, Moses, Aaron, and Miriam.

E. "'. . . for out of that well the flocks were watered:' from there each one drew water for his standard, tribe, and family."

F. "And the stone upon the well's mouth was great:"

H. (Reverting to Hama's statement:) "'. . . and put the stone back in its place upon the mouth of the well:' for the coming journeys."

The first interpretation (Section viii.2) applies the passage at hand to the life of Israel in the wilderness. The premise is the prevailing syllogism: Israel's future history is lived out, the first time around, in the lives of the patriarchs and matriarchs.

3. A. "'As he looked, he saw a well in the field:' refers to Zion.

B. "'. . . and lo, three flocks of sheep lying beside it:' refers to the three festivals.

C. "'. . . for out of that well the flocks were watered:' from there they drank of the holy spirit.

D. "'. . . The stone on the well's mouth was large:' this refers to the rejoicing of the house of the water-drawing."

E. Said R. Hoshaiah, "Why is it called 'the house of the water drawing'? Because from there they drink of the Holy Spirit."

F. "'. . . and when all the flocks were gathered there:' coming from 'the entrance of Hamath to the brook of Egypt' (1 Kgs. 8:66).

G. "'. . . the shepherds would roll the stone from the mouth of the well and water the sheep:' for from there they would drink of the Holy Spirit.

H. "'. . . and put the stone back in its place upon the mouth of the well:' leaving it in place until the coming festival."

Thus the second interpretation (Section viii.3) reads the verse in light of the Temple celebration of the Festival of Tabernacles.

4. A. "'. . . As he looked, he saw a well in the field:' this refers to Zion.

B. "'. . . and lo, three flocks of sheep lying beside it:' this refers to the three courts.

C. "'. . . for out of that well the flocks were watered:' for from there they would hear the ruling.
D. "'The stone on the well's mouth was large:' this refers to the high court that was in the chamber of the hewn stones.
E. "'. . . and when all the flocks were gathered there:' this refers to the courts in session in the Land of Israel.
F. "'. . . the shepherds would roll the stone from the mouth of the well and water the sheep:' for from there they would hear the ruling.
G. "'. . . and put the stone back in its place upon the mouth of the well:' for they would give and take until they had produced the ruling in all the required clarity."

The third interpretation (Section viii.4) reads the verse in light of the Israelite institution of justice and administration.

5. A. "'As he looked, he saw a well in the field:' this refers to Zion.
   B. "'. . . and lo, three flocks of sheep lying beside it:' this refers to the first three kingdoms (Babylonia, Media, Greece).
   C. "'. . . for out of that well the flocks were watered:' for they enriched the treasures that were laid up in the chambers of the Temple.
   D. "'. . . The stone on the well's mouth was large:' this refers to the merit attained by the patriarchs.
   E. "'. . . and when all the flocks were gathered there:' this refers to the wicked kingdom, which collects troops through levies from all the nations of the world.
   F. "'. . . the shepherds would roll the stone from the mouth of the well and water the sheep:' for they enriched the treasures that were laid up in the chambers of the Temple.
   G. "'. . . and put the stone back in its place upon the mouth of the well:' in the age to come the merit attained by the patriarchs will stand (in defense of Israel)."

So the fourth interpretation (Section viii.5) interweaves the themes of the Temple cult and the domination of the four monarchies.

6. A. "'As he looked, he saw a well in the field:' this refers to the Sanhedrin.
   B. "'. . . and lo, three flocks of sheep lying beside it:' this alludes to the three rows of disciples of sages that would go into session in their presence.
   C. "'for out of that well the flocks were watered:' for from there they would listen to the ruling of the law.
   D. "'. . . The stone on the well's mouth was large:' this refers to the most distinguished member of the court, who determines the law-decision.

E. "'... and when all the flocks were gathered there:' this refers to disciples of the sages in the Land of Israel.
F. "'... the shepherds would roll the stone from the mouth of the well and water the sheep:' for from there they would listen to the ruling of the law.
G. "'... and put the stone back in its place upon the mouth of the well:' for they would give and take until they had produced the ruling in all the required clarity."

The fifth interpretation (Section viii.6) again reads the verse in light of the Israelite institution of legal education and justice.

7. A. "'As he looked, he saw a well in the field:' this refers to the synagogue.
B. "'... and lo, three flocks of sheep lying beside it:' this refers to the three who are called to the reading of the Torah on weekdays.
C. "'... for out of that well the flocks were watered:' for from there they hear the reading of the Torah.
D. "'... The stone on the well's mouth was large:' this refers to the impulse to do evil.
E. "'... and when all the flocks were gathered there:' this refers to the congregation.
F. "'... the shepherds would roll the stone from the mouth of the well and water the sheep:' for from there they hear the reading of the Torah.
G. "'... and put the stone back in its place upon the mouth of the well:' for once they go forth (from the hearing of the reading of the torah) the impulse to do evil reverts to its place."

The sixth and last interpretation (Section viii.7) turns to the twin themes of the reading of the Torah in the synagogue and the evil impulse, temporarily driven off through the hearing of the Torah. The six themes read in response to the verse cover Israel in the wilderness, the Temple cult on festivals with special reference to Tabernacles, the judiciary and government, the history of Israel under the four kingdoms, the life of sages, and the ordinary folk and the synagogue. The whole is an astonishing repertoire of fundamental themes of the life of Israel: at its origins in the wilderness, in its cult, in its institutions based on the cult, in the history of the nations, and, finally, in the twin social estates of sages and ordinary folk, matched by the institutions of the master-disciple circle and the synagogue. The vision of Jacob at the well thus encompassed the whole of the social reality of Jacob's people, Israel. The labor of interpreting this same passage in the profound, typological context already established now goes forward.

Genesis Rabbah LXX:ix.1

A. R. Yohanan interpreted the statement in terms of Sinai:
B. " 'As he looked, he saw a well in the field:' this refers to Sinai.
C. " '... and lo, three flocks of sheep lying beside it:' these stand for the priests, Levites, and Israelites.
D. " '... for out of that well the flocks were watered:' for from there they heard the Ten Commandments.
E. " '... The stone on the well's mouth was large:' this refers to the Presence of God."
F. "... and when all the flocks were gathered there:"
G. R. Simeon b. Judah of Kefar Akum in the name of R. Simeon: "All of the flocks of Israel had to be present, for if any one of them had been lacking, they would not have been worthy of receiving the Torah."
H. (Returning to Yohanan's exposition:) " '... the shepherds would roll the stone from the mouth of the well and water the sheep:' for from there they heard the Ten Commandments.
I. " '... and put the stone back in its place upon the mouth of the well:' 'You yourselves have seen that I have talked with you from heaven' (Ex. 20:19)."

Yohanan's exposition adds what was left out, namely, reference to the revelation of the Torah at Sinai. Through the demonstration of the ubiquitous syllogism that Israel's history is the story of the lives of the founders, we now go over the same proposition again, with utterly fresh materials. This shows that the proposed syllogism reveals the deep structure of reality and provides the syntax that permits words to make diverse, yet intelligible statements. Once we have taken up this challenge, a still greater task requires us to make the same basic point in utterly different cases, and that allows us definitively to prove that syllogism as it is tested against diverse Scriptural cases.

Genesis Rabbah LXX:x.1

A. "Jacob said to them, 'My brothers, where do you come from?' They said, 'We are from Haran' (Gen. 29:40):
B. R. Yosé bar Haninah interpreted the verse at hand with reference to the Exile.
C. " 'Jacob said to them, "My brothers, where do you come from?"' They said, "We are from Haran:" that is, 'We are flying from the wrath of the Holy One, blessed be he.' (Here there is a play on the words for "Haran" and "wrath," which share the same consonants.)
D. " 'He said to them, "Do you know Laban the son of Nahor?"' The sense is this, 'Do you know him who is destined to bleach your sins as white as snow?' (Here there is a play on the words for "Laban" and "bleach," which share the same consonants.)

E. "'They said, "We know him." He said to them, "Is it well with him?" They said, "It is well."' On account of what sort of merit?

F. (Yosé continues his interpretation:) "'(The brothers go on,) ". . . and see, Rachel his daughter is coming with the sheep"' (Gen. 29:6–7).

G. "That is in line with this verse: 'Thus says the Lord, "A voice is heard in Ramah, lamentation and bitter weeping, Rachel weeping for her children. She refuses to be comforted." Thus says the Lord, "Refrain your voice from weeping . . . and there is hope for your future," says the Lord, and your children shall return to their own border"' (Jer. 31:15–16)."

In this case, the history of the redemption of Israel is located in the colloquy between Jacob and Laban's sons. The themes pour forth in profusion, forming propositions of a subordinate character.

Theological propositions of *Genesis Rabbah*

The propositions are divided among the principal category-formations of the Rabbinic theological structure. It is important to examine the details of the matter, since in Chapter Fifteen I propose that the Midrash compilations, while differentiated by logic, topic, and rhetoric, nonetheless participate in a common theology, governed by shared category-formations. Here we consider the category-formations of *Genesis Rabbah*.

God and man, man (Adam) and Israel, God and Israel

Given the narrative of the book of Genesis, we should not be surprised by evidence of an elaborate theological anthropology, which identifies what is implicit in the narrative, and which frames principles from the implications of the stories. And indeed, *Genesis Rabbah* forms a primary source of the Rabbinic anthropology, with its complete account of the history of mankind in its sequences: Adam and Eve in Eden; ten generations from Adam to Noah, the flood (the anti-Eden), then ten generations from Noah to Abraham, counterpart to Adam, a fresh start for mankind, and the consequent division of post-Flood mankind into the children of Noah and the children of Abraham.

God and man

God's relationship to man forms the primary category-formation of the Rabbinic theology set forth in the Midrash compilations. The propositions are many; the point, simple. All humanity is in God's likeness and comes from a single progenitor (*Gen. Rab.* XXIV:vii). Obedience is the mark of the virtuous person, rebellion defines sin (*Gen. Rab.* XXXIV:ii–iv). God particularly values the obedience of the martyrs (*Gen. Rab.* XXIV:ix). The difference between the wicked and the righteous is, the righteous control their impulses, the wicked are subordinate to them (Gen. Rab. XXXIV:x). But as man enjoys freedom of will, so God cannot be coerced, and he is invariably just (*Gen. Rab.* XXXIV:i). For God to commit injustice would be a profanation of the name of Heaven (*Gen. Rab.* XLIX:ix).

Adam and Israel

Israel forms God's stake in humanity, idolaters the component of humanity that hate God. In that context, however, Adam and Israel are comparable; both are quick to rebel and sin (*Gen. Rab.* XXVIII:v)). The Torah might have been given to Adam, not only to Moses. Indeed, God considered giving Adam the Torah, but when Adam could not keep even the six commandments assigned to him, God concluded that Adam could not keep the 613 commandments that the Torah put forth, so he decided to wait until Moses. So too Adam could have been the progenitor of the twelve tribes, but when Adam's son killed his brother, God gave up on the idea (*Gen. Rab.* XXIV:v). The world was created on account of the merit of Abraham (*Gen. Rab.* XII:ix).

On account of the sin of Adam and his heirs God departed from the world, but Abraham and his progeny returned God to the world. The principal location of the Presence of God was [meant to be] among the creatures down here. When the first man sinned, the Presence of God moved up to the first firmament. When Cain sinned, it went up to the second firmament. When the generation of Enosh sinned, it went up to the third firmament. When the generation of the Flood sinned, it went up to the fourth firmament. When the generation of the dispersion at the tower of Babel sinned, it went up to the fifth. On account of the Sodomites it went up to the sixth, and on account of the Egyptians in the time of Abraham it went up to the seventh. But, as a counterpart, there were seven righteous men who rose up: Abraham, Isaac, Jacob, Levi, Kohath, Amram, and Moses. They brought the Presence of God [by stages] down to earth. Abraham brought it from the seventh to the sixth, Isaac brought it from the sixth to the fifth, Jacob brought it from the fifth to the fourth, Levi brought it down from the fourth to the third, Kohath brought it down from the third to the second, Amram brought it down from the second to the first. Moses brought it down to earth (*Gen. Rab.* XIX:vii).

Adam and Israel set forth parallel histories, what happened to the one happened to the other as well. Thus:

Genesis Rabbah XIX:ix.2

A. R. Abbahu in the name of R. Yosé bar Haninah: "It is written, 'But they are like a man [Adam], they have transgressed the covenant' (Hos. 6:7).

B. "'They are like a man,' specifically, like the first man. [We shall now compare the story of the first man in Eden with the story of Israel in its land.]

C. "'In the case of the first man, I brought him into the garden of Eden, I commanded him, he violated my commandment, I judged him to be sent away and driven out, but I mourned for him, saying "How . . ."'[which begins the book of Lamentations, hence stands for a lament, but which, as we just saw, also is written with the consonants that also yield, 'Where are you'].

D. "'I brought him into the garden of Eden,' as it is written, 'And the Lord God took the man and put him into the garden of Eden' (Gen. 2:15).

E. "'I commanded him,' as it is written, 'And the Lord God commanded . . .' (Gen. 2:16).

F. "'And he violated my commandment,' as it is written, 'Did you eat from the tree concerning which I commanded you' (Gen. 3:11).

G. "'I judged him to be sent away,' as it is written, 'And the Lord God sent him from the garden of Eden' (Gen. 3:23).

H. "'And I judged him to be driven out.' 'And he drove out the man' (Gen. 3:24).

I. "'But I mourned for him, saying, "How . . ."' 'And he said to him, "Where are you"' (Gen. 3:9), and the word for 'where are you' is written, 'How . . .'

J. "'So too in the case of his descendants, [God continues to speak,] I brought them into the Land of Israel, I commanded them, they violated my commandment, I judged them to be sent out and driven away but I mourned for them, saying, "How. . . ."'

K. "'I brought them into the Land of Israel.' 'And I brought you into the land of Carmel' (Jer. 2:7).

L. "'I commanded them.' 'And you, command the children of Israel' (Ex. 27:20). 'Command the children of Israel' (Lev. 24:2).

M. "'They violated my commandment.' 'And all Israel have violated your Torah' (Dan. 9:11).

N. "'I judged them to be sent out.' 'Send them away, out of my sight and let them go forth' (Jer 15:1).

O. "'. . . and driven away.' 'From my house I shall drive them' (Hos. 9:15).

P. "'But I mourned for them, saying, "How. . . ."' 'How has the city sat solitary, that was full of people' (Lam. 1:1)."

God lamented driving Adam from Eden (*Gen. Rab.* XXI:ii).

God and the nations, Israel and the nations

The counterpart of Adam is Israel; the counterpart of Israel is the nations, made up of individuals. Israel alone forms a corporate moral entity. Abraham represents Israel. God's care of Abraham kept Abraham from danger and error, both in his father's house and afterward; and God cares for the nations and so sends them men who can teach them to do better (LII:xi). The nations of the world were given dominion with the advent of Isaac but lost it when they separated themselves at Sinai and did not accept the Torah (LIII:ix).

Just as in the case of a palm tree, there is nothing that is left as refuse, for the dates are eaten, the branches used for reciting the Hallel-psalms [on the festival of Tabernacles], the twigs used for *Sukkah*-roofing on the same festival, the bast is used for ropes, the leaves are used for besoms, the planed boards used for making ceilings for rooms, the same is so of Israel. There is none among them who lacks value. Some of them are masters of Scripture, some masters of Mishnah teachings, some masters of Talmud [study], some of them are masters of lore (XLI:i).

So much for Israel, what of the nations? The nations are murderous, Israel is docile; God will require the blood shed by the four kingdoms, Babylonia, Media, Greece, and Rome (XXXIV:xiii). The nations are answerable to God for how they treat Israel (XX:i). Israel's claim on the Land of Israel is validated by the account of Creation. It was God who made the world, and he has the right to dispose of it as he wishes (I:ii). The earth would be punished by reason of the deeds of man (II:ii). God was pleased in creation by the actions of nature, which gave praise, but found only rebellion from Man, thus Enosh, the generation of the Flood, the generation of the dispersion (V:i). The evil impulse lusts for Cain and his fellows, and the lust of God is only for Israel (XX:vii).

But while the nations are, in general, undifferentiated, genealogy singles out one nation as comparable to Israel, and that is Rome. Israel's counterpart and opposite among the nations is Rome, represented in Genesis by Esau, Jacob's twin. The one corresponds to the other, as exact opposite (LXIII:vi). Jacob's descendants would spread throughout the world, would endure by the merit of Torah-study, would benefit from humiliation by the nations and in their humility would triumph over the nations (LXIX:v). Jacob further foresaw the building, destruction, and restoration of the Temple (LXIX:vii). Esau will govern, then Jacob will take over (LXXV:iv). But God will embitter the rule of Edom/Esau/Rome, the Germans being feared by the Romans (LXXV:ix).

Israel's encounter with God through the Torah

The religious duties were given in the Torah only in order to purify mankind (XLIV:i). The Torah is not the only way to God. Reasoned argument opens the path as well. For example, Abraham reasoned his way to belief in one God: " 'Is it possible for the world to endure without someone in charge,' the Holy One, blessed be he, responded and looked out and said to him, 'I am the one in charge of the house, the lord of all the world'" (XXXIX:i). He was the first to reason in that way. He had no commandments to guide him, no revelation to instruct him (XXXIX:iii). He came at the end of the generations of Enosh, the Flood, and the Dispersion, the first point of light beyond the Flood itself (XXXIX:v). By accepting God's commandment without ado, he showed his perfect faith (XXXIX:ix).

The Torah is God's gift to the world, along with light and rain (VI:v). But one should not speculate about what the Torah itself does not reveal; rather, one should concentrate on what has happened since man was placed on earth (VIII:ii). Israel attains merit through Torah study, and thereby Israel is able to endure while the nations come to naught.

Genesis Rabbah XLI:ix.1

A. "I will make your descendants as the dust of the earth" (Gen. 13:16):
B. Just as the dust of the earth is from one end of the world to the other, so your children will be from one end of the world to the other.
C. Just as the dust of the earth is blessed only with water, so your children will be blessed only through the merit attained by study of the Torah, which is compared to water [hence: through water].
D. Just as the dust of the earth wears out metal utensils and yet endures forever, so Israel endures while the nations of the world come to an end.
E. Just as the dust of the world is treated as something on which to trample, so your children are treated as something to be trampled upon by the government.

The end of days

In the age to come both Israelites and gentiles will be afraid (XLVIII:vi). The future condition of the world is encompassed within creation, e.g., the destruction of the Temple in the time of Jeremiah (II:i). The nations will restore to the King-Messiah the gifts that Jacob gave to Esau (LXXVIII:xii). Every wound that God inflicts in this world he heals in the world to come.

Genesis Rabbah XCV:i.1

C. ...[..."Then the eyes of the blind shall be opened, then shall the lame man leap as a hart, and the tongue of the dumb shall sing" (Is. 35:5).]
G. All are healed, but just as a person goes out, so he comes back to life.
H. If he goes out blind, he comes back blind, if he goes out deaf, he comes back deaf, if he goes out dumb, he comes back dumb, if he goes out lame, he comes back lame.
I. Just as he is garbed when he goes out, so he is garbed when he comes back: "It is changed as clay under the seal, and they stand as in a garment" (Job 38:14).
L. And why is it the case that just as a person goes out, so he comes back to life?

M. It is so that the wicked of the world will not claim that, after they have died the Holy One, blessed be he, will heal them and afterward bring them back to life. It then would appear that these are not the ones who died, but others.

N. Accordingly, the Holy One, blessed be he, says, "If so, let them rise up out of the dust just as they went, and afterward I shall heal them."

O. Why so? "That you may know that . . . before me there was no God formed, neither shall any be after me" (Is. 43:10).

Conclusion

In *Genesis Rabbah* the sages show in detail the profound depths of the story of the creation of the world and Israel's founding family. Bringing their generative proposition about the character of the Scripture to the stories at hand, they systematically found in the details of the tales the history of the people Israel portrayed in the lives and deeds of the founders, the fathers and the mothers of this book of the Torah. It is no accident that the exegetes of the book of Genesis invoke large-scale constructions of history to make fundamental judgments about society—Israel's society. Nor is it merely happenstance that the exegetes bring into juxtaposition distinct facts of scriptural history or appeal to a typological reading of the humble details of the scriptural tale, for example the simple statement that the shepherds had brought their flocks to the well. A large proposition has governed the details of exegesis, and the individual verses commonly, though not always, address their facts in the proof of an encompassing hypothesis, a theorem concerning Israel's fate and faith. This is what we mean when we say that the Rabbinic sages wrote with Scripture—a dense and complex statement conveying a simple and coherent message.

4

Exodus in *Mekhilta attributed to R. Ishmael*

Reorganizing the Facts of Scripture into Coherent Expositions on Important Topics

Identifying *Mekhilta attributed to R. Ishmael*

The book of Exodus is mediated to Rabbinic Judaism by *Mekhilta attributed to R. Ishmael* (Mekhilta). By contrast to *Genesis Rabbah*, it is miscellaneous and does not set forth a coherent and systematic reading of the biblical book. That fact makes defining the document difficult. We cannot identify a coherent argument running through the expositions of diverse themes, such as we find in *Genesis Rabbah*. What we do encounter are expositions of topics, not systematic arguments on all-encompassing propositions.

The compilers and authors make no one point over and over again. They undertake no sustained, methodical analysis that joins bits and pieces of exegesis into a large-scale composition bearing a consistent meaning. They do not pursue a single range of problems in such a way as to demonstrate, in many ways and through discrete results, a single cogent position. Yet because of its very miscellaneous character, the document affords access to the unarticulated theology that animates the Rabbinic exegesis of Exodus.

While the date of the document is subject to debate, the consensus of scholarship today tends to favor ca. 250–300 C.E. But, unlike *Genesis Rabbah* in its context, none of the points of emphasis of Mekhilta can be correlated with particular concerns of that period.

The document seen in the aggregate presents a composite of three kinds of materials concerning the book of Exodus:

(1) a set of *ad hoc* and episodic exegeses of some, but not all, passages of Exodus;

(2) a group of propositional and argumentative essays in exegetical form, in which theological principles are set forth and demonstrated;

(3) topical compositions—what we might call articles—some of them sustained, many of them well-crafted, about important subjects.

The document covers Ex. 12:1–23:19, Ex. 31:12–13, and Ex. 35:1–3. It is comprised of nine free-standing tractates, Pisha (Ex. 12:1–13:16), Beshallah (Ex. 13–17, 14–31), Shirata (Ex. 15:1–21), Vayassa (Ex. 15:22–17:7), Amalek (Ex. 17:8–18:27), Bahodesh (Ex. 19:1–20:26), Neziqin (Ex. 21:1–22:23), Kaspa (Ex. 22:24–23:19), and Shabbata (Ex. 31:12–17 and 35:1–3). There are eighty-two sections, subdivided into paragraphs. The divisions of the book of Exodus into tractates bear no relationship to the prescribed lections read in the synagogue today.

An encyclopaedia of information, not a focused, argumentative statement

Seen as an exercise in writing with Scripture, Mekhilta is comparable to an encyclopaedia. A scriptural encyclopedia joins together expositions of topics, disquisitions on propositions, in general precipitated by the themes of scriptural narrative or the dictates of biblical law. It collects and arranges the exegeses (paraphrases or brief explanations of clauses of biblical verses) in accord with Scripture's order and program. The facts comprise a corpus of information, to which people require ready access. What is provided, then, is an encyclopedia of things one should know on themes Scripture dictates, and the sequence of topics and propositions follows the order demanded by Scripture.

Facts in support of a proposition

That is not to suggest that the compilers of the document have not undertaken to prove propositions. Episodically, they did. What they did not do was impose upon the reading of Exodus an all-encompassing viewpoint, a unitary perspective. But their topical expositions and ad hoc propositional arguments certainly show purpose. Scripture is searched for probative examples, and many are collected in what serves as a theological syllogism, as in the following demonstration that God humbles the arrogant in that very thing in which they take pride:

Mekhilta XXVII:ii.1, 4–7, 9–17

1. A. "I will sing to the Lord, for he is highly exalted; [the horse and his rider he has thrown into the sea]:"
4. A. Another teaching concerning "for he is highly exalted:"
   B. "He is exalted above all who take pride in themselves."
   C. For with that in which the nations of the world take pride before him he exacts punishment from them.

What follows is a series of cases, which are summarized below: the generation of the Flood, the generation of the Tower of Babel, and the men of Sodom, the Egyptians, Sisera, Samson, Absalom, Sennacherib, Nebuchadnezzar, Tyre, the nations of the world—all supply probative cases for that one proposition, beautifully articulated:

> 4. D. For so Scripture says in connection with the men of the generation of the flood, "Their bull genders . . . they send forth their little ones . . . they sing to the timbrel and harp and rejoice" (Job 21:10–12).
> 5. A. R. Yosé of Damascus says, "Since they set their eyes both above and below to express their lust. So the Holy One, blessed be he, opened up against them the springs above and below so as to destroy them.
> 6. A. And along these same lines, you found in connection with the men of the tower [of Babel], that with that in which they took pride before him he exacts punishment from them.
> 7. A. And along these same lines, you found in connection with the men of Sodom, that with that in which they took pride before him he exacts punishment from them.
> 9. A. So you find in the case of the Egyptians that with that in which they took pride before him he exacts punishment from them.
> 10. A. So you find in the case of Sisera that with that in which he took pride before him he exacts punishment from him.
> 11. A. So you find in the case of Samson that with that in which he took pride before him he exacts punishment from him.
> 12. A. So you find in the case of Absalom that with that in which he took pride before him he exacts punishment from him.
> 13. A. So you find in the case of Sennacherib that with that in which he took pride before him he exacts punishment from him.
> 14. A. So you find in the case of Nebuchadnezzar that with that in which he took pride before him he exacts punishment from him.
> 15. A. So you find in the case of Tyre that with that in which they took pride before him he exacts punishment from them.
> 16. A. So you find in the case of the prince of Tyre that with that in which he took pride before him he exacts punishment from him.
> 17. A. Lo, with that in which the nations of the world take pride before him he exacts punishment from them:"

We are not left in doubt as to the point of the collected cases: God's justice is exact, so that he exacts punishment by means of the very thing in which people take pride. But this proposition joins up with no others. No larger polemic animates the entire compilation, no recurrent proof of kindred propositions, along the lines of the one before us.

Where we find coherent components

That miscellaneous character of the whole tract should not obscure the fact that the parts really do form coherent statements, each on its own. Indeed, what makes the document interesting is the laconic and uncontroversial character of its discourse. Its framers clearly take for granted that what they are telling us are the established, accepted truths of the faith. That is why they can find it appropriate just to collect and present information, certain of the knowledge that everyone knows what they say is so. The main points that this Midrash compilation makes in its several parts may be conveniently divided into three classifications: (1) generalizations about the character of Scripture, (2) rules for correct conduct, and (3) theological teachings, with special reference to the relationship between Israel and God and the implications of that relationship for the fate of Israel among the nations. The first two are in volume and intellectual dimensions not imposing, the third is enormous and important, bearing the weight of the burden of our document. Here are some points of general intelligibility that register:

Traits of Scripture

The order in which Scripture sets forth two or more propositions does not necessarily indicate the priority assigned to those items. Scripture itself will dictate priority. Scripture uses euphemistic language. Scripture is not bound by temporal considerations, e.g., of sequence.

The moral life in Israel

When one party pays respect to another, they speak in harmony. With the measure with which one metes out to others is one's own reward meted out. When one welcomes a fellow it is as if one welcomed the face of the Presence of God. Do not favor either rich or poor in judging a case.

Theological convictions

These add up to a great collection of the basic theses of the theology of Rabbinic Judaism. They include the following mélange of points:

God and Israel

Through doing religious duties Israel was redeemed, and preparation of the rite well in advance was the religious duty to which redemption for Israel would serve as reward. What God says he will do, he does. Wherever Scripture indicates that God has said something, we can find in some other passage precisely where and what he had said. The upshot, of course, is that by carefully reading Scripture, we are able to identify the rules that govern history and salvation. The vindication of Moses's demands of Pharaoh turns the demands into prophecies of precisely what would come about. This is further underlined by the careful delineation of the degradation and humiliation of Pharaoh, portrayed as running about. And then comes the striking contrast between the reverence in which Israelites hold the rule of God and the humiliation of the Egyptian ruler. People get what is coming to them. Divine punishment is inexorable, so too divine reward. When God exacts punishment of the nations, his name is made great in the world. Merit is what saved Israel at the sea. The issue to be pursued is, what sort of merit, e.g., deriving from what actions or persons? The acts of healing of the Holy One, blessed be he, are not like the acts of healing of mortals. The redemption at the sea prefigures the redemption at the end of time. Faith in God is what saves Israel.

As we saw just now, God punishes the arrogant person by exacting a penalty precisely from that about which such a person takes pride. With that in which the nations of the world take pride before him he exacts punishment from them. Numerous cases on a long line of instances, based upon historical facts provided by Scripture, serve to demonstrate that proposition. Israel is unique among the nations. Mortals have the power to praise and glorify God. God takes many forms. The Lord is master of all media of war. The Lord needs none of those media. The Lord is a man of war, but the Lord is in no way comparable to a man of war, because he makes war in a supernatural way, specifically by retaining, even while making war, the attributes of mercy and humanity. God is just, and God's justice insures that the worthy are rewarded and the unworthy are penalized. God responds to human actions and attitudes. Those who oppose Israel are as though they opposed God. God is unique and God's salvation at the sea will be repeated at the end of time.

Israel's election

Israel gained great merit because it alone was willing to accept the Ten Commandments. The Israelites deserve praise for accepting the Torah. The "other gods" are not really gods at all. They are called "other" for various theological reasons. Suffering is precious and will not be rejected. One must not act in regard to God the way the outsiders treat their gods. They honor their gods in good times, not in bad, but Israel, exemplified by Job, honors God in bad time as much as in good. These fundamental principles of faith hardly exhaust the allusions to, or representations of, theological and normative statements in Mekhilta. They represent only those convictions that are spelled out in massive detail and argued with great force, the points of emphasis within a vast fabric of faith.

What we see is a reprise of Scripture's own doctrines, implicit or explicit, on the matters subject to discussion. Rabbinic Judaism in form and polemic claims to recapitulate the message of the written Torah, and through the Midrash process registers and establishes that claim. No wonder, then, that in Mekhilta we are dealing with a repertoire of established, normative dogmas of Rabbinic Judaism, defined as a recapitulation of Scripture. And that we may rely on Mekhilta for an account of that Judaism is further to be gainsaid. For nothing in the representation just now set forth points toward controversy or can be shown to contradict convictions contained within other documents. In Mekhilta we therefore deal with a compilation of authoritative teachings of Scripture, not a sustained argument particular to the Rabbinic sages to which Scripture contributes mere pretexts.

A sample passage

The *ad hoc,* topical exposition of the Torah's own truths is best exemplified in the document's presentation of the Ten Commandments. The presentation focuses upon clarification and amplification, but it is Scripture's statements, not the Rabbinic sages' program, that dictate the points that are to register.

Mekhilta LI:i.1, 4–5, 8–10

1. A. "[And God spoke all these words, saying,] 'I am the Lord your God, [who brought you out of the land of Egypt, out of the house of bondage]:'"
   B. How come the Ten Commandments were not stated at the very beginning of the Torah?
   C. The matter may be compared to the case of a king who came into a city. He said to the people, "May I rule over you?"
   D. They said to him, "Have you done us any good, that you should rule over us?"
   E. What did he then do? He built a wall for them, brought water for them, fought their battles.
   F. Then he said to them, "May I rule over you?"
   G. They said to him, "Yes, indeed."
   H. So the Omnipresent brought the Israelites out of Egypt, divided the sea for them, brought manna down for them, brought up the well for them, provided the quail for them, made war for them against Amalek.
   I. Then he said to them, "May I rule over you?"
   J. They said to him, "Yes, indeed."

The aim of the exegete here is to answer the question stated at the outset: why are the Ten Commandments situated where they are, and, given their primary importance, not earlier? The answer is cogent, but it leads to no further exposition, e.g., other passages that are situated out of the anticipated order or position.

The next noteworthy passage asks why the Ten Commandments begin with God's identifying himself with the language, "I am the Lord your God." The answer is compelling, but it does not join together with other propositions to register some point beyond any of them.

4. A. "I am the Lord your God:"
   B. Why is this stated? Since when he appeared at the sea, it was in the form of a mighty soldier making war, as it is said, "The Lord is a man of war" (Ex. 15:3),
   C. and when he appeared to them at Sinai, it was as an elder, full of mercy, as it is said, "And they saw the God of Israel" (Ex. 24:10)

D. and when they were redeemed, what does Scripture say? "And the like of the very heaven for clearness" (Ex. 24:10); "I beheld until thrones were placed and one that was ancient of days sat" (Dan. 7:9); "A fiery stream issued" (Dan. 7:10) —

E. [so God took on many forms.] It was, therefore, not to provide the nations of the world with an occasion to claim that there are two dominions in heaven,

F. that Scripture says, "I am the Lord your God [who brought you up out of the land of Egypt, out of the house of bondage]:"

G. [This then bears the message:] "I am the one in Egypt, I am the one at the sea, I am the one at Sinai; I am the one in the past and I am the one in the age to come, the one in this age is the one in the world to come: See now that I, even I, am he" (Dt. 32:39); "Even to old age I am the same" (Is. 46:4); "Thus says the Lord, the king of Israel and his redeemer, the Lord of hosts: 'I am the first and I am the last'" (Is. 44:6); "Who has wrought and done it? He who called the generations from the beginning. I the Lord who am the first and with the last I am the same" (Is. 41:4).

Now a contemporary issue is introduced, namely, the Minim, who try to prove on the basis of Scripture that there are two dominions in Heaven, not a single omnipotent God at all. So the main point now registers: God alone is in charge.

5. A. R. Nathan says, "In this connection we find a refutation of the minim, who maintain that there are two dominions.

B. "When the Holy One, blessed be he, went and said, 'I am the Lord your God, [who brought you out of the land of Egypt, out of the house of bondage],' who went and opposed him?

C. "If you maintain that it was in secret that the matter was carried out, is it not said, 'I have not spoken in secret' (Is. 45:19), 'I did not say to the children of Jacob' (Is. 45:19), that to these only will I give it.

D. "'They sought me in the desert' (Is. 45:19): did I not give it in public? And so too: 'I the Lord speak righteousness, I declare things that are right' (Is. 45:19)."

The same verse provokes a completely distinct exposition. It concerns the nations of the world and their response to God's self-manifestation at Sinai. Why did the nations not assemble, instead of Israel at Sinai, and why did they not accept the Torah? That question certainly is provoked by the narrative of Exodus:

8. A. The nations of the world were approached [to accept the Torah], so as not to give them an excuse to say, "If we had been approached, we should have accepted responsibility [for carrying out the Torah]."

B. Lo, they were approached but did not accept responsibility for them, as it is said, "The Lord came from Sinai" (Dt. 33:2).

9. A. ["The Lord came from Sinai" (Dt. 33:2):]
   B. [When the Omnipresent appeared to give the Torah to Israel, it was not to Israel alone that he revealed himself but to every nation.]
   C. First of all he came to the children of the wicked Esau. He said to them, "Will you accept the Torah?"
   D. They said to him, "What is written in it?"
   E. He said to them, "'You shall not murder' (Ex. 20:13)."
   F. They said to him, "The very being of 'those men' [namely, us] and of their father is to murder, for it is said, 'But the hands are the hands of Esau'(Gen. 27:22). 'By your sword you shall live' (Gen. 27:40)."
   G. So he went to the children of Ammon and Moab and said to them, "Will you accept the Torah?"
   H. They said to him, "What is written in it?"
   I. He said to them, "'You shall not commit adultery' (Ex. 20:13)."
   J. They said to him, "[The very essence of fornication belongs to them (us)], all of us are the children of fornication, for it is said, 'Thus were both the daughters of Lot with child by their fathers' (Gen. 19:36)."
   K. So he went to the children of Ishmael and said to them, "Will you accept the Torah?"
   L. They said to him, "What is written in it?"
   M. He said to them, "'You shall not steal' (Ex. 20:13)."
   N. They said to him, "This is the blessing that was stated to our father: 'And he shall be a wild ass of a man' (Gen. 16:12) 'For indeed I was stolen away out of the land of the Hebrews' (Gen. 49:15)."
   O. But when he came to the Israelites: "At his right hand was a fiery law for them" (Dt. 33:2).
   P. They all opened their mouths and said, "All that the Lord has spoke we shall do and we shall hear" (Ex. 24:7).
   Q. "He stood and measured the earth, he beheld and drove asunder the nations" (Hab. 3:6).

The nations of the world were offered the Torah and declined. The secondary exposition of that theme introduces the religious duties assigned after the flood to all humanity, that is, the children of Noah. How do the Ten Commandments pertain?

10. A. R. Simeon b. Eleazar says, "If the seven religious duties that were assigned to the children of Noah they could not uphold, how much the more so all the religious duties that are in the Torah!
    B. "The matter may be compared to the case of a king who set up two administrators, one in charge of the supply of straw, the other in charge of the supply of silver and gold.
    C. "The one in charge of the supply of straw was suspected of thievery, and he complained that he had not been appointed over the supply of silver and gold.

    D. "They said to him, 'Fool! If you have been suspected of stealing from the straw-supply, how are people going to entrust to you charge of the supply of silver and gold!'
    E. "Now this yields an argument a fortiori:
    F. "If the seven religious duties that were assigned to the children of Noah they could not uphold, how much the more so all the religious duties that are in the Torah!"

Enough of the exposition is in hand to show how *Mekhilta* encompasses well-crafted narratives and expositions. But we see no effort to compile them into a unified whole.

Our next sample passage shows how multiple meanings are discovered in a single passage. What is important to note is that all of them work with all others, and none contradicts any other. When, therefore, we review the range of possible interpretations, we see how a coherent theological perspective sustains a variety of detailed applications. If we translate the propositions inherent in the several readings of "You shall have no other gods before me" into abstract principles, we make good progress in reconstructing the theological structure and system that animate the Midrash method and its results.

Mekhilta LXII:i.1–7, 10

1. A. "You shall have no other gods before me" (Ex. 20:3):
   B. Why is this stated?
   C. Since it says, "I am the Lord your God."
   D. The matter may be compared to the case of mortal king who came to a town. His staff said to him, "Issue decrees for them."
   E. He said to them, "No. When they accept my dominion, then I shall issue decrees over them. For if they do not accept my dominion, how are they going to carry out my decrees?"
   F. So said the Omnipresent to Israel, "I am the Lord your God.
   G. "You shall have no other gods before me.
   H. "I am the one whose dominion you accepted upon yourselves in Egypt."
   I. They said to him, "Indeed so."
   J. "And just as you accepted my dominion upon yourself, now accept my decrees: 'You shall have no other gods before me.'"

When Israel accepted God's rule, it was with full knowledge and consent. First they accepted God's dominion, then his detailed decrees. The process is entirely rational, nothing arbitrary attaches to it.

2. A. ["The Lord spoke to Moses saying, 'Speak to the Israelite people and say to them, I am the Lord your God'" (Lev. 18:2):]

B. R. Simeon b. Yohai says, "That is in line with what is said elsewhere: 'I am the Lord your God [who brought you out of the land of Egypt, out of the house of bondage]' (Ex. 20:2).

C. "'Am I the Lord, whose sovereignty you took upon yourself in Sinai?'

D. "They said to him, 'Indeed.'

E. "'And just as you accepted my dominion upon yourself, now accept my decrees.'

F. "'You shall not copy the practices of the land of Egypt where you dwelt, or of the land of Canaan to which I am taking you; nor shall you follow their laws.'

G. "What is said here? 'I am the Lord your God [who brought you out of the land of Egypt, out of the house of bondage]' (Ex. 20:2).

H. "'Am I the Lord, whose sovereignty you took upon yourself?'

I. "They said to him, 'Indeed.'

J. "'And just as you accepted my dominion upon yourself, now accept my decrees.'

K. 'You shall have no other gods before me' (Ex. 20:3)."

The same issue persists: first the process of accepting God's dominion, then the decrees. Now the details begin: not to take up the practices of Canaan or continue those of Egypt. At issue, we shall now see, is graven images:

3. A. "You shall have [no other gods before me]" (Ex. 20:3):

B. Why is this stated?

C. Because it is said, "You shall not make for yourself a graven image [or any likeness of anything that is in heaven above, or that is in the earth beneath, or that is in the water under the earth; you shall not bow down to them or serve them]."

D. I know only that one may not make them. How do I know that as to one that is already made, one may not keep it?

E. Scripture says, "You shall have [no other gods before me]" (Ex. 20:3).

4. A. "other gods:"

B. Are they gods at all? Has it not already been stated, "And have cast their gods into the fire; for they were no gods, but the work of men's hands, wood and stone, therefore they have destroyed them" (Is. 37:19).

C. Why are they called "other gods" then?

D. It is because others call them gods.

5. A. Another comment on "other gods:"

B. They are Gods that hold back.

C. For they postpone [using the same letters as the word for "other"] goodness from coming into the world.

6. A. Another comment on "Other gods":

B. For they make those who worship them into other [strangers to the true God].

7. A. Another comment on "Other gods":
   B. They act like others [strangers] toward those who serve them.
   C. And so Scripture says, "Yes, though one cries to him, he cannot answer, nor save him out of his trouble" (Is. 46:7).
10. A. R. Eliezer says, "Why are they called 'other gods'?
    B. "For every day they make for themselves new gods.
    C. "How so? If one of them was of gold and the owner needs it, he makes it in silver instead, if it was in silver, he makes it over in copper, if it was copper, he makes it over in iron, if it was iron, he makes it over in tin, if it was tin and the owner needs it, he makes it over in lead, if it was lead and the owner needs it, he makes it over in wood.
    D. "So it is said, 'New gods that came newly up' (Dt. 32:17)."

The first implication of "other gods" is Halakhic: you may not make graven images, you also may not keep those made by others. Then the issue shifts to the theological problem: how can God refer to "other gods" as gods at all. That is addressed in Secion i.4. Section i.5 introduces a reading of the word "other" that removes any sense of divinity, God and other gods. Now the letters that spell "other" yield another meaning, "postpone, be late, be tardy," thus, gods that hold back goodness. Section 1.6 adds yet another meaning inherent in the same letters, "other" in the sense of "alien," thus, those that alienate men from God. Section i.7 moves along the same line, now, gods who are other, alien, to those that serve them and do not answer their prayers. Section 1.10 uses "other" in the sense of "replacement," "new," for the indicated purpose. Now we see the congruence of the various meanings sustained by the scriptural phrase and word-choice. The "other gods" are not gods at all; they are gods that interfere in God's blessings of the world; they alienate man from God; they are strangers to those that worship them. None of these propositions contradicts any other. And, it goes without saying, Scripture itself sustains them all.

One of the purposes of ad hoc exegesis is to raise possibilities that inhere in Scripture and to sort them out. In the following, we subject the language of Scripture to a close reading, asking whether, for example, a prohibition yields a remission, or whether you may not do this, but then again, you may do that. The response is to amass evidence of Scripture to close off all possibilities that may be imagined to inhere in the wording of the commandment.

Mekhilta LII:ii.1

A. "You shall not make for yourself a graven image:"
B. One shall not make one that is engraved, but may one make one that is solid?
C. Scripture says, "or any likeness of anything."
D. One should not make a solid one, but may one plant a tree for oneself as an idol?

E. Scripture says, "You shall not plant an Asherah for yourself" (Dt. 16:21).
F. One may not plant a tree for oneself as an idol, but perhaps one may make a tree into an idol?
G. Scripture says, "of any kind of tree."
H. One may not make an idol of a tree, but perhaps one may make one of a stone?
I. Scripture says, "Nor shall you place any figured stone."
J. One may not make an idol of stone, but perhaps one may make an idol of silver or gold?
K. Scripture says, "Gods of silver or gods of gold you shall not make for yourself."
L. One may not make an idol of silver or gold, but perhaps one may make one of copper, iron, tin, or lead?
M. Scripture says, "Nor make for yourselves molten gods" (Lev. 19:4).
N. One may not make for oneself any of these images.
O. But may one make an image of any figure?
P. Scripture says, "lest you deal corruptly and make for yourself a graven image, even the form of any figure" (Dt. 4:16).
Q. One may not make an image of a figure, but perhaps one may make an image of cattle or fowl?
R. Scripture says, "The likeness of any beast that is on the earth, the likeness of any winged fowl" (Dt. 4:17).
S. One may not make an image of cattle or fowl, but perhaps he may make an image of fish, locusts, unclean animals, or reptiles?
T. Scripture says, "The likeness of any thing that creeps on the ground, the likeness of any fish that is in the water" (Dt. 4:18).
U. One shall not make an image of any of these, but perhaps one may make an image of the sun, moon, stars, or planets?
V. Scripture says, "lest you lift up your eyes to heaven" (Dt. 4:18).
W. One may not make an image of any of these, but perhaps one may make an image of angels, cherubim, or Ophannim?
X. Scripture says, "of anything that is in heaven."
Y. Since Scripture says, "that is in heaven above, [or that is in the earth beneath, or that is in the water under the earth]," might one suppose that that involves only sun, moon stars, or planets?
Z. It says, "above," that is, not the image of angels, cherubim, or Ophannim.
AA. One may not make an image of any of these, but perhaps one may make an image of deeps and darkness?
BB. Scripture says, "or that is in the water under the earth."

This protracted exposition follows a variety of possibilities. It is inserted here because our base-text serves as part of the repertoire of proof-texts. But the collection produces the effect of broadening and deepening the prohibition of the making of a graven image.

The Ten Commandments are formed into two groups of five, facing one another, and how these opposites reciprocally impart meaning is articulated in a remarkably creative exegesis:

Mekhilta LIV:iii.1–6

1. A. "How were the Ten Commandments set forth?
   B. "There were five on one tablet, five on the other.
   C. "On the one was written, 'I am the Lord your God.'
   D. "and opposite it: 'You shall not murder.'
   E. "Scripture thus indicates that whoever sheds blood is regarded as though he had diminished the divine image.
   F. "The matter may be compared to the case of a mortal king who came into a town, and the people set up in his honor icons, and they made statues of him, and they minted coins in his honor.
   G. "After a while they overturned his icons, broke his statues, and invalidated his coins, so diminishing the image of the king.
   H. "Thus whoever sheds blood is regarded as though he had diminished the divine image, for it is said, 'Whoever sheds man's blood . . . for in the image of God he made man' (Gen. 9:6).
2. A. "On the one was written, 'You shall have no other god.'
   B. "and opposite it: 'You shall not commit adultery.'
   C. "Scripture thus indicates that whoever worships an idol is regarded as though he had committed adultery against the Omnipresent, for it is said, 'You wife that commits adultery, that takes strangers instead of your husband' (Ez. 16:32); 'And the Lord said to me, Go yet, love a woman beloved of her friend and an adulteress' (Hos. 3:1).
3. A. "On the one was written, 'You shall not take the name of the Lord your God in vain.'
   B. "and opposite it: 'You shall not steal.'
   C. "Scripture thus indicates that whoever steals in the end will end up taking a false oath: 'Will you steal, murder, commit adultery, and swear falsely:' (Jer. 7:9); 'Swearing and lying, killing and stealing, and committing adultery' (Hos. 4:2).
4. A. "On the one was written, 'Remember the Sabbath day to keep it holy.'
   B. "and opposite it: 'You shall not bear false witness.'
   C. "Scripture thus indicates that whoever violates the Sabbath is as though he had given testimony before the One who spoke and brought the world into being, indicating that he had not created his world in six days and not rested on the seventh, and whoever keeps the Sabbath day is as though he had given testimony before the One who spoke and brought the world into being, indicating that he had cre-

ated his world in six days and rested on the seventh: 'For you are my witnesses, says the Lord' (Is. 43:10).

5. A. "On the one was written, 'Honor your father and your mother.'
   B. "and opposite it: 'You shall not covet your neighbor's wife.'
   C. "Scripture thus indicates that whoever covets in the end will produce a son who curses his father and honors one who is not his father.
   D. "Thus the Ten Commandments were given, five on this tablet, and five on that," the words of R. Hananiah b. Gamaliel.
6. A. And sages say, "The ten were written on this tablet, and the ten on the other.
   B. "For it says, 'These words . . . and he wrote them upon two tablets' (Dt. 5:19); 'Your two breasts are like two fawns that are twins of a gazelle' (Song 4:5); 'His hands are as rods of gold set with beryl' (Song 5:15)."

This elegant construction is parachuted down, with no bearing on the exposition of a particular verse or phrase. It shows how the Rabbinic sages stood back from details and gained a perspective on the whole, which then infused their exposition of other details in a process of extension and amplification. Here are the matches:

(1) whoever sheds blood is regarded as though he had diminished the divine image,

(2) whoever worships an idol is regarded as though he had committed adultery against the Omnipresent,

(3) whoever steals in the end will end up taking a false oath,

(4) whoever violates the Sabbath is as though he had given testimony before the One who spoke and brought the world into being, indicating [falsely] that he had not created his world in six days and not rested on the seventh,

(5) whoever covets in the end will produce a son who curses his father and honors one who is not his father.

Here again, the Midrash process produces Midrash exegeses that express in detail a prevailing theological perspective.

When we translate the details into the generalizations that they sustain, we find ourselves in the heart of the Rabbinic system, which the sages claim also is what Scripture sets forth as well. Here we meet what is essential to Midrash exegesis: the claim that the interpretation is generated by Scripture, the reality that it rests upon the Rabbinic theological and legal structure and system, and the actuality that the latter recapitulates the former with remarkably slight variation.

5

Leviticus in *Sifra*

Mediating Between the Two Torahs, Oral and Written

The book of Leviticus is mediated to Judaism by two Rabbinic Midrash compilations. The first, *Sifra*, ca. 300 C.E., in the course of a systematic, verse-by-verse reading of Leviticus, asks about the relationship of the laws of the Mishnah and the Tosefta to the imperatives of Scripture set forth in Leviticus. The second, *Leviticus Rabbah*, ca. 450–500 C.E., forms large propositional expositions on Israel's social order from selected passages of Leviticus when read in light of other passages of Scripture altogether. Here we address the earlier document, then in Chapter Six, the later one.

The large issue of Leviticus

In *Sifra*, as in Mekhilta, the exposition of sequences of verses yields a highly coherent set of propositions. Given the focus of Leviticus on matters of Temple ritual—cultic cleanness to be preserved in the cult so that death is kept away from the source of life, cleanness to be observed by the priesthood, and sanctification to be aimed at by holy Israel—we should not miss the powerful theological substructure that sustains the reading of the book of Leviticus by the framers of *Sifra*. When at Lev. 19:2 God declares, "You shall be holy, for I the Lord your God am holy," the Rabbinic sages respond, in *Sifra*, with the question: "does God's holiness depend upon the Israelite's acts of sanctification?" This is a different question altogether from the familiar one of medieval and modern ethics, which differentiates between holiness and goodness. They answer that it does not.

Sifra CXCV:i.1–3

1. A. "And the Lord said to Moses, Say to all the congregation of the people of Israel, You shall be holy, [for I the Lord your God am holy. Every one of you shall revere his mother and his father, and you shall

keep my Sabbaths; I am the Lord your God. Do not turn to idols or make for yourselves molten gods; I am the Lord your God]" (Lev. 19:1–4):
- B. This teaches that this chapter was stated in the assembly of all Israel.
- C. And why was it stated in the assembly of all Israel?
- D. It is because most of the principles of the Torah depend upon its contents.
2. A. "You shall be holy:"
  - B. "You shall be separate."
3. A. "You shall be holy, for I the Lord your God am holy:"
  - B. That is to say, "if you sanctify yourselves, I shall credit it to you as though you had sanctified me, and if you do not sanctify yourselves, I shall hold that it is as if you have not sanctified me."
  - C. Or perhaps the sense is this: "If you sanctify me, then lo, I shall be sanctified, and if not, I shall not be sanctified"?
  - D. Scripture says, "For I . . . am holy," meaning, I remain in my state of sanctification, whether or not you sanctify me.
  - E. Abba Saul says, "The king has a retinue, and what is the task thereof? It is to imitate the king."

The normative reading of the commandment of holiness leaves no possibility of making the distinction deemed self-evident by any who frame the issue as I just did: is it good because God wants it, or does God want it because it is good? For *Sifra* such a distinction simply does not compute. How creatures are to imitate their creator is what is made explicit in Scripture, for Leviticus 19 immediately introduces, as concretizations of sanctification, a systematic articulation of the Ten Commandments: honor of parents, not making images of God, care for the poor, not stealing, not deceiving, not swearing falsely, fearing God by not insulting the deaf or placing a stumbling block before the blind (Lev. 19:14).

The systematic exposition of the realizations of holiness ends with the golden rule, "You shall not take vengeance or bear a grudge against your fellow. You shall love your neighbor as yourself, I am the Lord" (Lev. 19:18). The commandment to love is deemed fundamental by the great religions of the world, among them, Judaism. That is shown by the amplification of the passage in *Sifra:*

Sifra CC:iii.1–2, 4–7

1. A. "You shall not hate your brother in your heart, [but reasoning, you shall reason with your neighbor, lest you bear sin because of him. You shall not take vengeance or bear any grudge against the sons of your own people, but you shall love your neighbor as yourself: I am the Lord]" (Lev. 19:17–18).
  - B. Might one suppose that one should not curse him, set him straight, or contradict him?
  - C. Scripture says, "in your heart."

       D. I spoke only concerning hatred that is in the heart.
2. A. And how do we know that if one has rebuked him four or five times, he should still go and rebuke him again?
    B. Scripture says, "reasoning, you shall reason with your neighbor."
    C. Might one suppose that that is the case even if one rebukes him and his countenance blanches?
    D. Scripture says, "lest you bear sin."
4. A. "You shall not take vengeance [or bear any grudge]:"
    B. To what extent is the force of vengeance?
    C. If one says to him, "Lend me your sickle," and the other did not do so.
    D. On the next day, the other says to him, "Lend me your spade."
    E. The one then replies, "I am not going to lend it to you, because you didn't lend me your sickle."
    F. In that context, it is said, "You shall not take vengeance."
5. A. "... or bear any grudge:"
    B. To what extent is the force of a grudge?
    C. If one says to him, "Lend me your spade," but he did not do so.
    D. The next day the other one says to him, "Lend me your sickle,"
    E. and the other replies, "I am not like you, for you didn't lend me your spade [but here, take the sickle]!"
    F. In that context, it is said, "or bear any grudge."
6. A. "You shall not take vengeance or bear any grudge against the sons of your own people:"
    B. "You may take vengeance and bear a grudge against others."
7. A. "... but you shall love your neighbor as yourself: [I am the Lord]:"
    B. R. Aqiba says, "This is the encompassing principle of the Torah."
    C. Ben Azzai says, "'This is the book of the generations of Adam' (Gen. 5:1) is a still more encompassing principle."

Sanctification is not an end in itself but aims at a higher goal, which is love of neighbor. Among the great Rabbinic sages, Aqiba is joined by Hillel, who framed matters in negative terms and in Aramaic, "What is hateful to yourself, do not do to your fellow. That is the entire Torah. All the rest is commentary. Now go, study!" (*b. Šabbat* 30b). Clearly, *Sifra* takes as its assignment the exposition of the fundamental issues of Leviticus, with its theme of sanctification of Israel's social order. But that represents only part of its encompassing program. We shall focus on the principal part.

The rhetorical forms of *Sifra*'s exegesis of the language of Scripture

Three rhetorical forms dictate the entire rhetorical repertoire of this document. The first, the *dialectical*, is the demonstration that if we wish to classify things, we must follow the taxonomies dictated by Scripture rather than relying solely upon the traits of the things we wish to classify. The second, the *citation-form*, which we have already met, invokes the citation of passages of the Mishnah or the Tosefta in the setting of Scripture. The third is *commentary form*, in which a phrase of Scripture is followed by an amplificatory clause of some sort. The forms of the document admirably expressed the polemical purpose of the authorship at hand. What they wished to prove was that a taxonomy resting on the traits of things without reference to Scripture's classifications cannot serve. They further wished to restate the oral Torah in the setting of the written Torah. And, finally, they wished to accomplish the whole by rewriting the written Torah. The dialectical form accomplishes the first purpose, the citation-form the second, and the commentary form the third.

In the simple commentary form a verse, or an element of a verse, is cited, and then a very few words explain the meaning of that verse. Second come the complex forms, in which a simple exegesis is augmented in some important way, commonly by questions and answers, so that we have more than simply a verse and a brief exposition of its elements or of its meaning as a whole. The authorship of the *Sifra* time and again wishes to show that prior documents, the Mishnah or Tosefta, require the support of exegesis of Scripture for important propositions, presented in the Mishnah and the Tosefta not on the foundation of exegetical proof at all. In the main, moreover, the authorship of *Sifra* tends not to attribute its materials to specific authorities, and most of the pericopae containing attributions are shared with Mishnah and Tosefta. As we should expect, just as in *Mekhilta attributed to R. Ishmael*, *Sifra* contains a fair sample of pericopae which do not make use of the forms common in the exegesis of specific Scriptural verses and mostly do not pretend to explain the meaning of verses, but rather resort to forms typical of Mishnah and Tosefta.

When *Sifra* uses forms other than those in which its exegeses are routinely phrased, it commonly, though not always, draws upon materials also found in Mishnah and Tosefta. It is uncommon for *Sifra* to make use of non-exegetical forms for materials peculiar to its compilation. To state matters simply, *Sifra* quotes Mishnah or Tosefta, but its own materials follow its distinctive, exegetical forms. Let me now spell out what is in play in this matter.

Mediating between the two Torahs, oral and written

Unlike Mekhilta, *Sifra* holds together start to finish, not merely at specific points. The problem of the authors of *Sifra* concerns the relationship between the laws set forth in the Mishnah and their counterparts in Scripture, represented by Leviticus. The Mishnah stands for and contains both oral tradition and Scripture. In mythic terms, then, at issue in Mishnah-Scripture relations is the relationship between the oral and the written components of the one whole Torah of Moses, our rabbi, revealed by God at Sinai.

The Mishnah, a philosophical law code that came to closure at ca. 200 C.E., was regarded as the outcome of a long process of oral formulation and oral transmission. That is because tractate ʾAbot, about 250 C.E., accorded to the Mishnah the standing of revealed Torah, and is accomplished by establishing that principal authorities of the Mishnah stand in a chain of tradition extending backward to Sinai: "Moses received Torah at Sinai and handed it on to Joshua . . ." (m. ʾAbot 1:1), and onward to such figures as Shammai and Hillel, Gamaliel and Simeon his son, through to Judah the Patriarch and his sons, sponsors of the Mishnah itself. By that theory, the Mishnah, represented as the formalization of the oral tradition of Sinai, stands autonomous of Scripture. It is as much part of the Torah of Moses as Leviticus. That is how, in its contents, the Mishnah is represented as revealed Torah on its own, not requiring an elaborate structure of proof-texts to attain authority.

But what about that process of Midrash exegesis that drew from Scripture the lessons that the Rabbinic sages set forth? Does the Mishnah not derive its lessons from Scripture? The authorship of *Sifra* took the view that the Mishnah depends on Scripture, its laws deriving from the laws of Exodus, Leviticus, Numbers, and Deuteronomy. It maintained that the very category-formations of the Mishnah, which sustain the Mishnah's organization of data by topics, depend on the validation supplied by Scripture. The Mishnah at its foundations thus is claimed to have rested on Scripture, the oral part of the Torah upon the written part.

How did the framers of *Sifra* make their case stick? This was demonstrated, first, formally by provision of proof texts from Scripture for statements of the Mishnah—as is constantly done in the two Talmuds. Just now we saw a fine example of systematic exegesis of successive verses of Leviticus to yield lessons. It also was shown, second, through a profound analysis of the interior structure of thought: how do we know what categories join together discrete data into intelligible patterns? The Rabbinic sages' analysis of large segments of Leviticus in relationship to the Mishnah's topical organization of the laws is aimed at demonstrating the dependence of the Mishnah on Scripture for the very category-formations that impose sense and order on the free-standing facts of the Torah, as I shall explain.

Showing the relationship of the Mishnah to Scripture

The first task in establishing the priority of Scripture, the written Torah, over the Mishnah, the first written recording of the oral Torah, is the simplest. It is to link the two together and show how the Mishnah depends on Scripture. This is accomplished by citing a passage of the Mishnah and linking it to a passage of Scripture. In the following selection we follow the exegesis of the same Holiness-passage we noted above, and we see how the author cites passages of the Mishnah verbatim, showing how Scripture is extended and articulated by the Mishnah or its companion, the Tosefta (given in bold face type). What we see is how the Mishnah is cited verbatim and shown to depend on Scripture for full exposition of its law, as at 3.B below.

Sifra CXCIX:ii.1–7

1. A. "You shall not oppress your neighbor [or rob him]. The wages of a hired servant shall remain with you all night until the morning" (Lev. 19:13).
   B. Might one think [that that sort of harassment does not involve] even one's saying, "Mr. So-and-so is a very powerful man," while he is not a powerful man, "Mr. So-and-so is a sage," while he is not a sage, "Mr. So-and-so is rich," while he is not rich?
   C. Scripture says, ". . . or rob him." [Spreading lies, even to the man's advantage, is prohibited as harassment.]
2. A. What is particular about robbery is that it involves money, so oppression in context must involve something that involves money.
   B. What is then involved?
   C. It is the case of one who holds back the wages of a hired servant.
3. A. ["You shall not oppress your neighbor or rob him]. The wages of a hired servant shall not remain with you all night until the morning" (Lev. 19:13):
   B. I know only that the rule covers the fee owing to a human being. How do I know that the rental fee for a domesticated beast or for utensils is subject to the law, or the rent for use of real estate [M. Baba Mesia 9:12A]?
   C. Scripture says, "The wages . . . shall not remain with you all night until the morning,"
   D. meaning, the wages owing for anything.
4. A. "until morning:"
   B. **One violates the law in this connection [if he does not pay forthwith] only on account of the first night alone [T. Baba Mesia 10:2E].**
5. A. Might one suppose that one violates the law even if the worker does not come and lay claim for the fee [M. Baba Mesia 9:12F]?
   B. Scripture says, "with you,"
   C. I have spoken of a case only in which the money remains with you at your pleasure. [But if it is at the pleasure of the other, you do not violate the law.]
6. A. Might one suppose that even if the employer gave him a draft on a storekeeper or a money changer [M. Baba Mesia 9:12G–H], one might violate the law in question?
   B. Scripture says, "shall not remain *with you* all night."
7. A. "The wages of a hired servant shall not remain with you all night until the morning:"

B. I know only that a day-worker collects his wage any time of the night [M. Baba Mesia 9:11A].
C. How do I know that a night-worker collects his wage any time of the day [M. Baba Mesia 9:11B]?
D. Scripture says, "On his day you will pay his wage" (Dt. 24:15).

The exposition of Lev. 19:13 does two things. First, it amplifies Scripture's own statement. That is the purpose of Section ii.1 and ii.2, with their extension of Scripture's rules. The point of interest here comes at Section ii.3, which cites Lev. 19:13 and asks how the case of the cited passage of the Mishnah or the Tosefta pertains. That is, may one postpone handing over the payment for renting the specified property, a domesticated beast for labor, utensils for a craft, or even the rent for the use of real estate? Scripture yields those secondary matters as well. Section ii.4 carries us to a rule of the Tosefta, which is linked to the clause of Scripture to which it is attached. Section ii.5 opens the question of whether the law operates automatically, or whether the worker has to lay claim for his salary. Scripture answers that question in line with the cited passage of the Mishnah. Sections ii.6 and ii.7 go through the same process. So, in all, we see how *Sifra's* framers have clarified the relationship of the Mishnah and the Tosefta to Scripture by citing the latter lawbooks and linking their details to statements of Scripture.

Using logic to criticize reason in the name of revelation

There is a much more profound critique in play. For what we have seen to this point are formal proofs, and there is no pretense at getting to the foundations of the matter: the very thought processes that sustain the Mishnah and how these are subordinated to the decrees of Scripture. The Mishnah presents itself as a highly orderly document, in which topics are categorized by their traits. Classes of objects or actions that bear the same indicative traits, e.g., traits of purpose or of normal use, form a single classification and are subject to the same rule, and those that do not share those traits belong in some other classification. These classifications then are arranged in a hierarchy. And since the Mishnah executes a vast labor of hierarchical classification, its entire system and structure rest on that claim that all things bear within themselves the markers of their own classification.

To dispose of the Mishnah's claims that its category-formations are autonomous and that its hierarchy is obligatory, *Sifra* advances a systematic proof. Time and again it demonstrates that reason is not reliable, and only Scripture's designation of category-formations serves.

This formidable theological exercise in the criticism of reason in the name of revelation was carried out in two ways. First, it involved systematically demolishing the logic that sustains an autonomous Mishnah, a philosophical logic that appeals to the intrinsic traits of things to accomplish classification and hierarchization. Secondly, it was done by demonstrating that the Mishnah's identification of the correct classification *depends* on Scripture in particular. By composing a document that for very long stretches simply cannot have been put together without the Mishnah and at the same time subjecting the generative logical principles of the Mishnah to devastating critique, that same authorship took up its position. The Mishnah depended upon Scripture not only for details of the law but for the very principles of organizing the laws into a rational structure of category-formations: its topical tractates, which impose order on Scripture's indifference, in setting forth the laws, to subject-matter. (A good instance of that indifference is in Leviticus chapter Nineteen, which we have considered; a broad range of subjects is covered, under the organizing rubric of sanctification. Another is the Ten Commandments, which hold together for other than topical considerations.)

Classifying things by appeal to their intrinsic traits versus sorting things out by the direction of Scripture

To understand this point, we need to dwell for another moment on the character of the Mishnah. In the Mishnah we seek connection between fact and fact, sentence and sentence, by comparing and contrasting two things, seeing how they are like and not alike. If they are alike, they follow a common rule. If not, they follow opposed rules. An object's intrinsic traits and its teleology—the purpose served by the object through those traits—govern. Once we find regularities, we propose rules. Accordingly, as to the species of the genus, so far as they are alike, they share the same rule. So far as they are not alike, each follows a rule contrary to that governing the other. The framers of the Mishnah effect their taxonomy—their classification-system and the definition of their category-formations—through the traits of things: their purpose, their indicative qualities.

The authorship of *Sifra* insists that the source of classification is Scripture. *Sifra's* authorship time and again demonstrates that classification of cases within common rules—the very heart of the Halakhic enterprise—cannot be carried out without Scripture's taxonomy, and, it must follow, hierarchical arguments based on extra-scriptural taxonomies always fail.

Sifra's rhetorical exegesis follows a standard redactional process. Scripture will be cited. Then a statement will be made about its meaning, or a statement of law correlative to that Scripture will be given. That statement sometimes cites the Mishnah, often verbatim. Finally, the author of *Sifra* invariably states, "Now is that not (merely) logical?" And the force of that statement will be, "Can this position not be gained through the working of mere logic, based upon facts supplied (to be sure) by Scripture?" But the answer always is that it is not (merely) logical, but that only Scripture can correct the flaws of mere logic. The polemical power of *Sifra* lies in its repetitive demonstration that the stated position, citation of a Mishnah-pericope, is not only not the product of logic, but is, and only can be, the product of exegesis of Scripture. The Mishnah is shown to be subordinated to Scripture and validated only through Scripture.

Classifying not by traits of things but by Scripture's own categories

Here is a simple example of the alternative mode of classification, one that does not appeal to the traits of things but to the utilization of names defined by Scripture. What we see is how by naming things in a particular way, Scripture orders all things, classifying and, in the nature of things, also hierarchizing them—one example among many of how our authorship conceives the right way of logical thought to proceed:

Sifra VII:v.1–2

1. A. "... and Aaron's sons the priests shall present the blood and throw the blood (round about against the altar that is at the door of the tent of meeting):"
   B. Why does Scripture make use of the word "blood" twice (instead of using a pronoun)?
   C. (It is for the following purpose:) How on the basis of Scripture do you know that if blood deriving from one burnt offering was confused with blood deriving from another burnt offering, blood deriving from one burnt offering with blood deriving from a beast that has been substituted therefor, blood deriving from a burnt offering with blood deriving from an unconsecrated beast, the mixture should nonetheless be presented?
   D. It is because Scripture makes use of the word "blood" twice (instead of using a pronoun).

Section v.1 sets the stage, simply pointing out that the use of the word "blood" twice encompasses a case in which blood in two distinct classifications is somehow mixed in the conduct of the cult. In such a case it is quite proper to pour out the mixture of blood deriving from distinct sources, e.g., beasts that have served different, but comparable purposes. We then systemically work out the limits of that rule, showing how comparability works, then pointing to cases in which comparability is set aside.

2. A. Is it possible to suppose that while if blood deriving from beasts in the specified classifications, (the blood of the sacrifice) is to be presented (on the altar, as a valid offering), for the simple reason that if the several beasts while alive had been confused with one another, they might be offered up,
   B. but how do we know that even if the blood of a burnt offering were confused with that of a beast killed as a guilt offering (it is to be offered up)?

C. I shall concede the case of the mixture of the blood of a burnt offering confused with that of a beast killed as a guilt offering; it is to be presented, for both this one and that one fall into the classification of Most Holy Things.
D. But how do I know that if the blood of a burnt offering were confused with the blood of a beast slaughtered in the classification of peace-offerings or of a thanksgiving offering (the mixture is to be presented)?

We now differentiate, by indicative traits, those things that initially seemed to form a single classification. The differentiation is a systematic and orderly concession of part, only to distinguish another part, of a common whole:

E. I shall concede the case of the mixture of the blood of a burnt offering confused with that of a beast slaughtered in the classification of peace-offerings or of a thanksgiving offering (it is to be presented), because the beasts in both classifications produce blood that has to be sprinkled four times.
F. But how do I know that if the blood of a burnt offering were confused with the blood of a beast slaughtered in the classification of a firstling or a beast that was counted as the tenth (that is, it is to serve as the tithe of that herd or flock) or of a beast designated as a Passover (it is to be presented)?
G. I shall concede the case of the mixture of the blood of a burnt offering confused with that of a beast slaughtered in the classification of firstling or a beast that was counted as a tenth or of a beast designated as a Passover (it is to be presented), because Scripture uses the word "blood" two times.
H. Then while I may make that concession, might I also suppose that if the blood of a burnt offering was confused with the blood of beasts that had suffered an invalidation, it also may be offered up?

Now comes the final solution: Scripture excludes the case, imposing its own classification upon all the data. Without Scripture, taxonomic logic produces only chaos.

I. Scripture says, ". . . its blood" (thus excluding such a case).

The process resumes:

J. Then I shall concede the case of a mixture of the blood of a valid burnt offering with the blood of beasts that had suffered an invalidation, which blood is not valid to be presented at all.
K. But how do I know that if such blood were mixed with the blood deriving from beasts set aside as sin-offerings to be offered on the inner altar (it is not to be offered up)?

L. I can concede that the blood of a burnt offering that has been mixed with the blood deriving from beasts set aside as sin-offerings to be offered on the inner altar is not to be offered up, for the one is offered on the inner altar, and the other on the outer altar (the burnt offering brought as a free will offering, under discussion here, is slaughtered at the altar ". . . that is at the door of the tent of meeting," not at the inner altar).

M. But how do I know that even if the blood of a burnt offering was confused with the blood of sin-offerings that are to be slaughtered at the outer altar, it is not to be offered up?

N. Scripture says, ". . . its blood" (thus excluding such a case).

In place of the rejecting of arguments resting on classifying species into a common genus, we demonstrate how classification really is to be carried on. It is through the imposition upon data of the categories dictated by Scripture: Scripture's use of language. That is the force of this powerful exercise. Throughout the exposition, at the crucial point we invoke the formulation of Scripture, subordinating logic, or, in this instance, the process of classification of like species according to Scriptural categories. I cannot imagine a more successful demonstration of what the framers wish to say.

What is the point? We wish to classify matters by reference to reason. But time and again, distinctions are made that reason does not sort out. "I can concede this, but how about that?" "I concede that, but how do I know about the other thing?" Indicative traits leave areas of doubt. Scripture alone indicates what is included and what is excluded in the classification of "blood." It does so by using the word "blood" twice, and that deals with blood in two distinct classifications and indicates that the different types of blood may be poured out en masse on the altar.

What can we do by appeal to Scripture that we cannot do if we do not rely on Scripture? It is to establish the possibility of polythetic classification. We can appeal to shared traits of otherwise distinct taxonomies and so transform species into a common genus for a given purpose. *Sifra's* authors maintain that only Scripture makes that initiative feasible. Because of Scripture's provision of taxonomies, we are able to undertake the science of making lists, including hierarchical classification, in the right way. Without them we face chaos. And they flow from the source, the mind of the Creator, who saw the genera, whereas logic on its own analyzes only points of differentiation. Let me now generalize on the case just now reviewed.

How does *Sifra*'s authorship reject the principles of the logic of hierarchical classification as these are worked out by the framers of the Mishnah?

It is a critique of designating classifications of things without Scriptural warrant. For it is not the principle that like things follow the same rule that is at stake.

Sifra shares that principle implicitly. What *Sifra*'s authorship disputes is that we can classify things on our own by appeal to the traits or indicative characteristics, that is, utterly without reference to Scripture. The argument is simple. On our own, we cannot classify species into genera. Everything is different from everything else in some way. But Scripture tells us what things are alike and for what purposes. Hence Scripture dictates the definitive classifications, not our unaided discernment of traits in the things themselves. When we see the nature of the critique, we shall have a clear picture of what is at stake when we examine, in some detail, precisely how the Mishnah's logic works.

The argument of *Sifra*'s authorship is that traits does not permit us definitively to classify species into a common genus. There always are traits distinctive to a species, but without the revelation of the Torah, we are not able to effect any generic classification at all. We are left only with the species, but with no genus, all cases, no rules. Time and again, we can easily demonstrate things have so many and such diverse and contradictory indicative traits that, comparing one thing to another, we can always distinguish one species from another. Though we may find something in common, we also can discern some other unshared trait characteristic.

Consequently, we also can show that the hierarchical logic on which we rely, the argument *a fortiori* or *qol vehomer*, has no force. For if on the basis of one set of traits that yield a given classification we place into hierarchical order two or more items, on the basis of a different set of traits, we have either a different classification altogether, or, much more commonly, simply a different hierarchy. So the attack on the way in which the Mishnah's authorship has done its work appeals not merely to the limitations of classification solely on the basis of traits. The more telling argument addresses what is, to those who seek to order and regularize data, the source of power and compelling proof: hierarchization. That is why, throughout, we must designate the Mishnah's mode of the science of list making—German *Listenwissenschaft*—a logic of hierarchical classification. Things are not merely like or unlike, therefore following one rule or its opposite. Things also are weightier or less weighty, and that particular point of likeness of difference generates the logical force of the science of making lists.

The source of valid category-formations

Sifra's authorship affirms taxonomic logic when applied to the right categories. It systematically demonstrates the affirmative case, that the science of making lists is a self-evidently valid mode of demonstrating the truth of propositions. But *the* source of the correct classification of things is Scripture and only Scripture. Without Scripture's intervention into the taxonomy of the world, we should have no knowledge at all of how things should be classified and therefore by which rules they are governed.

Sifra is careful not to criticize the Mishnah. Its position, as we have already seen, favors restating the Mishnah or the Tosefta within the context of Scripture, not rejecting the conclusions of the Mishnah, let alone its authority. Consequently, when we find a critique of applied reason divorced from Scripture, we rarely uncover an explicit critique of the Mishnah, and when we find a citation of the Mishnah, we rarely uncover linkage to the ubiquitous principle that Scripture forms the source of all classification and hierarchy. When the Mishnah is cited by our authorship, it will be presented as part of the factual substrate of the Torah. When the logic operative throughout the Mishnah is subjected to criticism, the language of the Mishnah will rarely, if ever, be cited in context.

The operative question in critiquing the logic of the list-making science as applied by the framers of the Mishnah ordinarily is, "is it not a matter of logic?" Then the sorts of arguments against taxonomy pursued outside of the framework of Scripture's classifications will follow. When, by contrast, the authorship of *Sifra* wishes to introduce into the context that it has already approved a verbatim passage of the Mishnah, it will ordinarily, though not always, use, *mikan amru*, which, in context, means, "in this connection sages have said." It is fact that when *Sifra*'s intent is to demolish improper reasoning, the Mishnah's rules in its own language rarely, if ever, are cited. When the authorship of *Sifra* wishes to incorporate paragraphs of the Mishnah into their re-presentation of the Torah, they will do so either without fanfare, as in the passage we have examined, or by the neutral joining-language "in this connection (sages) have said."

At issue: not the Mishnah but the meaning of the Torah

At stake is the character of the Torah. In insisting, in agreement with the framers of the Mishnah, that there are not only cases but also rules, not only species but also genera, the authorship of *Sifra* also made its case in behalf of the Torah as a the source of essential philosophical knowledge, comparable to the knowledge attained through natural philosophy. I may phrase what is at issue in this way: exactly what do we want to learn from, or discern within the Torah? What is at stake in finding the properties and origins of hierarchical classification?

In their delineation of correct hierarchical logic, our authorship uncovered within the Torah (written and oral Torah alike) an adumbration of the working of the mind of God. That is because the premise of all discourse is that the Torah was written by God and dictated by God to Moses at Sinai. The whole then affords access to God's mind through the analysis of the principles inherent in God's wording of matters. And that will in the end explain why our authorship for its part has entered into the Torah long passages of not merely clarification but active intrusion, making itself a participant in the dialogue. The authorship of *Sifra* proposed to regain access to the modes of thought that guided the formation of the Torah, oral and written alike: comparison and contrast in a particular way, identification of categories in a specified manner. Since those were the modes of thought that, in our authorship's conception, dictated the structure of intellect upon which the oral and written Torah rested, a simple conclusion is the only possible one.

The wording is the key to the thinking. Hence from the language of the Torah we may learn the rules that govern the logic of God's own intellect. In their analysis of the deepest structures of intellect embodied in the Torah, the authorship of *Sifra* presumed to enter into the mind of God, showing how God's mind, or logic worked when God formed the Torah. But in discerning how God's mind worked, the intellectuals who created *Sifra* claimed for themselves a place in that very process of thought that had given birth to the Torah. Our authorship could rewrite the Torah because, knowing how the Torah originally was written, they too could write (though not reveal) the Torah .

What is at stake? At stake is the possibility of doing precisely what the framers of the Mishnah wish to do, that is, to join together masses of diverse data into a single, encompassing statement, in order to show the rule that inheres in diverse cases. The whole holds together, because Scripture makes possible the statement of all things within a single rule. That is, as we have noted, precisely what the framers of the Mishnah proposed to accomplish. Our authorship maintains that only by appeal to the Torah is this feat of learning possible. If, then, we wish to understand all things all together and all at once under a single encompassing rule, we had best revert to the Torah, with its account of the rightful names, positions, and order, imputed to all things. The creation account of Genesis states in narrative form what *Sifra* sets forth in exegetical form and through the analysis of logic.

6

Leviticus in *Leviticus Rabbah*

Turning Scripture's Laws into the Design of Holy Israel's Social Order

Thirty-seven propositions

Leviticus Rabbah, closed in the mid-fifth century, ca. 450 C.E., sets forth, in the thirty-seven *parashiyyot* or chapters into which the document is divided, thirty-seven well-crafted propositions, e.g., wine is wicked, God favors the pursued over the pursuer, Moses was a unique prophet, and the like. The framers of the document made no pretense at a systematic exegesis of sequences of verses of Scripture, abandoning the verse by verse mode of organizing discourse characteristic of *Sifra* and the two *Sifrés, Genesis Rabbah,* and the like. They struck out on their own to compose a means of expressing their ideas in a more systematic and cogent way.

The focus of *Leviticus Rabbah* and its laws of history is upon the society of Israel, its national fate and moral condition. Indeed, nearly all of the *parashiyyot* of *Leviticus Rabbah* turn out to deal with the national, social condition of Israel, and this in three contexts: (1) Israel's setting in the history of the nations, (2) the sanctified character of the inner life of Israel itself, (3) the future, salvific history of Israel. So the biblical book that deals with the tabernacle, identified by the sages as the holy Temple, now is shown to address the holy people.

As mediated by *Leviticus Rabbah,* Leviticus really discusses not the consecration of the cult but the sanctification of the nation—its conformity to God's will laid forth in the Torah, and God's rules. So when we review the document as a whole and ask what is that something else that the base text is supposed to address, it turns out that the sanctification of the cult stands for the salvation of the nation. So the nation now is like the cult then, the ordinary Israelite now like the priest then. The holy way of life lived now, through acts in response to the divine imperative, corresponds to the holy rites then. The process of metamorphosis is full, rich, complete. Everything stands for something else, and the something else repeatedly turns out to be the nation. This is what our document spells out in exquisite detail, yet never losing the main point.

From commentary to propositional statements

The framers of *Leviticus Rabbah* in their principal components treat topics, not particular verses. They make freestanding generalizations. They express cogent propositions through extended compositions. Earlier, in *Genesis Rabbah*, as we have seen, sages' insights were attached to verses of Scripture. Discourse was episodic, not systematic. That is to say, the sequence of verses of Genesis and their contents played a massive role in the larger-scale organization of *Genesis Rabbah* and in the expression of its propositions.

Here, by contrast, the authors of *Leviticus Rabbah* so collected and arranged their materials that an abstract proposition emerges independent of the sequence of verses of the book of Leviticus. That proposition is not expressed only or mainly through episodic restatements, assigned, as I said, to an order established by a base text (whether Genesis or Leviticus or a Mishnah-tractate for that matter). Rather it emerges through a logic of coherent discourse of its own: proposition, evidence, argument. What is new in *Leviticus Rabbah*, therefore, is the move from an essentially exegetical mode of logical discourse to a fundamentally philosophical one. It is the shift from discourse framed around an established text to syllogistic argument organized around a proposed theorem or proposition.

How *Leviticus Rabbah* expounds its ideas

A single example of how *Leviticus Rabbah*'s framers compose their ideas into a demonstration of an articulated proposition suffices. The proposition is that God favors the pursued over the pursuer; the context in which the proposition is important exegetically comes at the end: God wants as offerings on the altar beasts that are pursued, not pursuers, in the animal kingdom: a bull, sheep, lamb, not a lion, wolf, or leopard. The generalization is set forth, and then Scripture supplies probative cases, which are assembled not for exegetical purposes but as established facts, proving a larger point:

Leviticus Rabbah XXVII:v.1–2

1. A. "God seeks what has been driven away" (Qoh. 3:15).
   B. R. Huna in the name of R. Joseph said, "It is always the case that 'God seeks what has been driven away' [favoring the victim].
   C. "You find when a righteous man pursues a righteous man, 'God seeks what has been driven away.'

D. "When a wicked man pursues a wicked man, 'God seeks what has been driven away.'
E. "All the more so when a wicked man pursues a righteous man, 'God seeks what has been driven away.'
F. "[The same principle applies] even when you come around to a case in which a righteous man pursues a wicked man, 'God seeks what has been driven away.'"

2. A. R. Yosé b. R. Yudan in the name of R. Yosé b. R. Nehorai says, "It is always the case that the Holy One, blessed be he, demands an accounting for the blood of those who have been pursued from the hand of the pursuer.
B. "Abel was pursued by Cain, and God sought [an accounting for] the pursued: 'And the Lord looked [favorably] upon Abel and his meal offering' (Gen. 4:4).
C. "Noah was pursued by his generation, and God sought [an accounting for] the pursued: 'You and all your household shall come into the ark' (Gen. 7:1). And it says, 'For this is like the days of Noah to me, as I swore [that the waters of Noah should no more go over the earth]' (Is. 54:9).
D. "Abraham was pursued by Nimrod, 'and God seeks what has been driven away': 'You are the Lord, the God who chose Abram and brought him out of Ur' (Neh. 9:7).
E. "Isaac was pursued by Ishmael, 'and God seeks what has been driven away': 'For through Isaac will seed be called for you' (Gen. 21:12).
F. "Jacob was pursued by Esau, 'and God seeks what has been driven away': 'For the Lord has chosen Jacob, Israel for his prized possession' (Ps. 135:4).
G. "Moses was pursued by Pharaoh, 'and God seeks what has been driven away': 'Had not Moses His chosen stood in the breach before Him' (Ps. 106:23).
H. "David was pursued by Saul, 'and God seeks what has been driven away': 'And he chose David, his servant' (Ps. 78:70).
I. "Israel was pursued by the nations, 'and God seeks what has been driven away': 'And you has the Lord chosen to be a people to him' (Deut. 14:2).
J. "And the rule applies also to the matter of offerings. A bull is pursued by a lion, a sheep is pursued by a wolf, a goat is pursued by a leopard.
K. "Therefore the Holy One, blessed be he, has said, 'Do not make offerings before me from those animals that pursue, but from those that are pursued: When a bull, a sheep, or a goat is born'" (Lev. 22:27).

Section v.1B–F states the proposition, and then in Section v.2B–I we are given the cases of Abel, Noah, Abraham, Isaac, Jacob, Moses, David, culminating in God's favor shown to persecuted Israel. So the proposition is both spelled out and then illustrated from Scripture. Then in Section v.2J–K we revert to the issue of Leviticus: the selection of animals for the altar. That forms the climax and definitive proof.

Compositions ordered by proposition rarely find a place in the documents that came to closure before *Leviticus Rabbah,* for example, *Mekhilta, Sifra,* and (as we shall see in the next two chapters) the two *Sifrés,* not to mention *Genesis Rabbah.* The method of *Leviticus Rabbah* requires an articulate presentation of an idea, which is amplified and validated by reference to facts—verses—of Scripture.

A new method for a new message

In reading the Scriptural rules of sanctification of the priesthood, Temple, and offerings to yield the message of the salvation of all Israel, the framers of *Leviticus Rabbah* produced a fresh message through a new medium. Now things are made to stand for more than themselves. Leviticus became the story of how Israel, when it was purified from social sin and sanctified, would be saved. As the regularities logged in for the preference of the pursued show, the message of *Leviticus Rabbah* is that from the probative cases of Scripture the laws of history may be known, which is precisely the premise of *Genesis Rabbah.* What is new is that these laws focus upon the holy life of the community. They do not derive only from the signals contained within the patriarchs' lives and actions. From narrative concerning individuals, therefore, attention turns to rules governing the entire community, so the quest for history's laws here shifts to the laws of sanctification contained within Leviticus.

The new message then is clear. If Israel—the pursued, not the pursuer—obeys the laws of society aimed at Israel's sanctification, the foreordained history, resting on the merit of the ancestors, will unfold as Israel hopes. So there is no secret to the meaning of the events of the day, and Israel, for its part, can affect its destiny and effect salvation. The authorship of *Leviticus Rabbah* has thus joined into temporal sequence two great motifs, (1) sanctification and then (2) salvation, by reading a biblical book, Leviticus, that is devoted to sanctification in the light of the requirements of the salvation. In this way they made their fundamental point, which is that *salvation at the end of history depends upon sanctification in the here and now.*

Finding the pattern

To prove these points, the authors of the compositions make lists of facts of Scripture or of nature (e.g., the character of classifications of beasts) that bear the same traits and yield rules. These demonstrations then show the working of rules of history. It follows that the mode of thought brought to bear upon the theme of history remains exactly the same as in the Mishnah and in *Sifra:* list-making, with data exhibiting similar taxonomic traits drawn together into lists based on common traits or definitions. These lists then, through the power of repetition, make a single enormous point or prove a social law of history. The catalogues of exemplary heroes and historical events serve a further purpose. They provide a model of how contemporary events are to be absorbed into the biblical paradigm. Since biblical events exemplify the recurrent happenings of sin and redemption, forgiveness and atonement, they lose their one-time character. At the same time and in the same way, current events find a place within the ancient, but eternally present, paradigmatic scheme. So no new historical events, other than exemplary episodes in lives of heroes, demand narration because, through what is said about the past, what was happening in the times of the framers of *Leviticus Rabbah* would also come under consideration.

Patterning the social order and transcending history

This mode of dealing with biblical history and contemporary events produces reciprocal effects. The first is the mythicization of biblical stories, their removal from the framework of ongoing, unique patterns of history and sequences of events and their transformation into models, accounts of things that happen all the time. The second is that contemporary events too lose all of their immediacy, one-time-ness, and specificity and enter the paradigmatic framework of established mythic existence. In simple language: the past is ever-present, the present forms a recapitulation of the past. So (1) the Scripture's myth happens every day, and (2) every day produces re-enactment of the Scripture's myth.

That is how and why the focus of *Leviticus Rabbah*'s laws of history is upon the society of Israel, its national fate and moral condition. Indeed, nearly all of the *parashiyyot* of *Leviticus Rabbah* turn out to deal with the national, social condition of Israel, and this in three contexts: (1) Israel's setting in the history of the nations, (2) the sanctified character of the inner life of Israel itself, and (3) the future, salvific history of Israel. So the biblical book that deals with the tabernacle in the wilderness, which sages understood to form the model for the holy Temple later on built in Jerusalem, now is shown to address the life of the holy people.

That is no paradox, rather a logical next step in the exploration of sanctification. Leviticus really discusses not the consecration of the cult but the sanctification of the nation—its conformity to God's will laid forth in the Torah, and God's rules. *Leviticus Rabbah* shifts the character of the organizing categories, so that the nation now is like the cult then, the ordinary Israelite now like the priest then.

It is a paradox that the message of *Leviticus Rabbah* attaches itself to the book of Leviticus, as if that book had come from prophecy and addressed the issue of salvation. But it came from the priesthood and spoke of sanctification. The paradoxical syllogism—the as-if reading, the opposite of how things seem—of the composers of *Leviticus Rabbah* therefore reaches simple formulation. In the very setting of sanctification the authors find the promise of salvation. In the topics of the cult and the priesthood they uncover the national and social issues of the moral life and redemptive hope of Israel. The repeated comparison and contrast of priesthood and prophecy, sanctification and salvation, turn out to produce a complement, which comes to most perfect union in *Leviticus Rabbah*.

An example of the socialization of purity-taboos

These rather abstract remarks require a concrete example. It derives from the reading of Leviticus 11:4–8, the animals Israel may and may not eat. These are taken to represent the nations, and Israel's relationships with the nations then determine those animals that are suitable and those that are not. I give only part of the immense, systematic passage, which suffices to show how the laws of sanctification of Leviticus are transformed into rules governing Israel's social order in history.

Leviticus Rabbah XIII:v.9–13

9. A. Moses foresaw what the evil kingdoms would do [to Israel].
    B. "The camel, rock badger, and hare" (Deut. 14:7). [Compare: "Nevertheless, among those that chew the cud or part the hoof, you shall not eat these: the camel, because it chews the cud but does not part the hoof, is unclean to you. The rock badger, because it chews the cud but does not part the hoof, is unclean to you. And the hare, because it chews the cud but does not part the hoof, is unclean to you, and the pig, because it parts the hoof and is cloven-footed, but does not chew the cud, is unclean to you" (Lev. 11:4–8).]
    C. The camel (gāmāl) refers to Babylonia, [in line with the following verse of Scripture: "O daughter of Babylonia, you who are to be devastated!] Happy will be he who requites (gāmāl) you, with what you have done to us" (Ps. 147:8).
    D. "The rock badger" (Deut. 14:7)—this refers to Media.
    H. "The hare" (Deut 14:7)—this refers to Greece. The mother of King Ptolemy was named "Hare" [in Greek: lagos].
    I. "The pig" (Deut. 14:7)—this refers to Edom [Rome].
    J. Moses made mention of the first three in a single verse and the final one in a verse by itself (Deut. 14:7, 8). Why so?
    K. R. Yohanan and R. Simeon b. Laqish.
    L. R. Yohanan said, "It is because [the pig] is equivalent to the other three."
    M. And R. Simeon b. Laqish said, "It is because it outweighs them."
    N. R. Yohanan objected to R. Simeon b. Laqish, "Prophesy, therefore, son of man, clap your hands [and let the sword come down twice, yea thrice]" (Ez. 21:14).

O. And how does R. Simeon b. Laqish interpret the same passage? He notes that [the threefold sword] is doubled (Ez. 21:14).

10. A. (Gen. R. 65:1:) R. Phineas and R. Hilqiah in the name of R. Simon: "Among all the prophets, only two of them revealed [the true evil of Rome], Assaf and Moses.
B. "Assaf said, 'The pig out of the wood ravages it' (Ps. 80:14).
C. "Moses said, 'And the pig, [because it parts the hoof and is cloven-footed but does not chew the cud] ' (Lev. 11:7).
D. "Why is [Rome] compared to a pig?
E. "It is to teach you the following: Just as, when a pig crouches and produces its hooves, it is as if to say, 'See how I am clean [since I have a cloven hoof],' so this evil kingdom acts arrogantly, seizes by violence, and steals, and then gives the appearance of establishing a tribunal for justice."

11. A. Another interpretation: "The camel" (Lev. 11:4).
B. This refers to Babylonia.
C. "Because it chews the cud (*ma'alāh/gērāh*) [but does not part the hoof]" (Lev. 11:4).
D. For it brings forth praises [*(meqallēs)* with its throat] of the Holy One, blessed be he. [The Hebrew words for "chew the cud"—bring up cud—are now understood to mean "give praise." *gārāh* is connected with *gārôn*, throat, hence, "bring forth (sounds of praise through) the throat."]
E. R. Berekhiah and R. Helbo in the name of R. Ishmael b. R. Nahman: "Whatever [praise of God] David [in writing a psalm] treated singly [item by item], that wicked man [Nebuchadnezzar] lumped together in a single verse.
F. " 'Now I, Nebuchadnezzar, praise and extol and honor the King of heaven, [for all his works are right and his ways are just, and those who walk in pride he is able to abase' (Dan. 4:37).
G. [Nebuchadnezzar said only the word], " 'Praise'—[but David devoted the following entire Psalm to praise] : 'O Jerusalem, praise the Lord' (Ps. 147:12).
H. " 'Extol'—'I shall extol you, O Lord, for you have brought me low' (Ps. 30:2).
I. " 'Honor the king of heaven'—'The Lord reigns, let the peoples tremble! [He sits enthroned upon the cherubim, let the earth quake]' (Ps. 99:1).
J. " 'For all his works are right'—'For the sake of thy steadfast love and thy faithfulness' (Ps. 115:1).
K. " 'And his ways are just'—'He will judge the peoples with equity' (Ps. 96:10)
L. " 'And those who walk in pride'—'The Lord reigns, he is robed in majesty, [the Lord is robed, he is girded with strength]' (Ps. 93:1).

M. "'He is able to abase'—'All the horns of the wicked he will cut off'" (Ps. 75:11).
N. "The rock badger" (Lev. 11:5)—this refers to Media.
O. "For it chews the cud"—for it gives praise to the Holy One, blessed be he: "Thus says Cyrus, king of Persia, 'All the kingdoms of the earth has the Lord, the God of the heaven, given me'" (Ezra 1:2).
P. "The hare"—this refers to Greece.
Q. "For it chews the cud"—for it gives praise to the Holy One, blessed be he.
R. Alexander the Macedonian, when he saw Simeon the Righteous, said, "Blessed be the God of Simeon the Righteous."
S. "The pig" (Lev. 11:7)—this refers to Edom.
T. "For it does not chew the cud"—for it does not give praise to the Holy One, blessed be he.
U. And it is not enough that it does not give praise, but it blasphemes and swears violently, saying, "Whom do I have in heaven, and with you I want nothing on earth" (Ps. 73:25).

12. A. Another interpretation [of *gērah*, cud, now with reference to *gēr*, stranger:]
B. "The camel" (Lev. 11:4)—this refers to Babylonia.
C. "For it chews the cud" [now: brings up the stranger]—for it exalts righteous men: "And Daniel was in the gate of the [Babylonian] king" (Dan. 2:49).
D. "The rock badger" (Lev. 11:5)—this refers to Media.
E. "For it brings up the stranger"—for it exalts righteous men: "Mordecai sat at the gate of the king [of Media]" (Est. 2:19).
F. "The hare" (Lev. 11:6)—this refers to Greece.
G. "For it brings up the stranger"—for it exalts the righteous.
H. When Alexander of Macedonia, [a Greek,] saw Simeon the Righteous, he would rise up on his feet. They said to him, "Can't you see Jews [elsewhere], that you stand up before this Jew [and honor him]?"
I. He said to them, "When I go forth to battle, I see something like this man's visage, and I conquer."
J. "The pig" (Lev. 11:7)—this refers to Rome.
K. "But it does not bring up the stranger"—for it does not exalt the righteous.
L. And it is not enough that it does not exalt them, but it kills them.
M. That is in line with the following verse of Scripture: "I was angry with my people, I profaned my heritage; I gave them into your hand, [you showed them no mercy; on the aged you made your yoke exceedingly heavy]" (Is. 47:6).
N. This refers to R. Aqiba and his colleagues.

13. A. Another interpretation [now treating "bring up the cud" *(GR)* as "bring along in its train" *(GRR)*]:
B. "The camel" (Lev. 11:4)—this refers to Babylonia.

C. "Which brings along in its train"—for it brought along another kingdom after it.
D. "The rock badger" (Lev. 11:5)—this refers to Media.
E. "Which brings along in its train"—for it brought along another kingdom after it.
F. "The hare" (Lev. 11:6)—this refers to Greece.
G. "Which brings along in its train"—for it brought along another kingdom after it.
H. "The pig" (Lev. 11:7)—this refers to Rome.
I. "Which does not bring along in its train"—for it did not bring along another kingdom after it.
J. And why is it then called "pig" (HZYR)? For it restores (MHZRT) the crown to the one who truly should have it [namely, Israel, whose dominion will begin when the rule of Rome ends].
K. That is in line with the following verse of Scripture: "And saviors will come up on Mount Zion to judge the Mountain of Esau [Rome], and the kingdom will then belong to the Lord" (Ob. 1:21).

The food taboos differentiate Israel from gentiles. Hence the discussion of the food taboos will introduce the theme of the antipathy of the gentiles for Israel, on the one side, and the gentiles' hostile actions against the Israelites, on the other. Israel, of course, stands for a nation, and as such it suffers because of the hostility of other nations. There is no hint that individual Israelites play a role in the complaint of the framers. The nations mentioned are Babylonia, Media, Greece, and Rome, the latter time and again differentiated from the first three. The matter unfolds rather majestically, introducing first one theme—the nations' role in the history of Israel, their hostile treatment of Israel—and then the next—the food taboos—finally bringing the two themes together.

The climax identifies each of the successive kingdoms with the four explicitly tabooed animals of Lev. 11:1–8: camel, rock badger, hare, pig. Then, as we see, the reasons for the taboo assigned to each of them are worked out, in a triple sequence of word-plays, with special reference to the secondary possibilities presented by the words for "chew the cud," "bring up gērāh." So while the first impression is that a diverse set of materials has been strung together, upon a closer glance we see quite the opposite: a purposive and careful arrangement of distinct propositions, each leading to, and intensifying the force of, the next. That is why at the climax comes the messianic reference to Israel's ultimate inheritance of the power and dominion of Rome. Let us briefly survey the individual components.

Section v.9B starts us at Deut. 14:7, rather than Lev. 11:4ff., taking that simple list of three forbidden beasts and conducting the expected exegesis. Section v.9C–F then explain why each of the beasts stands for the several kingdoms. Section v.10 then takes up the comparison of Rome to the pig. It is formally different from Section v.9, but necessary to complete its theme and thought. Section v.11 then reverts to Lev. 11:4, a whole new exposition, now beginning a series of exegeses of the language for "chewing" or "bringing up" the cud *(GRH)*. The basic pattern is shown in Sections v.11A–D, N–T. Section v.11E–M really does not belong. Section v.12 follows a very strict formal pattern and contains no interpolations. Only Section v.12N is tacked on. Section v.12L is integral, as shown in Section v.13K. Section v.13, for its part, adheres still more closely to the basic pattern since it exhibits a formulaic quality in its language. That Sections v.11–13 constitute a single carefully worked out exposition of a single idea in a single pattern seems to me self-evident. But these materials reach their climax at Section v.13J–K. And, in my view, the framer of the whole, Sections v.1–10, then v.11–13, had exactly that goal in mind. So while, as is commonly the case, the composite contains miscellaneous materials, framed by diverse hands at different times, the judgment of the final compositor is everywhere expressed, and the impact of his viewpoint cannot be missed.

Philosophy executed through Scripture

What we have in *Leviticus Rabbah* is the result of the mode of thought not of prophets or historians, but of philosophers and scientists. The framers propose not to lay down, but to discover, rules governing Israel's life. As we find the rules of nature by identifying and classifying facts of natural life, so we find rules of society by identifying and classifying the facts of Israel's social life. In both modes of inquiry we make sense of things by bringing together like specimens and finding out whether they form a species, then bringing together like species and finding out whether they form a genus—in all, classifying data and identifying the rules that make possible the classification.

That sort of thinking lies at the deepest level of list-making, which offers a proposition and facts (for social rules) as much as a genus and its species (for rules of nature). Once discovered, the social rules of Israel's national life yield explicit statements, such as that God hates the arrogant and loves the humble. The logical status of these statements, in context, is as secure and unassailable as the logical status of statements about physics, ethics, or politics, as these emerge in philosophical thought. What differentiates the statements is not their logical status—as sound, scientific philosophy—but only their subject matter, on the one side, and distinctive rhetoric, on the other.

Modes of thought of *Leviticus Rabbah*

To summarize:

(1) The principal mode of thought required one thing to be read in terms of another, one verse in light of a different verse (or topic, theme, symbol, idea), one situation in light of another.

(2) The principal subject of thought is the moral condition of Israel, on the one side, and the salvation of Israel, on the other.

(3) The single unifying proposition—the syllogism at the document's deepest structure—is that Israel's salvation depends upon its moral condition.

What makes *Leviticus Rabbah* cogent

It follows that *Leviticus Rabbah* constitutes not merely diverse thoughts but a single, sustained composition. The authors do so through a rich tapestry of unstated propositions that are only illustrated, delineated at the outset, by the statement of some propositions. And these also are illustrated. It is, in a word, a "syllogism by example"—that is, by repeated appeal to facts—rather than by argument alone. For in context, an example constitutes a fact. The source of many examples or facts is Scripture, the foundation of all reality. Accordingly, in the context of Israelite life and culture, in which Scripture recorded facts, we have a severely logical, because entirely factual, statement of how rightly organized and classified facts sustain a proposition. In context that proposition is presented as rigorously and critically as the social rules of discourse allowed.

In this document the authorship chose in Leviticus itself an isolated verse here, an odd phrase there. These then presented the pretext for propositional discourse commonly quite out of phase with the cited passage. The verses that are quoted ordinarily shift from the meanings they convey to the implications they contain, speaking about something, anything, other than what they seem to be saying. So the *as-if* frame of mind brought to Scripture precipitates renewal of Scripture, requiring the seeing of everything with fresh eyes. And the result of the new vision was a re-imagining of the social world envisioned by the document at hand, I mean, the everyday world of Israel in its Land in that same difficult time at which *Genesis Rabbah* was taking shape, sometime in the fifth century and the first century after the conversion of Constantine and the beginning of the Christian chapter of Western civilization. For what the sages now proposed was a reconstruction of existence along the lines of the ancient design of Scripture as they read it. What that meant was that, from a sequence of one-time and linear events, everything that happened was turned into a repetition of known and already experienced paradigms, hence, once more, a mythic being. The source and core of the myth derive from Scripture—Scripture reread, renewed, reconstructed along with the society that revered Scripture.

The message of *Leviticus Rabbah* in detail

The recurrent message of the document may be stated in a brief way.

Israel and God

God loves Israel, so gave them the Torah, which defines their life and governs their welfare. Israel is alone in its category *(sui generis)*, so what is a virtue to Israel is a vice to the nations, life-giving to Israel, poison to the gentiles. True, Israel sins, but God forgives that sin, having punished the nation on account of it. Such a process has yet to come to an end, but it will culminate in Israel's complete regeneration. Meanwhile, Israel's assurance of God's love lies in the many expressions of special concern, for even the humblest and most ordinary aspects of the national life: the food the nation eats, the sexual practices by which it procreates. These life-sustaining, life-transmitting activities draw God's special interest, as a mark of his general love for Israel. Israel then is supposed to achieve its life in conformity with the marks of God's love.

Israel and the Nations

These indications moreover signify the character of Israel's difficulty, namely, subordination to the nations in general, but to Rome in particular. Both food laws and skin diseases stand for the nations. There is yet another category of sin, also collective and generative of collective punishment, and that is social sin. The moral character of Israel's life, the treatment of people by one another, the practice of gossip and small-scale thuggery—these too draw down divine penalty. The nation's fate therefore corresponds to its moral condition. The moral condition, however, emerges not only from the current generation. Israel's richest hope lies in the merit of the ancestors, thus in the Scriptural record of the merits attained by the founders of the nation, those who originally brought it into being and gave it life.

The world to come will right all presently unbalanced relationships. What is good will go forward, what is bad will come to an end. The simple message is that the things people revere, the cult and its majestic course through the year, will go on; Jerusalem will come back, so too the Temple, in all their glory. Israel will be saved through the merit of the ancestors, atonement, study of Torah, practice of religious duties. The prevalence of the eschatological dimension in the formal structures, with its messianic and other expressions, here finds its counterpart in the repetition of the same few symbols in the expression of doctrine.

Israel's life

The theme of the moral life of Israel produces propositions concerning not only the individual but, more important, the social virtues that the community as a whole must exhibit. First of all, the message to the individual constitutes a revision, for this context, of the address to the nation: humility as against arrogance, obedience as against sin, constant concern not to follow one's natural inclination to do evil or to overcome the natural limitations of the human condition. Israel must accept its fate, obey and rely on the merits accrued through the ages and

God's special love. The individual must conform, in ordinary affairs, to this same paradigm of patience and submission. Great men and women, that is, individual heroes within the established paradigm, conform to that same pattern, exemplifying the national virtues. Among these, Moses stands out; he has no equal. The special position of the humble Moses is complemented by the patriarchs and by David, all of whom knew how to please God and left as an inheritance to Israel the merit they had thereby attained.

If we now ask about further recurring themes or topics, there is one so commonplace that we should have to list the majority of paragraphs of discourse in order to provide a complete list. It is the list of events in Israel's history, meaning, in this context, Israel's history solely in scriptural times, down through the return to Zion. The one-time events of the generation of the flood, Sodom and Gomorrah, the patriarchs and the sojourn in Egypt, the exodus, the revelation of the Torah at Sinai, the golden calf, the Davidic monarchy and the building of the Temple, Sennacherib, Hezekiah, and the destruction of northern Israel, Nebuchadnezzar and the destruction of the Temple in 586, the life of Israel in Babylonian captivity, Daniel and his associates, Mordecai and Haman—these events occur over and over again. They turn out to serve as paradigms of sin and atonement, steadfastness and divine intervention, and equivalent lessons.

We find, in fact, a fairly standard repertoire of scriptural heroes or villains, on the one side, and conventional lists of Israel's enemies and their actions and downfall, on the other. The boastful, for instance, include the generation of the flood, Sodom and Gomorrah, Pharaoh, Sisera, Sennacherib, Nebuchadnezzar, the wicked empire (Rome)—contrasted to Israel, "despised and humble in this world." The four kingdoms recur again and again, always ending, with Rome, with the repeated message that after Rome will come Israel. But Israel has to make this happen through its faith and submission to God's will. Lists of enemies ring the changes on Cain, the Sodomites, Pharaoh, Sennacherib, Nebuchadnezzar, Haman.

Does *Leviticus Rabbah* form a theological statement on its own?

A rapid reprise shows that *Leviticus Rabbah* makes a cogent theological statement, but not a free-standing one; it is Scripture's, improved and embellished. The reprise follows.

God has made himself known to man in the Torah, which Israel accepted, and the nations rejected. The Torah contains God's design for creation and reveals the future. God is just and merciful. God judges man, Israel knows the power of repentance and atonement. God punishes Israel through its subjugation to the nations, and that leads Israel to repent and atone, and God forgives Israel. In the end God will judge all humanity, and, having atoned through death, all Israel—those who know God and accept his sovereignty—will rise from the grave, stand in judgment, and enter Eden for eternal life. These propositions cover most of the theological compositions and composites of *Leviticus Rabbah* and of the other Midrash-compilations already examined in this project. And, it is self-evident, they also represent no more, and no less, than the story that Scripture tells.

So *Leviticus Rabbah* does not form a theological statement on its own. That is so, even though the theological statement that it makes can be read autonomously to yield a system quite like the one just now set forth in the context of Scripture. That is, we can compose a cogent theological system entirely within the framework of our document. But, when we do, we find ourselves recapitulating that encompassing theological system, vastly transcending the limits of *Leviticus Rabbah*, that the system of Scripture itself sets forth. The whole is embodied in a story. The category-formations within which the discrete data of the document find their place yield a coherent story, tracking that of Genesis through Kings as read by the Prophets. It is the story of God's yearning for Israel, within mankind, because of Israel's willingness, stated at Sinai, to know God in the Torah and freely to choose to accept God's dominion in the Torah. At Sinai too, Israel sinned and rebelled. God punished Israel but forgives repentant Israel when Israel atones. Israel's situation even now replicates the paradigm of sin and suffering, punishment, atonement, and forgiveness. And ultimately, God will redeem Israel from the nations where, by reason of sin, Israel has been scattered, just as God redeemed Israel from Egypt. It is Scripture's story, when Scripture is read forward from Creation to the here and now of contemporary Israel of the Rabbinic sages. Exemplified by *Leviticus Rabbah*, Midrash method forms no more than a recapitulation of Scripture's message—and no less than that. It embodies the claim of the Rabbinic sages to recapitulate in the documents of oral tradition the message and meaning of the written Torah.

7

Numbers in *Sifré to Numbers*

Systematically Reading and Expounding Scripture's Narratives in Accord with the Rabbinic Model

Numbers in Judaism

The book of Numbers is mediated to Judaism by *Sifré to Numbers,* ca. 300 C.E., a miscellaneous reading of most of the book of Numbers attributed to the same Tannaite authorities that are responsible for the Mishnah and Tosefta, *Mekhilta attributed to R. Ishmael, Sifra,* and *Sifré to Deuteronomy* as well. The compositions that comprise *Sifré to Numbers* yield no propositional program. But the recurrent proofs that yield one and the same implication do accumulate. When we see what is implicit in the various exegetical exercises, we find a clear-cut message. Then, predictably, it is only when we examine the rhetorical plan that this propositional program emerges.

Affinities with *Sifra* and *Sifré to Deuteronomy*

That rhetorical plan, common to *Sifra, Sifré to Numbers,* and *Sifré to Deuteronomy,* shows that the exegetes, while working verse by verse, in fact have brought a considerable program to the reading of the books of Leviticus, Numbers, and Deuteronomy. The authorships of *Sifra* and the two Sifrés share that program: cite a verse of Scripture and then a passage of the Mishnah. The aim is familiar from *Sifra:* logic alone cannot suffice. So all law and its category-formations must in the end derive from the written part of the Torah. Then the single sustained proposition of the several writings is that truth derives from Scripture, not from reason unaided by revelation.

The proposition in all three writings concerns the interplay of the Oral Torah, represented by the Mishnah, with the written Torah, represented by the book of Leviticus or Numbers or Deuteronomy. That question demanded, in the Rabbinic sages' view, not an answer comprising mere generalities. They wished to show their results through details, masses of details, and, like the rigorous philosophers that they were, they argued essentially through an inductive procedure, amassing evidence that in its accumulation made the intended point.

So much for rhetoric, what about topic?

As with *Sifra*, therefore, *Sifré to Numbers* follows no topical program distinct from that of Scripture, which is systematically clarified. An interest in the relations to Scripture of the Mishnah and Tosefta, a concern with the dialectics as we found characteristic of *Sifra*—these occur episodically, but scarcely define the character of the document. As with *Sifra*, here too, the sole point of coherence for the discrete sentences or paragraphs derives from the base-verse of Scripture that is subject to commentary. At the same time, if we examine the incremental message, the cumulative effect of the formal traits of speech and thought revealed in the uniform rhetoric and syntax of the document, we may discern a propositional program that is implicit in the rhetoric and logic of the compilation. What is required here is the articulation of the general consequences of numerous specific exegetical exercises. By the very labor of explaining the meaning of verses of Scripture, the Rabbinic exegetes laid claim to participate in the work of revelation. And by distinguishing their contribution from the received text of the Torah, they clarified their place within the process of revelation.

What then is the documentary message?

(1) Beginning at all points with a verse of Scripture, sages demonstrate that only by starting with the word-choices and propositions of that verse of Scripture can all further interpretation commence.

(2) Consequently, man has a place in the process of revealing the Torah of Sinai, which comes to expression in the careful separation of the cited verse of the written Torah from the contribution of the contemporary exegete. In that formal preference too, the authorship made a major point and established—if implicitly—a central syllogism: God's will follows the rules of reason. Man can investigate the consequences of reason as expressed in God's will. Therefore man can join in the labor of exploring God's will in the Torah.

(3) A further formal preference in all three documents, in addition to the exegetical form, makes the same point. This familiar, other form involves citation of a passage of the Mishnah followed by an extensive discourse on how the verse of Scripture that pertains to the topic of that Mishnah-passage must contribute its facts, revealed at Sinai, if we wish to know the truth. Reason alone, which is systematically tested through a sequence of propositions shown to fail, will not suffice.

Formal traits of the commentary

Let us now characterize the formal exegetical traits of *Sifré to Numbers* as a commentary, since it is here that we identify the implicit propositional program of the document's compilers and the writers of the bulk of its compositions. These we reduce to two classifications, extrinsic and intrinsic exegesis, a purely formal distinction solely based on the point of origin of the theme, problem, or polemic under disussion:

(1) exegesis of a verse in the book of Numbers in terms of the theme or problems of that verse, hence, intrinsic exegesis;

(2) exegesis of a verse in Numbers in terms of a theme or polemic not particular to that verse, hence, extrinsic exegesis.

The forms of extrinsic exegesis

The implicit message of the external category proves simple to define, since the several extrinsic classifications turn out to form a cogent polemic. Let me state the recurrent polemic of external exegesis.

The syllogistic composition

Scripture supplies hard facts, which, properly classified, generate syllogisms. By collecting and classifying facts of Scripture, therefore, we may produce firm laws of history, society, and Israel's everyday life. The diverse compositions, which compile verses from various books of the Scriptures in a list of evidence for a given proposition, make that one point. And given their power and cogency, they make the point stick.

The fallibility of reason unguided by scriptural exegesis

Scripture alone supplies a reliable basis for speculation. Laws cannot be generated by reason or logic unguided by Scripture. Efforts at classification and contrastive-analogical exegesis, in which Scripture does not supply the solution to all problems, prove few and far between. This polemic forms the complement of the point above. So when extrinsic issues intervene in the exegetical process, they coalesce to make a single point. Scripture stands paramount; logic, reason, analytical processes of classification and differentiation, secondary. Reason not built on scriptural foundations yields uncertain results. The Mishnah itself demands scriptural bases.

The forms of intrinsic exegesis

What about the polemic present in the intrinsic exegetical exercises? This clearly does not allow for ready characterization.

The limitations of logic unguided by revelation

Intrinsic exegetical exercises focus on the use of logic, specifically, the logic of classification, comparison and contrast of species of a genus, in the explanation of the meaning of verses of the book of Numbers. The internal dialectical mode, moving from point to point as logic dictates, underlines the main point already stated: logic produces possibilities, Scripture chooses among them. Again, the question, "What is the purpose of this passage?" commonly produces an answer generated by further verses of Scripture, e.g., this passage clarifies what otherwise would be confusing only on the basis of other verses. *So Scripture produces problems of confusion and duplication, and Scripture—not logic, not differentiation, not classification—solves those problems. Scripture is complete, harmonious, perfect.* Logic not only does not generate truth beyond the limits of Scripture but also plays no important role in the harmonization of difficulties yielded by what appear to be duplications or disharmonies. These forms of internal exegesis then make the same point that the extrinsic ones do.

Citation of a verse and a gloss thereon

This is the single most profuse category of exegesis. We have treated that form as simple and undifferentiated: (1) a verse or a clause of Scripture, followed by (2) a brief statement of its meaning. Since there is no unifying polemic in favor of, or against, a given proposition, this most common form of exegesis also proves to be the least pointed: X bears this meaning, Y bears that meaning, or, as we have seen, citation of verse X, followed by (what this means is).... Whether simple or elaborate, the result is the same.

The implicit proposition in the exegetical exercise of *Sifré to Numbers*

What can be at issue when no polemic expressed in the formal traits of syntax and logic finds its way to the surface? What does the exegete do when he merely clarifies a phrase? Or, to frame the question more logically: what premises must validate the exegete's *intervention,* that is, the willingness to undertake to explain the meaning of a verse of Scripture? The answer is that man's independent judgment bears weight and produces meaning. Man therefore may join in the process of receiving the Torah and expounding it. God's revelation to Moses at Sinai requires man's intervention. Man has the role, and the right, to say what that revelation means. Man's mind corresponds to God's.

The critical point is that what validates the exegete's entry into the process of revelation is *the correspondence between the logic of his mind and the logic of the document.* Only if man thinks in accord with the logic of the revealed Torah can his thought-processes contribute to clarifying the unfolding of God's will in the Torah. Man is able to join in the discourse of the Torah because he speaks the same language of thought: syntax and grammar cohere at the deepest levels of his intellect.

Since a shared logic of syntax and grammar joins man's mind to the mind of God as revealed in the Torah, he can explain the meaning of a sentence of the Torah. So he too can amplify, clarify, expand, revise, rework: that is to say, create a commentary. So the work of commenting upon the written Torah bears profound consequence for the revelation of the Torah, the sage becoming partner with God in the giving of the Torah. By reaching such a conclusion, we find ourselves repeating the main point that *Sifra* yields in the description of Rabbinic literature as a whole.

A sample of *Sifré to Numbers*

What we see in Sifré Numbers' reading of Num. 7:1ff. is what we should by now expect: a systematic and close reading, verse by verse, with slight attention to issues of coherence with large-scale meaning: exegesis pure and simple.

Sifré to Numbers XLIV:i.1–ii.3

i. 1. A. "(On the day when Moses had finished setting up the tabernacle and had anointed and consecrated it with all its furnishings and had anointed and consecrated the altar with all its utensils) the leaders of Israel (heads of their fathers' houses, the leaders of the tribes, who were over those who were numbered) offered and brought their offerings before the Lord, six covered wagons and twelve oxen, a wagon for every two of the leaders, and for each one an ox, they offered them before the tabernacle. Then the Lord said to Moses, 'Accept these from them, that they may be used in doing the service of the tent of meeting, and give them to the Levites, to each man according to his service.' So Moses took the wagons and the oxen and gave them to the Levites)" (Num. 7:1–6):

    B. Scripture indicates that for each of the seven days of consecrating the tabernacle, Moses would set up the tabernacle, and every morning he would anoint it and dismantle it. But on that day he set it up and anointed it, but he did not dismantle it. (On the prior days he set up the tabernacle and dismantled it. On the eighth day, he set it up but did not dismantle it.)

C. R. Yosé b. R. Judah: "Also on the eighth day he set it up and dismantled it, for it is said, 'And in the first month in the second year on the first day of the month the tabernacle was erected' (Ex. 30:17). On the basis of that verse we learn that on the twenty-third day of Adar, Aaron and his sons, the tabernacle and the utensils were anointed."

i. 2. A. On the first day of the month the tabernacle was set up, on the second the red cow was burned (for the purification rite required at Num. 19), on the third day water was sprinkled from it in lieu of the second act of sprinkling, the Levites were shaved.

B. On that same day the Presence of God rested in the tabernacle, as it is said, "Then the cloud covered the tent of meeting, and the glory of the Lord filled the tabernacle, and Moses was not able to enter the tent of meeting, because the cloud abode upon it" (Ex. 40:34).

C. On that same day the heads offered their offerings, as it is said, "He who offered his offering the first day . . ." (Num. 7:12). Scripture uses the word "first" only in a setting when "first" introduces all of the days of the year.

D. On that day fire came down from heaven and consumed the offerings, as it is said, "And fire came forth from before the Lord and consumed the burnt offering and the fat upon the altar" (Lev. 9:24).

E. On that day the sons of Aaron offered strange fire, as it is said, "Now Nadab and Abihu, the sons of Aaron, each took his censer and put fire in it . . . and offered unholy fire before the Lord, such as he had not commanded them" (Lev. 10:1).

F. "And they died before the Lord . . ." (Lev. 10:2): they died before the Lord, but they fell outside (of the tabernacle, not imparting corpse uncleanness to it).

G. How so? They were on their way out.

H. R. Yosé says, "An angel sustained them, as they died, until they got out, and they fell in the courtyard, as it is said, 'And Moses called Mishael and Elzaphan, the sons of Uzziel the uncle of Aaron, and said to them, "Draw near, carry your brethren from before the sanctuary out of the camp"' (Lev. 10:4). What is stated is not, 'From before the Lord,' but, 'from before the sanctuary.'"

I. R. Ishmael says, "The context indicates the true state of affairs, as it is said, 'And they died before the Lord,' meaning, they died inside and fell inside. How did they get out? People dragged them with iron ropes."

The expansion and amplification of the base verse comprise Section i.1. Beginning with Section i.2, we deal with the other events of that same day, surveying the several distinct narratives that deal with the same issue, Ex. 40, Lev. 9–10, and so on. This produces the effect of unifying the diverse scriptural accounts into one tale, an important and powerful exegetical result. One of the persistent contributions of our exegetes is to collect and harmonize a diversity of verses taken to refer to the same day, event, or rule. These yield a generalization out of the cited cases.

ii. 1. A. "... and had anointed and consecrated it with all its furnishings and had anointed and consecrated the altar with all its utensils:"
   B. Might I infer that as each utensil was anointed, it was sanctified?
   C. Scripture says, "... and had anointed and consecrated it with all its furnishings and had anointed and consecrated the altar with all its utensils," meaning that not one of them was sanctified until all of them had been anointed. (The process proceeded by stages.)

ii. 2. A. "... and had anointed and consecrated it with all its furnishings and had anointed and consecrated the altar with all its utensils:"
   B. The anointing was done both inside and outside (of the utensil).
   C. R. Josiah says, "Utensils meant to hold liquids were anointed inside and outside, but utensils meant to hold dry stuffs were anointed on the inside but not anointed on the outside."
   D. R. Jonathan says, "Utensils meant to hold liquids were anointed inside and not outside, but utensils meant to hold dry stuffs not anointed.
   E. "You may know that they were not consecrated, for it is said, 'You shall bring from your dwellings two loaves of bread to be waved, made of two-tenths of an ephah' (Lev. 23:17). Then when do they belong to the Lord? Only after they are baked." (The bread was baked in utensils at home, so the utensils were not consecrated.)

ii. 3. A. Rabbi says, "Why is it said, '... and had anointed and consecrated it'? And is it not already stated, '... and had anointed and consecrated it'?
   B. "This indicates that with the anointing of these utensils all future utensils were sanctified (so that the sanctification of the tabernacle enjoyed permanence and a future tabernacle or Temple did not require a rite of sanctification once again)."

Section ii.1 clarifies the rite of sanctification, aiming at the notion that the act of consecration covered everything at once, leading to the final conclusion that that act also covered utensils later on to be used in the cult. Section ii.3 goes over that same ground. Section ii.2 deals with its own issue, pursuing the exegesis of the verse at hand. Its interest in the consecration of the utensils is entirely congruent with Section 3, because it wants to know the status of utensils outside of the cult, concluding that while they serve the purpose of the cult as specified, still, they are not deemed to have been consecrated.

Sifré to Numbers XLV:i.1–ii.4

i. 1. A. "(On the day when Moses had finished setting up the tabernacle and had anointed and consecrated it with all its furnishings and had anointed and consecrated the altar with all its utensils) the leaders of Israel (heads of their fathers' houses, the leaders of the tribes, who were over those who were numbered) offered and brought their offerings before the Lord, six covered wagons and twelve oxen, a wagon for every two of the leaders, and for each one an ox, they offered them be-

fore the tabernacle. Then the Lord said to Moses, 'Accept these from them, that they may be used in doing the service of the tent of meeting, and give them to the Levites, to each man according to his service.' So Moses took the wagons and the oxen and gave them to the Levites" (Num. 7:1–6):
- B. May I infer that they had been ordinary people who were elevated.
- C. Scripture says, "heads of their fathers' houses."
- D. And they were not merely, "heads of their fathers' houses," but also "the leaders of the tribes, who were over those who were numbered."
- E. They were leaders, sons of leaders.

i. 2. A. "... the leaders of the tribes, who were over those who were numbered:"
- B. They were the same ones who had been appointed over them in Egypt, as it is said, "And the leaders of the children of Israel smote . . ." (Ex. 5:14).

The interest is in showing the distinguished origins of the Israelite leadership.

ii. 1. A. "... six covered wagons (and twelve oxen, a wagon for every two of the leaders, and for each one an ox, they offered them before the tabernacle):"
- B. The word "covered" means only "decorated," for they lacked for nothing.
- C. Rabbi says, "The word 'covered' means only 'canopied,' and even though there is no firm proof for that proposition, there is at least some indication of it: 'And they shall bring all your brethren from all the nations as an offering to the Lord, upon horses and in chariots and in litters and upon mules and upon dromedaries to my holy mountain, Jerusalem, says the Lord' (Is. 66:20)."

ii. 2. A. "... six covered wagons and twelve oxen, a wagon for every two of the leaders, and for each one an ox, they offered them before the tabernacle."
- B. May I infer that there was a wagon for each one?
- C. Scripture says, "... a wagon for every two of the leaders."
- D. May I infer there was an ox for every two of the leaders?
- E. Scripture says, "... and for each one an ox."

ii. 3. A. They came and took up positions before the tabernacle, but Moses did not accept anything from them, until it was stated to him by the mouth of the Holy One, "Accept these from them, that they may be used in doing the service of the tent of meeting."
- B. Lo, mortals thus brought their judgment into accord with the judgment on high.

ii. 4. A. R. Nathan says, "And why in the present matter did the princes bring voluntary gifts first (rather than waiting for the community to do so), while in the work of the making of the tabernacle they in fact did not

        volunteer to begin with (but let the community give and only afterward they made their contribution)?
- B. "Well, this is how the leaders had earlier reasoned matters out: 'Let the community contribute what they will, and what is still needed after they have given we shall make up.'
- C. "When the princes realized that the community had provided all that was needed, as it is said, 'And the work was sufficient,' (Ex. 34:4), the princes said, 'What is left for us to do?'
- D. "So the princes brought the precious stones for the ephod.
- E. "That is why, in the present case, the princes brought their voluntary offering first (so as not to be left out)."

Section ii.1 provides the explanation of a word, and Section ii.2 proceeds to a phrase. Section ii.3 restates what the text says and explains its implications, and Section ii.4 draws into relationship two distinct accounts of gifts to the sanctuary, explaining in a striking way the difference in the detail of the two pictures.

Sifré to Numbers XLVI:i.1–ii.2

i.   1. A. "So Moses took the wagons and the oxen and gave them to the Levites" (Num. 7:1–6):
          B. Lo, Moses took them and divided them up on his own initiative.

i.   2. A. "The two wagons and the four oxen he gave to the sons of Gershom, and the four wagons and the eight oxen he gave to the sons of Merari,"
          B. Because Eleazar had sixteen sons, and Ithamar, eight.
          C. As it is said, "The male heads of families proved to be more numerous in the line of Eleazar than in that of Ithamar, so that sixteen heads of families were grouped under the line of Eleazar and eight under that of Ithamar. He organized them by drawing lots among them, for there were sacred officers and offices of God in the line of Eleazar and in that of Ithamar" (1 Chr. 24:4–6).

Section i.1 draws its own conclusions from the cited verse, and Section i.2 proceeds to relate the present division to the materials available elsewhere, a common exegetical interest.

ii. 1. A. "He gave none to the Kohathites, because the service laid upon them was that of the holy things: these they had to carry themselves on their shoulders" (Num. 7:9):
          B. R. Nathan, "On the basis of what is said here we see what David missed, for the Levites did not bear the ark, but they bore the wagon, as it is said, 'They mounted the ark of God on a new cart and conveyed it from the house of Abinadab on the hill' (1 Sam. 6:3).
          C. "'The Lord was angry with Uzzah and struck him down there for his rash act, so he died there beside the ark of God' (2 Sam. 6:7).

D. "'David was vexed because the Lord's anger had broken out upon Uzzah, and he called the place Perez-uzzah, the name it still bears' (2 Sam 6:8).

E. "Ahitophel said to David, 'Should you not have learned the lesson of Moses, your master, for the Levites bore the ark only on their shoulders, as it says, "He gave none to the Kohathites, because the service laid upon them was that of the holy things: these they had to carry themselves on their shoulders."'

F. "Lo, David then sent and had it carried by shoulder, as it is said, 'And David summoned Zadok and Abiathar the priests, together with the Levites, Uriel, Asaiah, Joel, Shemaiah, Eliel, and Amminadab, and said to them, You who are heads of families of the Levites, hallow yourselves, you and your kinsmen, and bring up the ark of the Lord, the God of Israel, to the place which I have prepared for it. . . . So the priests and the Levites hallowed themselves to bring up the ark of the Lord, the God of Israel, and the Levites carried the ark of God, bearing it on their shoulders with poles, as Moses had prescribed at the command of the Lord' (1 Chr. 15:11–15)."

ii. 2. A. "This was their order of duty for the discharge of their service when they entered the house of the Lord, according to the rule prescribed for them by their ancestor Aaron, who had received his instructions from the Lord, the God of Israel" (1 Chr. 24:19):

B. Where did he give a commandment? He gave nothing at all to the sons of Kohath. So lo, the sons of the Levites in no way innovated, but everything was done on the instructions of Moses, and Moses did everything at the instructions of the Almighty.

Section ii.1 is important in underlining David's error in not following the precedent established here by Moses and the Levites, that the ark be carried on their shoulders. David then corrected himself, following the proper precedent. Section ii.2 then emphasizes that the precedent established by the base verse guided the Levites later on. What we see then is a harmonization of diverse materials on the same important theme.

Sifré to Numbers XLVII:i.1–2

1. A. "And the leaders presented offerings for the dedication of the altar on the day it was anointed; and the leaders offered their offering before the altar. And the Lord said to Moses, 'They shall offer their offerings, one leader each day, for the dedication of the altar.' He who offered his offering the first day was Nahshon the son of Amminadab of the tribe of Judah; and his offering was one silver plate whose weight was a hundred and thirty shekels, one silver basin of seventy shekels according to the shekel of the sanctuary, both of them full of fine flour mixed with oil for a cereal offering; one golden dish of ten

shekels, full of incense; one young bull, one ram, one male lamb a year old, for a burnt offering; one male goat for a sin offering; and for the sacrifice of peace offerings, two oxen, five rams, five male goats, and five male lambs a year old. This was the offering of Nahshon the son of Amminadab)" (Num. 7:10–17):
- B. The Scripture thus indicates that just as the princes made voluntary gifts for the work of building the tabernacle, so they did for the dedication of the tabernacle.
2. A. "And the leaders offered offerings for the dedication of the altar . . . and the leaders offered their offering before the altar:"
- B. They came and stood before the altar, but Moses did not accept the offerings from them, until he was so instructed by the word of the Holy One: "Let them make their offerings for the dedication of the altar."
- C. Moses still did not know the proper manner in which they were to make their offerings, whether by the order dictated for the journeys, whether by the order dictated by the generations in which the tribal founders had been born, until he was instructed by the explicit statement of the Holy One, blessed be he, "Let them offer in accord with the order governing their journeys," as it is said, "And it came to pass." For the words "and it came to pass" indicate solely what was said to Moses on the authority of the Holy One, so they offered in accord with the order governing their journeys.
- D. But Moses still did not know how the princes were to make their offerings, specifically, whether it was to be done all at once, or each one on his own day, until he was so instructed that each was to offer on his own day, as it is said, "They shall offer their offerings, one leader each day, for the dedication of the altar."
- E. The princes make voluntary offerings, but ordinary people do not do so. Why then does Scripture say, "They shall offer their offerings, one leader each day, for the dedication of the altar" (specifying that the princes did it, when we know that only they could do it)
- F. It was because Nahshon was a king, and he made the offering first. So people should not say, "Lo, because I made the offering first, I shall make an offering with everyone else, day by day." Therefore it is said, "They shall offer their offerings, *one leader* each day, for the dedication of the altar."

We begin with the simple clarification of the donation of the princes, not only for building the tabernacle, but also for dedicating the altar. Then, Section i.2 emphasizes that each detail of the process of dedication was dictated by divine instructions. This would highlight the polemic that the original work of sanctification imparted to the cult an indelible character of holiness. It is difficult to find a single point that does not begin in the amplification of the statements of Scripture.

Sifré to Numbers's theology

Sifré to Numbers stands out in the Rabbinic Midrash compilations for a remarkable fact. The document scarcely acknowledges the Rabbinic theological structure and system that animate the other Midrash compilations of the formative age. It contains such a negligible quantity of theological compositions and a corpus of such marginal and episodic quality, that we cannot make any claims about the presence of a theological system that is realized there. The few theological category-formations of *Sifré to Numbers* are however shared among the other Midrash-compilations: *Pesiqta deRab Kahana, Genesis Rabbah, Song of Songs Rabbah, Leviticus Rabbah, Lamentations Rabbati, Ruth Rabbah, Esther Rabbah I, Sifra,* and *Sifré to Deuteronomy*. To the extent that *Sifré to Numbers* contains theological statements at all, familiar category-formations do accommodate those statements. That is to claim very little.

God and man, God and Israel

The main point in the Midrash compilations just now listed, including this one, is that God's relationships with mankind in general ("the nations") and God's relationships with Israel in particular are complementary. The nations rejected, Israel accepted, God's dominion embodied in the Torah, and the rest follows. But *Sifré to Numbers* contains remarkably little reflection on God's relationship with the gentiles. Its focus throughout is on God's love for Israel. The framers then take for granted that the gentiles have marked themselves as God's enemies. In the next rubric, we see the consequence: the nations also mark themselves as Israel's enemies.

The principal point is familiar: God loves and yearns for Israel. The correlation of God's love for Israel and God's enduring presence within Israel extends even to Israel's uncleanness and sinfulness. God so loves Israel that even though they contract uncleanness, his presence remains with them (*Sifré to Numbers* I:x.1). And sin is the cause of that uncleanness (I:x.2–3). But, also, Israel did as Moses instructed them (I:xi.1). Israel is so precious that God dwells among them even when they are unclean. God accompanies Israel into Exile, to Egypt, Babylonia, Elam, Edom; and God will return with them when they come back to the Land (CLXI:iii.2). Why does God so love Israel? It is because Israel accepted the Torah and carry out God's will.

But Israel does the opposite as well. When the Israelites carry out the will of the Omnipresent, then, ". . . the Lord [will] lift up his countenance upon you." But when the Israelites do not carry out the will of the Omnipresent, then, ". . . [he] will not lift up a face and show favoritism" (Deut. 10:17). So Israel's deeds make the difference (XLII:i.2). When Israel (XLII:i.2) obeys the word of the Lord their God, then all the blessings promised in the Torah come upon them. These blessings include property and good health; the blessing keeps Israel from the evil impulse. It prevents others from ruling over Israel and keeps Israel from demons.

God will keep the covenant he made with the fathers of Israel. Israel is subject to a foreordained end. God will keep the soul of the Israelite at the hour of death and guard him in the world to come (XI:i.1–10). A mark of God's grace is to make a person pleasing to other people (XLI:ii.2). It is further by giving the Israelite knowledge, understanding, enlightenment, virtue and wisdom (XLI:ii.4), and mastery of the Torah (XLI:ii.4). Various cases prove that gentiles who bring themselves near to God are themselves brought closer by God, and all the more so an Israelite who carries out the Torah will be drawn nearer to God by God's own intervention (LXXVIII:i.1).

The next category-formation, showing the parallel relationships of the gentiles with God and with Israel, completes the one significant theological program that *Sifré to Numbers* sets forth.

God and the nations, Israel and the nations

The logic of the first theological category-formation dictates its continuation: the correlation of relationships, the nations' with God, the nations' with Israel, Israel's with God, God's with both other parties. The nations who hate Israel hate God. Those who support Israel support God. Whoever hates Israel is as if he hates God, whoever rose up against Israel is as if he rose up against God, whoever lays hands on Israel is as if he lays hands on the apple of God's eye. So too, whoever helps Israel is as if he helps God. Israel's suffering is suffering for God too. Everywhere Israel went into exile, God went into exile with them. And when they come back, God's presence will return with them (LXXXIV:iv.1). But in *Sifré to Numbers,* the specific stories about the nations and Israel, e.g., Balaam's blessing, do not yield data that sustain weighty propositions pertinent to these matters. And that failure in an important component of the exposition of Numbers matches the still more striking one we shall encounter in a moment.

Israel's encounter with God through the Torah

Here is an example of a theological category-formation well-attested in other documents yet scarcely noted in *Sifré to Numbers.* An Israelite cannot pick and choose among the commandments but must accept and keep them all (CXII:iv.2). One who studies the Torah but does not repeat it for others despises the word of the Lord (CXII:iv.3). This is a trivial point, hardly comparable to assertions elsewhere that through Torah-study Israel meets God.

Divine justice and mercy

The issue of justice, which shapes the generative logic of the entire Rabbinic theological system and structure, surfaces only rarely. A single point registers, the priority of mercy over justice in God's ultimate dispensation. God's attribute of bestowing mercy outweighs his attribute of bestowing justice (VIII:viii.1–2). A mark of divine justice is that the punishment commences with the limb that began the transgression. This therefore yields an argument *a fortiori:* If punishment is exacted beginning from the limb with which she began to commit the transgression, then when good, which is the greater, is bestowed, how much the more so! (XVIII:i.1). But well might we claim, the main point has been missed, when we realize, the document does not contain speculation, systematic or even episodic, on the justice of the disposition of the wife accused of infidelity. And, beyond that point, the entire issue of divine justice, raised by that matter, is not treated.

Midrash compilation without theology?

If the only Rabbinic document in our hands were *Sifré to Numbers,* we should find the reconstruction of the Rabbinic theological system exceedingly difficult. All we should find plausible is that the Rabbinic exegetes drew as appropriate on the theological category-formations of Scripture. For it is Scripture that originally draws the monumental parallels between Adam and Israel, Adam's relationship with God and Israel's relationship with God, and it is in Scripture that the Rabbinic sages learn to see God's enemies as Israel's enemies, and Israel's as God's. In that context, the original judgment—that *Sifré to Numbers* neither adumbrates nor is animated by a theological system—takes on weight and meaning.

8

Deuteronomy in *Sifré to Deuteronomy*

Turning Scripture's Cases into Laws, and Laws into an Entire Social System

The book of Deuteronomy reaches Judaism through *Sifré to Deuteronomy*, attributed to Tannaite authorities, a commentary to the book of Deuteronomy that reached closure at ca. 300 C.E. Out of that book's singleton cases and ad hoc rules, the Rabbinic sages seek generalizations and governing principles. These concern Israel's social order. But the same process extends to the laws of history. Since in the book of Deuteronomy, Moses explicitly sets forth a vision of Israel's future, sages in *Sifré to Deuteronomy* examined that vision to uncover not only rules for the social order but also laws yielding extrapolations, in order to explain what happens next. Like *Sifra* and *Sifré to Numbers*, *Sifré to Deuteronomy* therefore pursues a diverse topical program in order to demonstrate a few fundamental propositions.

What is particular to *Sifré to Deuteronomy*?

What is particular to that document is not specific doctrines but rather the systematic mode of methodical analysis, in which it does two things. First, the compilers take the details of cases and carefully re-frame them into rules pertaining to all cases. The authorship therefore asks those questions of susceptibility to generalization ("generalizability") that first-class philosophical minds raise.

Second, they provide answers to those questions by showing the two possibilities that arise: either the law is limited to the case and to all cases that replicate this one; or the law derives from the principles exemplified, in detail, in the case at hand. Essentially, as a matter of both logic and topical program, our authorship has reread the legal portions of the book of Deuteronomy, Deut 12–26, and turned Scripture into what we now know as the orderly and encompassing law code supplied by the Mishnah. To state matters simply, this authorship "mishnaizes" Scripture: treats cases as exemplary of laws.

What of *Sifra*'s "Is it not a matter of logic?"

We find in *Sifra* and in *Sifré to Numbers* no parallel to the systematic inquiry into generalizability conducted by *Sifré to Deuteronomy*. But in other aspects, the three principal Tannaitic Midrash compilations intersect. In the two Sifrés and *Sifra* we find a recurrent motif of how the written component of the Torah serves as the sole source of final truth. Logic or reason untested against Scripture produces flawed and unreliable results. The Torah, read as rabbis read it, and that alone, proves paramount. Reason on its own is subordinate. There are governing category-formations, rules and regularities, but reason alone will not show us what they are. A systematic and reasoned reading of the written Torah—joined to a sifting of its cases in search of the regularities and points of law and order—are what will identify the prevailing rule.

The upshot is simply stated: any rule of the Mishnah and its account of the here and now of everyday life rests upon the Torah, not upon (mere) logic. Any rule of Israel's history, past, present, and future, likewise derives from a search for regularities and points of order identified not by logic alone, but by logic addressed to the Torah. These are the modes of gaining truth that apply equally to Mishnah and Scripture. There is logic, applied reason and practical wisdom, such as sages exhibit; there is the corpus of facts supplied by Scripture, read as sages read it. These two together form God's statement upon the world today.

The four components of the topical program of the document

The topical program of *Sifré to Deuteronomy* agrees in its fundamental propositions with programs of other authorships—beginning with those of Scripture, indeed with Deuteronomy itself. Moses himself will have found entirely familiar such notions of *Sifré to Deuteronomy* as the conditional character of Israel's possession of the land of Israel, the centrality of the covenant in Israel's relationship with God and with the other nations of the world, the decisive role of the covenant in determining its own destiny, and the covenantal responsibilities and standing of Israel's leadership—surely a considerable motif in the very structure of the book of Deuteronomy itself, beginning and end in particular.

Four principal topics encompass the propositions of *Sifré to Deuteronomy*, of which the first three correspond to the three relationships into which Israel enters: with Heaven, on earth, and within. These yield systematic statements that concern the relationships between Israel and God, with special reference to the covenant, the Torah, and the land; Israel and the nations, with interest in Israel's history, past, present, and future, and how that cycle is to be known; Israel on its own terms, with focus upon Israel's distinctive leadership. The fourth rubric encompasses not specific *ad hoc* propositions, that form aggregates of proofs of large truths, but, rather, prevailing modes of thought, demonstrating the inner structure of intellect, in our document yielding the formation, out of the cases of Scripture, of encompassing rules.

Israel and God—the implications of the covenant

The basic proposition, spelled out in detail, is that Israel stands in a special relationship with God, and that relationship is defined by the contract, or covenant, that God made with Israel. The covenant comes to particular expression in *Sifré to Deuteronomy* in two matters: first, the land; second, the Torah. Each marks Israel as different from all other nations, on the one side, and as selected by God, on the other. In these propositions, sages situate Israel in the realm of heaven, finding on earth the stigmata of covenanted election and the concomitant requirement of loyalty and obedience to the covenant.

First comes the definition of those traits of God that our authorship finds pertinent. God sits in judgment upon the world, and his judgment is true and righteous. God punishes faithlessness. But God's fundamental and definitive trait is mercy. The way of God is to be merciful and gracious. The basic relationship of Israel to God is one of God's grace for Israel. God's loyalty to Israel endures, even when Israel sins. When Israel forgets God, God is pained. Israel's leaders, whatever their excellence, plead with God only for grace, not on the basis of their own merit. Correct attitudes in prayer derive from the need for grace, Israel having slight merit on its own account. Israel should follow only God, carrying out religious deeds as the covenant requires, in accord with the instructions of prophets. Israel should show mercy to others, in the model of God's merciful character.

Second, the contract, or covenant, produces the result that God has acquired Israel, which God created. The reason is that only Israel accepted the Torah, among all the nations, and that is why God made the covenant with Israel in particular. Why is the covenant made only with Israel? The gentiles did not accept the Torah, while Israel did, and that has made all the difference. Israel recognized God forthwith; the very peace of the world and of nature depends upon God's giving the Torah to Israel. That is why Israel is the sole nation worthy of dwelling in the palace of God and that is the basis for the covenant too. The covenant secures for Israel an enduring relationship of grace with God. The covenant cannot be revoked and endures forever. The covenant, the terms of which are specified in the Torah, has two stipulations: if you do well, you will bear a blessing, and if not, you will bear a curse.

That is the singular mark of the covenant between God and Israel. A mark of the covenant is the liberation from Egypt, and that sufficed to impose upon Israel God's claim for their obedience. An important sign of the covenant is the possession of the land. Part of the covenant is the recognition of the merit of the ancestors. In judging the descendants of the patriarchs and matriarchs, God promised, in making the covenant, recognition of the meritorious deeds of the ancestors. The conquest of the land and inheriting it are marks of the covenant, which Israel will find easy because of God's favor. The inheritance of the land is a mark of merit, inherited from the ancestors. The land is higher than all others and more choice. All religious duties are important, those that seem trivial as much as those held to be weightier.

God always loves Israel. That is why Israel should carry out the religious duties of the Torah with full assent. All religious duties are equally precious. Israel must be whole-hearted in its relationship with God. If it is, then its share is with God, and if not, then not. Israel may hate God, but the right attitude toward God is love, and Israel should love God with a whole heart. The reason that Israel rebels against God is prosperity, for with prosperity people become arrogant and believe that their prosperity derives from their own efforts. But that is not so, and God punishes people who thus rebel to show them that they depend solely upon God. When Israel practices idolatry, God punishes them, e.g., through exile, through famine, through drought, and the like. Whether or not Israel knows or likes the fact, it is the fact that Israel has no choice but to accept God's will and fulfill the covenant.

Heaven and earth respond to the condition of Israel and therefore carry out the stipulations of the covenant. If Israel does not carry out religious duties concerning heaven, then heaven bears witness against them. This witness centers on the land of Israel in particular. Possession of the land is conditional, not absolute. It begins with grace, not merit. It is defined by the stipulation that Israel observe the covenant, in which case Israel will retain the land. If Israel violates the covenant, Israel will lose the land. When Israel inherits the land, in obedience to the covenant and as an act of grace bestowed by God, it will build the Temple, where Israel's sins will find atonement. The conquest of the land itself is subject to stipulations, just as possession of the land, as an act of God's grace, is marked by religious obligations. If Israel rebels or rejects the Torah, it will lose the land, just as the Canaanites did for their idolatry.

The land is not the only, or the most important, mark of the covenant. Israel's possession of the Torah preeminently shows that it stands in a special relationship to God. The Torah is the source of life for Israel. It belongs to everyone, not only the aristocracy. Children should start studying the Torah at the earliest age possible. The study of the Torah is part of the fulfillment of the covenant. Even the most arid details of the Torah contain lessons, and if one studies the Torah, the reward comes both in this world and in the world to come.

The possession of the Torah imposes a particular requirement, involving an action. The most important task of every male Israelite is to study the Torah, which involves memorizing, and not forgetting, each lesson. This must go on every day and all the time. Study of the Torah should be one's main obligation, prior to all others. The correct motive is not for the sake of gain, but for the love of God and the desire for knowledge of God's will. People must direct heart, eyes, ears, to teachings of the Torah. Study of the Torah transforms human relationships, so that strangers become the children of the master of the Torah whom they serve as disciples. However unimportant the teaching or the teacher, all is as if on the authority of Moses at Sinai. When a person departs from the Torah, that person becomes an idolater. Study of the Torah prevents idolatry.

Israel and the nations—the meaning of history

The covenant, through the Torah of Sinai, governs not only the ongoing life of Israel but also the state of human affairs universally. The history of Israel forms a pattern or paradigm, in that what happened in the beginning prefigures what will happen at the end of time. Events of Genesis are reenacted both in middle-history, between the beginning and the end, and also at the end of times. So the traits of the tribal founders dictated the history of their families to both the here and now and also to the eschatological age. Moses was shown the whole of Israel's history, past, present, future. The times of the patriarchs are reenacted in the end of days. That shows how Israel's history runs in patterns, so that events of ancient times prefigure events now. The prophets, beginning with Moses, describe those patterns. What happens now bears close ties to what is going to happen. The prophetic promises too were realized in Temple times, and will be realized at the end of time.

The periods in the history of Israel, marked by the Exodus and wandering, the inheritance of the Land and the building of the Temple, the destruction—all are part of a divine plan. In this age Rome rules, but in the age to come, marked by the study of the Torah and the offering of sacrifices in the Temple cult, Israel will be in charge. That is the fundamental pattern and meaning of history. The Holy Spirit makes possible actions that bear consequences only much later in time. The prefiguring of history forms the dominant motif in Israel's contemporary life, and reenacting what has already been forms a constant. Israel therefore should believe, if not in what is coming, then in what has already been. The very names of places in the land attest to the continuity of Israel's history, which follows rules that do not change. The main point is that while Israel will be punished in the worst possible way, Israel will not be wiped out.

But the pattern of Israel's history should not mislead. Events follow a pattern, but knowledge of that pattern, which is provided by the Torah, permits Israel both to understand and also to affect its own destiny. Specifically, Israel controls its own destiny through its conduct with God. Israel's history is the working out of the effects of Israel's conduct, moderated by the merit of the ancestors. Abraham effected a change in God's relationship to the world. But merit, which makes history, is attained by one's own deeds as well. The effect of merit, in the nation's standing among the other nations, is simple. When Israel enjoys merit, it gives testimony against itself, but when not, then the most despised nation testifies against it.

But God is with Israel in time of trouble. When Israel sins, it suffers. When it repents and is forgiven, it is redeemed. For example, Israel's wandering in the wilderness took place because of the failure of Israel to attain merit. Sin is what causes the wandering in the wilderness. People rebel because they are prosperous. The merit of the ancestors works in history to Israel's benefit. What Israel does not merit on its own, at a given time, the merit of the ancestors may secure in any event. The best way to deal with Israel's powerlessness is through Torah-study; the vigor of engagement with Torah-study compensates for weakness.

It goes without saying that Israel's history follows a set time, e.g., at the fulfillment of a set period of time, an awaited event will take place. The prophets prophesy concerning the coming of the day of the Lord. Accordingly, nothing is haphazard, and all things happen in accord with a plan. That plan encompasses this world, the time of the Messiah, and the world to come, in that order. God will personally exact vengeance at the end of time. God also will raise the dead. Israel has overcome difficult times and can continue to do so. The task ahead is easier than the tasks already accomplished. Israel's punishment is only once, while the punishment coming upon the nations is unremitting. Peace is worthwhile and everyone needs it. Israel's history ends in the world to come or in the days of the Messiah. The righteous inherit the Garden of Eden. The righteous in the age to come will be joyful.

God acts in history and does so publicly, in full light of day. That is to show the nations who is in charge. The Torah is what distinguishes Israel from the nations. All the nations had every opportunity to understand and accept the Torah, and all declined it; that is why Israel was selected. And that demonstrates the importance of both covenant and the Torah, the medium of the covenant. The nations even had a prophet, comparable to Moses, who was Balaam. The nations have no important role in history, except as God assigns them a role in relationship to Israel's conduct. The nations are estranged from God by idolatry. That is what prevents goodness from coming into the world. The name of God rests upon Israel in greatest measure. Idolators do not control heaven. The greatest sin an Israelite can commit is idolatry, and those who entice Israel to idolatry are deprived of the ordinary protections of the law. God is violently angry at the nations because of idolatry. As to the nations' relationships with Israel, they are guided by Israel's condition. When Israel is weak, the nations take advantage, when strong, they are sycophantic. God did not apportion love to the nations of the world as he did to Israel.

Israel at home—the community and its governance

A mark of God's favor is that Israel has (or, has had and will have) a government of its own. Part of the covenantal relationship requires Israel to follow leaders whom God has chosen and instructed, such as Moses and the prophets. Accordingly, Israel is to establish a government and follow sound public policy. Its leaders are chosen by God. Israel's leaders, e.g., prophets, are God's servants, and that is a mark of the praise that is owing to them. They are to be in the model of Moses, humble, choice, select, well-known. Moses was the right one to bestow a blessing, Israel were the right ones to receive the blessing.

Yet all leaders are mortal, even Moses died. The saints are leaders ready to give their lives for Israel. The greatest of them enjoy exceptionally long life. But the sins of the people are blamed on their leaders. The leaders depend on the people to keep the Torah, and Moses thanked them in advance for keeping the Torah after he died. The leaders were to be patient and honest, to give a full hearing to all sides, and to make just decisions in a broad range of matters. To stand before the judge is to stand before God. God makes sure that Israel does not lack for leadership. The basic task of the leader is both to rebuke and also to console the people.

The rulers of Israel are servants of God. The prophets exemplify these leaders, in the model of Moses, and Israel's rulers act only on the instruction of prophets. Their authority rests solely on God's favor and grace. At the instance of God, the leaders of Israel speak, in particular, words of admonition. These are delivered before death, when the whole picture is clear, so that people can draw the necessary conclusions. These words, when Moses spoke them, covered the entire history of the community of Israel. The leaders of Israel admonish the entire community at once. No one is excepted. But the Israelites can deal with the admonition. They draw the correct conclusions. Repentance overcomes sin, as at the sin of the golden calf. The Israelites were contentious, nitpickers, litigious, and, in general, gave Moses a difficult time. Their descendants should learn not to do so. Israel should remain united and obedient to its leaders. The task of the community is to remain united. When the Israelites are of one opinion below, God's name is glorified above.

The laws and law—the structure of intellect

The explicit propositional program of *Sifré to Deuteronomy* is joined by two implicit propositions concerning modes of correct analysis and inquiry that pertain to the Torah. The first, familiar from the other Tannaitic compilations, is that pure reason does not suffice to produce reliable results. Only through linking our conclusions to verses of Scripture may we come to final and fixed conclusions.

The second is the more important: the demonstration that many things conform to a single structure and pattern. We can show this uniformity of the law by addressing the same questions to disparate cases and, in so doing, composing general laws that transcend cases and form of data a cogent system. What is striking, then, is the power of a single set of questions to reshape and reorganize diverse data into a single construction of questions and answers, all things fitting together into a single, remarkably well-composed structure. Not only so, but we uncover a single program, an effort to ask whether a case of Scripture imposes a rule that limits or imparts a rule that augments the application of the law at hand: a fact or an example susceptible of extension. The size, the repetitious quality, the obsessive interest in augmentation and restriction, generalization and limitation to particular cases—these traits of logic and their concomitant propositional results form the centerpiece of the whole.

A sample passage

Here is a sustained abstract of the document, already introduced in Chapter Two, which puts on display its modes of discourse and their results. We start with an example of the methodical inquiry into how cases yield rules, only the category is meanings of words and phrases, not generalizations of cases into laws:

Sifré to Deuteronomy I:i.1–5

1. A. "These are the words that Moses spoke to all Israel in Transjordan, in the wilderness, that is to say in the Arabah, opposite Suph, between Paran on the one side and Tophel, Laban, Hazeroth, and Dizahab, on the other" (Dt. 1:1):
   B. "These are the words that Moses spoke" (Dt. 1:1): Did Moses prophesy only these alone? Did he not write the entire Torah?
   C. For it is said, "And Moses wrote this Torah" (Dt. 31:9).
   D. Why then does Scripture say, "These are the words that Moses spoke" (Dt. 1:1)?
   E. It teaches that [when Scripture speaks of the words that one spoke, it refers in particular to] the words of admonition.
   F. So it is said (by Moses), "But Jeshurun waxed fat and kicked" (Dt. 32:15).
2. A. So too you may point to the following:
   B. "The words of Amos, who was among the herdsman of Tekoa, which he saw concerning Israel in the days of Uzziah, king of Judah, and in the days of Jeroboam, son of Joash, king of Israel, two years before the earthquake" (Amos 1:1):
   C. Did Amos prophesy only concerning these kings alone? Did he not prophesy concerning a greater number of kings than any other?
   D. Why then does Scripture say, "These are the words of Amos, (who was among the herdsman of Tekoa, which he saw concerning Israel in the days of Uzziah, king of Judah, and in the days of Jeroboam, son of Joash, king of Israel, two years before the earthquake)" (Amos 1:1)
   E. It teaches that (when Scripture speaks of the words that one spoke, it refers in particular to) the words of admonition.
   F. And how do we know that they were words of admonition?
   G. As it is said, "Hear this word, you cows of Bashan, who are in the mountain of Samaria, who oppress the poor, crush the needy, and say to their husbands, 'Bring, that we may feast'" (Amos 4:1).
   H. "And say to their husbands, 'Bring, that we may feast'" speaks of their courts (of justice).
3. A. So too you may point to the following:
   B. "And these are the words that the Lord spoke concerning Israel and Judah" (Jer. 30:4).
   C. Did Jeremiah prophesy only these words of prophecy alone? Did he not write two complete scrolls?
   D. For it is said, "Thus far are the words of Jeremiah" (Jer. 51:64)
   E. Why then does Scripture say, "And these are the words (that the Lord spoke concerning Israel and Judah)" (Jer. 30:4)?

F. It teaches that (when the verse says, "And these are the words that the Lord spoke concerning Israel and Judah" [Jer. 30:4]), it speaks in particular of the words of admonition.
   G. And how do we know that they were words of admonition?
   H. In accord with this verse: "For thus says the Lord, 'We have heard a voice of trembling, of fear and not of peace. Ask you now and see whether a man does labor with a child? Why do I see every man with his hands on his loins, as a woman in labor? and all faces turn pale? Alas, for the day is great, there is none like it, and it is a time of trouble for Jacob, but out of it he shall be saved'" (Jer. 30:5–7).
4. A. So too you may point to the following:
   B. "And these are the last words of David" (2 Sam. 23:1).
   C. And did David prophesy only these alone? And has it furthermore not been said, "The spirit of the Lord spoke through me, and his word was on my tongue" (2 Sam. 23:2)?
   D. Why then does it say, "And these are the last words of David" (2 Sam. 23:1)?
   E. It teaches that, (when the verse says, "And these are the last words of David" [2 Sam. 23:1]), it refers to words of admonition.
   F. And how do we know that they were words of admonition?
   G. In accord with this verse: "But the ungodly are as thorns thrust away, all of them, for they cannot be taken with the hand" (2 Sam. 23:6).
5. A. So too you may point to the following:
   B. "The words of Qohelet, son of David, king in Jerusalem" (Qoh. 1:1).
   C. Now did Solomon prophesy only these words? Did he not write three and a half scrolls of his wisdom in proverbs?
   D. Why then does it say, "The words of Qohelet, son of David, king in Jerusalem" (Qoh. 1:1)?
   E. It teaches that (when the verse says, "The words of Qohelet, son of David, king in Jerusalem" [Qoh. 1:1]), it refers to words of admonition.
   F. And how do we know that they were words of admonition?
   G. In accord with this verse: "The sun also rises, and the sun goes down . . . the wind goes toward the south and turns around to the north, it turns round continually in its circuit, and the wind returns again— that is, east and west (to its circuits. All the rivers run into the sea)" (Qoh. 1:5–7).
   H. (Solomon) calls sun, moon, and sea "the wicked" for (the wicked) have no reward (coming back to them).

I repeat here what was said in chapter two. The focus is upon the exegesis of the opening word of Deuteronomy, "words. . . ." The problem is carefully stated. And yet, without the arrangement within what is going to be a commentary on Deuteronomy, we should have no reason to regard the composition as exegetical at all. In fact, it is a syllogism, aiming at proving a particular proposition concerning word-usages. Standing by itself, what we have is simply a very carefully formalized syllogism that makes a philological point, which is that the word "words of . . . ," bears the sense of "admonition" or "rebuke." Five proofs are offered. We know that we reach the end of the exposition when, at I.5.H, there is a minor gloss, departing from the consistent form. That is a common mode of signaling the conclusion of discourse on a given point. We now take up a passage we have seen in another connection.

Sifré to Deuteronomy I:ii.1–2

1. A. ". . . to all Israel:"
   B. (Moses spoke to the entire community all at once, for) had he admonished only part of them, those who were out at the market would have said, "Is this what you heard from the son of Amram? And did you not give him such-and-such an answer? If we had been there, we should have answered him four or five times for every word he said!"
2. A. Another matter concerning ". . . to all Israel:"
   B. This teaches that Moses collected all of them together, from the greatest to the least of them, and he said to them, "Lo, I shall admonish you. Whoever has an answer—let him come and say it."

We proceed to the next word in the base verse, but now our comment is particular to the verse. The explanation of why Moses spoke to everyone is then clear. On the one hand, Section ii.1 indicates that it was to make certain that there was no one left out. On the other, Section ii.2 indicates that it was to make certain that everyone had a say. These two points then complement one another.

Sifré to Deuteronomy I:iii.1–2

1. A. Another matter concerning ". . . to all Israel:"
   B. This teaches that all of them were subject to admonition but quite able to deal with the admonition.
2. A. Said R. Tarfon, "By the Temple service! (I do not believe) that there is anyone in this generation who can administer an admonition."
   B. Said R. Eleazar ben Azariah, "By the Temple service! (I do not believe) that there is anyone in this generation who can accept admonition."
   C. Said R. Aqiba, "By the Temple service! (I do not believe) that there is anyone in this generation who knows how to give an admonition."
   D. Said R. Yohanan ben Nuri, "I call to give testimony against me heaven and earth (if it is not the case that) more than five times was R. Aqiba criticized before Rabban Gamaliel in Yabneh, for I would lay complaints against him, and (Gamaliel therefore) criticized him. Nonetheless, I know that (each such criticism) added to (Aqiba's) love for me.
   E. "This carries out the verse, 'Do not criticize a scorner, lest he hate you, but reprove a wise person, and he will love you' (Prov. 9:8)."

Sections I:iii.1 and I:iii.2 are quite separate units of thought, each making its own point. Shall we say that all we have, at *Sifré* I:i–iii, is a sequence of three quite disparate propositions? In that case, the authorship before us has presented nothing more than a scrapbook of relevant comments on discrete clauses. I think otherwise. It seems to me that in I:i–iii as the distinct and complete units of thought unfold we have a proposition, fully exposed, composed by the setting forth of two distinct facts, which serve as established propositions to yield the syllogism of Section I:iii. But the syllogism is not made explicitly, rather it is placed on display by the (mere) juxtaposition of section I:i and section I:ii and then the final proposition, I:iii.1, followed by a story making the same point as the proposition. The exegesis now joins the (established) facts (1) that Moses rebuked Israel and (2) that all Israel was involved. The point is (3) that Israel was able to deal with the admonition and did not reject it. Section I:iii.2 then contains a story that makes explicit and underlines the virtue spun out of the verse. Aqiba embodies that virtue, the capacity—the wisdom—to accept rebuke. The upshot, then, is that the authorship wished to make a single point in assembling into a single carefully ordered sequence I:i–iii, and it did so by presenting two distinct propositions, at I:i and I:ii; and then, at I:iii, recast the whole by making a point drawing upon the two original, autonomous proofs. Joining I:i and I:ii then led directly to the proposition at which the authorship was aiming. We have much more than an assembly of information on diverse traits or points of verses, read word by word. It is, rather, a purposeful composition, made up of what clearly are already-available materials.

Sifré to Deuteronomy I:iv.1–x.4

iv. 1. A. "On the other side of the Jordan" (Dt. 1:1):
   B. This teaches that he admonished them concerning things that they had done on the other side of the Jordan.
v. 1. A. "In the wilderness" (Dt. 1:1):
   B. This teaches that he admonished them concerning things that they had done in the wilderness.
  2. A. Another matter concerning "In the wilderness" (Dt. 1:1):
   B. This teaches that they would take their little sons and daughters and toss them into Moses's bosom and say to him, "Son of Amram, what ration have you prepared for these? What living have you prepared for these?"
   C. R. Judah says, "Lo, Scripture says (to make this same point), 'And the children of Israel said to them, "Would that we had died by the hand of the Lord in the land of Egypt (when we sat by the fleshpots, when we ate bread . . . for you have brought us forth to this wilderness to kill the whole assembly with hunger)" (Ex. 16:3).'"
  3. A. Another matter concerning "In the wilderness" (Dt. 1:1):
   B. This encompasses everything that they had done in the wilderness.
vi. 1. A. "In the Plain" (Dt. 1:1):
   B. This teaches that he admonished them concerning things that they had done in the Plains of Moab.

C. So Scripture says, "And Israel dwelt in Shittim (and the people began to commit harlotry with the daughters of Moab" [Num. 25:1]).

vii. 1. A. "Over against Suph (the sea)" (Dt. 1:1):
B. This teaches that he admonished them concerning things that they had done at the sea.
C. For they rebelled at the sea and turned their back on Moses' days.
2. A. R. Judah says, "They rebelled at the sea, and they rebelled within the sea.
B. "And so Scripture says, 'They rebelled at the sea, even in the sea itself' (Ps. 106:7)."
3. A. Is it possible to suppose that he admonished them only at the outset of a journey? How do we know that he did so between one journey and the next?
B. Scripture says, "Between Paran and Tophel" (Dt. 1:1).
4. A. "Between Paran and Tophel" (Dt. 1:1):
B. The word Tophel bears the sense of disparaging words with which they disparaged the manna.
C. And so does Scripture say, "And our soul loathed this light bread" (Num. 21:5).
D. (God) said to them, "Fools! Even royalty choose for themselves only light bread, so that none of them should suffer from vomiting or diarrhea. For your part, against that very act of kindness that I have done for you, you bring complaints before me.
E. "It is only that you continue to walk in the foolishness of your father, for I said, 'I will make a help meet for him' (Gen. 2:18), while he said, 'The woman whom you gave to be with me gave me of the tree and I ate' (Gen. 3:12)."

The words of admonition, now fully exposed, apply to a variety of actions of the people. That is the main point of I:iv–vii. The matter is stated in a simple way at I:iv, v.1 (with an illustration at I:v.2), I:v.3, I:vi, I:vii. After the five illustrations of the proposition that the admonition covered the entire past, we proceed to a secondary expansion, I:vii.2–3, which itself is amplified at I:vii.4. The main structure is clear, and the proposition is continuous with the one with which we began: Moses admonished all Israel, which could take the criticism, and covered the entire list of areas where they had sinned, which then accounts for the specification of the various locations mentioned by Deut 1:1. When we realize what is to come, we understand the full power of the proposition, which is syllogistic, though in exegetical form. It is to indicate the character and encompassing program of the book of Deuteronomy—nothing less.

viii. 1. A. "And Hazeroth" (Dt. 1:1):
B. (God) said to them, "Ought you not to have learned from what I did to Miriam in Hazeroth?
C. "If to that righteous woman, Miriam, I did not show favor in judgment, all the more so to other people!"

2. A. Another matter: now if Miriam, who gossiped only against her brother, who was younger than herself, was punished in this way, one who gossips against someone greater than himself all the more so!
   3. A. Another matter: Now if Miriam, whom when she spoke, no person heard, but only the Omnipresent alone, in line with this verse, "And the Lord heard . . . ," (Num. 12:2), was punished, one who speaks ill of his fellow in public all the more so!

The basic point is made at the outset and the case is then amplified. The sin concerning which Moses now admonished the people was that of gossiping, and the connection to Miriam is explicit. The argument that each place-name concerns a particular sin thus is carried forward. The entire discourse exhibits remarkable cogency.

ix. 1. A. "And Dizahab" (Dt. 1:1):
   B. (Since the place name means, "of gold," what he was) saying to them (was this:) "Lo, everything you did is forgiven. But the deed concerning the golden calf is worst of them all."
   2. A. R. Judah would say, "There is a parable. To what may the case be compared? To one who made a lot of trouble for his fellow. In the end he added yet another. He said to him, 'Lo, everything you did is forgiven. But this is the worst of them all.'
   B. "So said the Omnipresent to Israel, 'Lo, everything you did is forgiven. But the deed concerning the golden calf is worst of them all.'"

The place-name calls to mind the sin of the golden calf. This is made explicit as a generalization in section I:ix.1, and then, in section I:ix.2, Judah restates the matter as a story.

x. 1. A. R. Simeon says, "There is a parable. To what may the case (of Israel's making the calf of gold) be compared? To one who extended hospitality to sages and their disciples, and everyone praised him.
   B. "Gentiles came, and he extended hospitality to them. Thieves came and he extended hospitality to them.
   C. "People said, 'That is so-and-so's nature—to extend hospitality (indiscriminately) to anyone at all.'
   D. "So did Moses say to Israel, '(Dizahab, meaning, enough gold, yields the sense) There is enough gold for the tabernacle, enough gold also for the calf!'"
   2. A. R. Benaiah says, "The Israelites have worshipped idolatry. Lo, they are liable to extermination. Let the gold of the tabernacle come and effect atonement for the gold of the calf."
   3. A. R. Yosé b. Haninah says, "'And you shall make an ark cover of pure gold' (Ex. 25:17).

B. "Let the gold of the ark cover come and effect atonement for the gold of the calf."
4. A. R. Judah says, "Lo, Scripture states, 'In the wilderness, in the plain.'
   B. "These are the ten trials that our fathers inflicted upon the Omnipresent in the wilderness.
   C. "And these are they: two at the sea, two involving water, two involving manna, two involving quails, one involving the calf, and one involving the spies in the wilderness."
   D. Said to him R. Yosé b. Dormasqit, "Judah, my honored friend, why do you distort verses of Scripture for us? I call to testify against me heaven and earth that we have made the circuit of all of these places, and each of the places is called only on account of an event that took place there (and not, as you say, to call to mind Israel's sin).
   E. "And so Scripture says, 'And the herdsmen of Gerar strove with the herdsmen of Isaac, saying, "The water is ours." And he called the name of the well Esek, because they contended with him' (Gen. 26:29). 'And he called it Shibah' (Gen. 26:33)."

Section I:x.1–3 carries forward the matter of DiZahab—"of gold"—and amplifies upon the theme, not the proposition at hand. Section I:x.4 then presents a striking restatement of the basic proposition, which has been spelled out and restated in so many ways. It turns out that Judah takes the position implicit throughout and made explicit in section I:x.4. There is then a contrary position, at section I:x.4D. We see, therefore, how the framers have drawn upon diverse materials to present a single, cogent syllogism, the one then stated in most succinct form by Judah. The contrary syllogism, that of Yosé, is not spelled out, since amplification is hardly possible. Once we maintain that each place has meaning only for what happened in that particular spot, the verse no longer bears the deeper meaning announced at the outset—admonition or rebuke, specifically for actions that took place in various settings and that are called to mind by the list of words (no longer place-names) of Deut 1:1.

The Rabbinic reading of Deuteronomy

Apart from its interest in deriving the law out of the laws, I find nothing in *Sifré to Deuteronomy* that stands out of phase with the results already set forth for the other Midrash-compilations. A cogent theological system and structure now turn out to sustain the Midrash-compilations, early and late, Halakhic and Aggadic. The theological category-formations that emerge by inductive inquiry are consistent. The differences between and among the Midrash compilations are formal, logical, and topical, but not theological. And, we see time and again, when it comes to theology, Midrash exegesis recapitulates Scripture's theology.

9

Esther in *Esther Rabbah I*

A Woman Saves Israel

Of indeterminate date and venue, *Esther Rabbah I,* covering the book of Esther's first two chapters, sets forth only one message, and it is reworked in just a few ways. The document's statement concerns God's relationships with the nations, and why Israel is ruled by wicked kingdoms such as Persia. The message is that the nations are swine, their rulers fools, and Israel is subjugated to them, though it should not be, only because of its own sins. No other explanation serves to account for Israel's situation, which defines the paradox and anomaly that prevail in world order. But just as God saved Israel in the past, so the salvation that Israel can attain will recapitulate the pattern of former times.

On the stated theme, Israel among the nations, therefore, the Rabbinic sages set forth a proposition entirely familiar from the books of Deuteronomy through Kings, on the one side, and much of prophetic literature, on the other. Israel is responsible for its own condition, brought about by Israel's rebellion against God's will. All the Rabbinic sages add is, God's will *as expressed in the Torah*. But Moses as the Rabbinic sages knew him in Scripture will not have differed.

The three principal propositions of *Esther Rabbah I*

The principal theological propositions of *Esther Rabbah I* fit into the standard category-formations of Rabbinic Judaism in the various Midrash compilations. The data, when sifted for coherence and cogency, break down into three principal categories and messages.

God and man, God and Israel

God relates to man in a rational way; man can discern the rules that govern. Such is the case with the anomaly that Israel is subjugated to pagan empires. First, how is Israel elect? It is by reason of the Torah. The nations rejected the Torah (*Es-

ther Rabbah I I:i.8). Israel accepted it, and that accounts for God's relationship with each classification of mankind. God's special relationship to Israel comes about by reason of Israel's loyalty to him. Second, why are the nations rejected? God's estrangement from the nations is because of the nations' rebellion, expressed through idolatry.

Mordecai stands for Israel, Haman for the nations. The difference is, who knows and worships God, and who worships idols? Out of loyalty to God, Mordecai refused to bow down to the idol that Haman wore, because he held that there is a Lord exalted above all who exalt, whom he would not abandon. Because Mordecai affirmed the unity of God before everyone in the world, he was called a Judaean, unique (XXXVI:ii.4). Aware of the offerings in the Temple, God regards Israel as his children, companions, beloved, sons of Abraham (XXIII:ii.16). Disobeying the prophet's instructions, originating with God, led to Israel's crisis in the time of Haman (V:i.1).

God's actions are always appropriate and proportionate. He designed for every one what was suitable, e.g., Adam was first of all creatures, Cain of Murders, Abel of Victims, Ahasuerus the first of those who sell people at a price, Haman the first of those who buy people at a price, and so on (VIII:i.1). These represent details that gain cogency within the encompassing structure of Rabbinic theology.

God and the nations, Israel and the nations

The relationship between the nations and God runs parallel to the relationship between the nations and Israel. What the nations do to Israel they do because God not only allows them, but because they thereby carry out God's plan. Esther tells the story of a wicked government, prepared to sell Israel to the highest bidder and to wipe them out. Haman wishes to kill all the Jews and take over their property. How this can have come about requires us to invoke the prophetic-Rabbinic doctrine of divine governance of Israel's affairs. God rewards Israel's adherence to the Torah and punishes Israel's rebellion against the Torah, and that is accomplished through the instrumentality of the gentiles—here, Haman. But in the exposition before us, Israel is not described as sinners subject to punishment, only as victims subject to an unhappy turn in politics, the advent of a wicked ruler.

God's relationship to the nations corresponds to his relationship to Israel. For he uses the nations, particularly the four empires, as media for the penalization of Israel. When Israel sins by rebellion, God punished the people by bringing troubles upon them, and these troubles are inflicted by the nations. So the degree to which the nations prosper forms an indicator of the degree to which Israel has sinned. Under the four empires, Babylonia, Media, Greece, Rome, or in this age and in the age of the Messiah, this age marked by Vespasian, Trajan, Haman, and "the Romans," and the age to come by Gog and Magog, God remains devoted to his covenant with Israel (II:i.1).

God's plan is always known; nothing happens outside of his supervision and intent. The prophets prophesied concerning Israel's history under the four empires, Babylonia, Media, Greece, and Rome. In all four ages, God answered Israel when called upon (III:i.1, 2, 4, 5–7). In particular God warned about the coming of Ahasuerus and the events that would take place under the Medians. Thus Isaiah predicted what would come to pass only after the time of the Babylonians, in the area of Media and Persia (IX:i.1,3). The nations are paid back for what they have done. They make parties while God's house is in ruins, and there will be recompense in full measure for that (XI:i.1). When the Israelites make merry, they praise God. When the nations make merry, they are light-headed and lewd (XX:i.1).

Divine justice and mercy

If God is represented in the Torah as all-powerful, just, and merciful, in the narrative expounded here God plays a remarkably casual role, just as in the book of Esther itself God scarcely makes an appearance. It is, in that sense, a secular story, appealing to the courage of the woman and the wisdom of the sage, not to divine intervention at any finite point. I find no passage in which God's justice and mercy enter in, though they are the premise of the entire narrative. But Israel's triumph over Haman is not explained by God's direct intervention as an act of mercy, nor is Haman's plan to destroy Israel represented as an act of divine punishment of a particular sin or of a sinful attitude in general. So the Midrash compilation hews closely to the scriptural account in paying only limited attention to the established theme of God's justice and mercy.

The message of *Esther Rabbah I*

Esther Rabbah I finds in the book of Esther the perennial problem of Israel's condition among the nations and solves that problem in an ad hoc exercise, drawing only the most general conclusions from the Jews' salvation from their enemies. Perhaps Haman's plan, exceeding in intent any hostility characteristic of the nations, Babylonia, Media, Greece, Rome, rendered implausible any appeal to God's plan executed by the wicked courtier. After all, God called upon the nations to punish Israel and bring about Israel's repentance and reconciliation—not to exterminate Israel altogether! In the context of the prophetic-Rabbinic theology of history that everywhere governs in the Midrash compilations, such a scheme defied all rational explanation, violated all norms of reasonable behavior, whether by the nations or by God in relationship to Israel.

The context of *Esther Rabbah I*

Beyond the sequence of amplified details, there is a large motif not to be missed: the intense engagement with the other, the outsider, embodied by the woman. Israel's salvation from its enemy comes from that unexpected source. And it is not God's intervention but the sage's acuity and the woman's courage that form the center of the recapitulated story. So *Esther Rabbah I* in the end does not merely review the theology of Deuteronomy and prophesy about sin and suffering, atonement and reconciliation, in response to Israel's suffering inflicted by the nations. Rather, when all is said and done, there really is a simple message. It is that the Torah (as exemplified by the sage) makes the outsider into an insider, the woman into a heroic leader. As we shall see in the next chapter, that is precisely the same message—the power of the Torah to transform the outsider—that predominates in *Ruth Rabbah*. Just as in the book of Ruth as amplified by *Ruth Rabbah* we see how the Moabite is turned into an Israelite, the offspring of the outsider into the Messiah, so in Esther and *Esther Rabbah I* the woman, marginal to Israel's families as an orphan, raised by a bachelor-uncle, saves Israel. And—heightening the paradox—she does so by placing herself outside of the range of Israelite family conduct, engaging in sexual relations outside of the normal marriage and marrying a gentile. I cannot conceive of more striking incongruities than these. Indeed, these paradoxes come about only on the condition that the Torah govern.

A sample passage

Since the entire document is organized following the sequence of the verses of the book of Esther, that defines the framework of the outline. To show the non-documentary components of the whole, I use indentation. That is, where I find reason to remove a composition or composite from the mainstream of the document's flow, I indent the entry; that signals the judgment that an entry is secondary and intruded or otherwise impedes the systematic and orderly progress of the whole. These are the principal media by which I identify the components of the document and so identify the aberrational or extra-documentary compositions and composites. We consider the opening composite. In the following, a base-verse, Esther 1:1, is expounded in dialogue with another verse, taken from a different book altogether and deemed to illuminate the context in which the base-verse is to be interpreted.

Esther Rabbah I I:i.1–11

1. A. "Now it came to pass in the days of Ahasuerus, the Ahasuerus who reigned from India to Ethiopia over one hundred and twenty-seven provinces," (Esth. 1:1).

    A. Rab commenced (his exposition of Esther 1:1) by introducing the following verse of Scripture: "And your life shall hang in doubt before you; (night and day you shall be in dread, and have no assurance of your life. In the morning, you shall say, 'Would it were evening!' and at evening you shall say, 'Would it were morning!' because of the dread which your heart shall fear and the sights which your eyes shall see. And the Lord will bring you back in ships to Egypt, a journey which I promise that you should never make again; and there you shall offer yourselves for sale to your enemies as male and female slaves, but no man will buy you)" (Dt. 28:66–68).

Rab implicitly invokes Moses' vision of what will happen to Israel if Israel rebels against God's Torah and suffers punishment. So he explicitly reads the narrative of Esther in the context of the Deuteronomic-prophetic-Rabbinic theology of history that, overall, plays no vital role in the narrative of the book of Esther or in *Esther Rabbah I*.

To understand this document, we pay attention to its primary components and distinguish those that represent secondary amplifications or insertions or other sorts of intruded compositions and composites. These, as I said, are marked off through indentation; what is at the margin is what is primary to the document and what bears its message. Since what follows ignores Rab's opening, I treat it as aberrational, But we note that the compiler had a fine reason to include the additional material. There is a systematic exposition of the intersecting verse, so the composition belongs, not within the text (by our standards) but as a footnote or appendix, now marked as such. The cited verse of Deuteronomy now is interpreted in its own terms, out of relationship with the opening line of Esther.

> B. Rabbis and R. Berekhiah:
> C. Rabbis say, "'And your life shall hang in doubt before you:' this is one who buys wheat for a year (rather than raising his own).
> D. "'night and day you shall be in dread:' this is one who buys wheat in the market (a week at a time).
> E. "'and have no assurance of your life:' this is one who buys wheat from the baker (for a day or two at a time)."
> F. R. Berekhiah said, "'And your life shall hang in doubt before you:' this is one who buys wheat for three years.
> G. "'night and day you shall be in dread:' this is one who buys wheat for a year.
> H. "'and have no assurance of your life:' this is one who buys wheat in the market."
> I. Rabbis reply to R. Berekhiah, "What is the rule as to one who buys bread from a baker?"
> J. He said to them, "The Torah does not speak of corpses."
> 2. A. Another interpretation of the verse, "And your life shall hang in doubt before you; night and day you shall be in dread, and have no assurance of your life:"
> B. "And your life shall hang in doubt before you:" this is one who is in prison in Caesarea.
> C. "night and day you shall be in dread:" this is one who is taken out for trial.
> D. "and have no assurance of your life:" this is one who is taken out to be executed.

The task of the composition before us (now ignoring the intruded composition) is to show how the passage of Deuteronomy illuminates, and is illuminated by, the narrative of Esther. Here we find the intersecting-verse/base-verse composition at its most powerful. Now we revert to Rab's comment on the cited intersecting verse, now in relationship to the present context.

> 3. A. Rab interpreted the verse to speak of the time of Haman.
> B. "'And your life shall hang in doubt before you:' this speaks of the twenty-four hours from the removal of the ring.
> C. "'night and day you shall be in dread:' this speaks of the time that the letters were sent forth.
> D. "'and have no assurance of your life:' this was when the enemies of the Jews were told to be 'ready against that day' (Est. 3:14)."
> E. "In the morning, you shall say, 'Would it were evening!' and at evening you shall say, 'Would it were morning!'":
> F. "In the morning," of Babylonia, "you shall say, 'Would it were evening!'"
> G. "In the morning," of Media, "you shall say, 'Would it were evening!'"
> H. "In the morning," of Greece, "you shall say, 'Would it were evening!'"
> I. "In the morning," of Edom, "you shall say, 'Would it were evening!'"
> J. Another interpretation of the verse: "In the morning, you shall say, 'Would it were evening!' and at evening you shall say, 'Would it were morning!'"
> K. "In the morning" of Babylonia, "you shall say, 'Would it were the evening of Media!'"
> L. "In the morning," of Media, "you shall say, 'Would it were evening of Greece!'"
> M. "In the morning," of Greece, "you shall say, 'Would it were evening of Edom!'"
> N. Why so? "because of the dread which your heart shall fear and the sights which your eyes shall see."

Everything that follows expounds the intersecting verse in its own terms, rather than in relationship to Rab's program in citing it. The sequence of world-empires that ruled Israel is rehearsed: Babylonia, Media, Greece, Edom/Rome, just as we saw at *Genesis Rabbah* and successive Midrash compilations. What is implicit is always that the fifth and final empire is Israel.

We now see the full extent to which our document bears a large burden of secondary accretions, an internal commentary of its own.

> 4. A. "And the Lord will bring you back in ships to Egypt:"
> B. Said R. Isaac, "'in ships' (spelled not with the silent alef but with the silent ayin) can be read 'by reason of poverty and good deeds.'"
> 5. A. "And the Lord will bring you back in ships to Egypt:"
> B. Why Egypt?

C. Because it is ugly and wicked for a slave to return to his original master.

From the cited verse, we turn to a generalization that utilizes the verse but does not focus upon it.

6. A. Said R. Simeon b. Yohai, "In three passages God warned the Israelites not to go back to Egypt:
   B. "'For since you have seen the Egyptians today, you shall see them again no more' (Ex. 14:13).
   C. "'The Lord has said to you, You shall not return any more by that way' (Dt. 17:16).
   D. "'And the Lord will bring you back in ships to Egypt, a journey which I promise that you should never make again.'
   E. "They disobeyed all three and were punished on three counts:
   F. "in the days of Sennacherib: 'Woe to them who go down to Egypt for help' (Is. 31:1). Then: 'Now the Egyptians are men and not God' (Is. 31:3).
   G. "in the days of Yohanan b. Koreah: 'Then it shall come to pass that the sword which you fear shall overtake you there in the land of Egypt' (Jer. 42:16).
   H. "The third time in the days of Trajan, may his bones be pulverized."

Next comes a free-standing composition, inserted as a topical footnote to the closing line of the foregoing.

7. A. The wife of Trajan—may his bones be pulverized—gave birth to a child on the ninth of Ab, while the Jews were observing rites of mourning, and the child died on Hanukkah.
   B. They said to one another, "What shall we do? Shall we kindle the Hanukkah lights or not?"
   C. They said, "Let us light them, and what will be will be."
   D. They went and slandered the Jews to him, saying to his wife, "When your son was born, these Jews went into mourning, and when he died, they lit their lamps."
   E. She sent and said to her husband, "Instead of conquering the barbarians, come and conquer these Jews, who have rebelled against you."
   F. He had made a calculation that the trip would take ten days but the winds carried him and brought him in five days.
   G. He came into the synagogue and found the Jews occupied with this verse of Scripture: "The Lord will bring a nation against you from afar, from the end of the earth, as the vulture swoops down" (Dt. 28:49).

H. He said to them, "I am the vulture who expected the trip to last ten days but who was brought by the fair wind in five."

I. He surrounded them with his legions and slaughtered them.

We revert to the exegesis of the cited verse, and the composition bears several further compositions, all formed into a topical composite, as is clear.

8. A. "(there you shall offer yourselves for sale to your enemies as male and female slaves), but no man will buy you. (These are the words of the covenant which the Lord commanded Moses to make with the people of Israel [Dt. 28:69/29:1]):"

B. Why is there none to buy?

C. Rab said, "Because you did not acquire the words of the covenant ('These are the words of the covenant'); none among you purchased the words of the five books of the Torah, and the letters of the word for buy has the numerical value of five."

D. Said R. Samuel b. Nahman, "Because I made the rounds of all the nations of the world, and none among them would buy the words of Torah as you do ('These are the words of the covenant')."

E. Said R. Simeon b. Yohai, "You can acquire rights of ownership to members of the nations of the world, as it says, 'Moreover of the children of the strangers that sojourn among you, of them may you buy' (Lev. 25:45),

F. "but they cannot acquire rights of ownership to you. Why not? Because you acquired 'these the words of the covenant.' And the nations? They did not acquire 'these the words of the covenant' ('These are the words of the covenant')."

G. Said R. Jonathan, "Because you have patrons, and what are they? 'These are the words of the covenant.'

H. "You are crown property. If a man buys a slave from crown property, is not his life forfeit?

I. "So said Ahasuerus to his wife, 'Behold, I have given Esther the house of Haman' (Est. 8:7)."

J. On this matter said R. Judah b. R. Simon, "This was the penalty for having laid hands on the crown property."

9. A. Said R. Isaac, "There was a precedent in Pruspiah of a woman who would ransom captives. A captive woman came and she ransomed her, so too a second. When she ran out of money and could not buy any more, soldiers forthwith surrounded her and killed her.

B. Why so?

C. To warn bandits in the future (not to kidnap Jews, since no one would buy them; hence this curse is in a way a blessing in disguise, so Simon, *Midrash Rabbah Esther* [London, 1948] p. 5, n. 1).

10. A. (Another comment on the verse, "there you shall offer yourselves for sale to your enemies as male and female slaves, but no man will buy you:")
B. R. Levi and R. Isaac:
C. R. Levi says, "Who will buy a companion for himself knowing that on the next day he is going to be put to death? Who is going to take a woman and on the next day she is going to be put to death?"
D. R. Isaac said, "For slave-boys and slave-girls you will not be purchased, but you will be purchased 'to be destroyed, to be slain, and to perish.'
E. "For that is what Esther said to Ahasuerus: 'For we are sold . . . to be destroyed, to be slain, and to perish. But if we had been sold for bondmen and bondwomen, I would have held my peace' (Est. 7:4).
F. "For so did our master, Moses, write for us in the Torah: 'there you shall offer yourselves for sale to your enemies as male and female slaves, but no man will buy you.' Did he intend to say, 'You shall sell yourselves to be destroyed, to be slain, and to perish'? (Surely not.)"

Now we revert to the base-verse, for the first time.

11. A. "Now it came to pass in the days of Ahasuerus, the Ahasuerus who reigned from India to Ethiopia over one hundred and twenty-seven provinces:")
B. When they saw this, they all began to cry, "Woe?"
C. "Now it came to pass" (since the word in Hebrew for "now it came to pass" can yield the word "woe," hence the sense of the words, 'Now it came to pass in the days of Ahasuerus' is this:) "Woe for that which was in the days of Ahasuerus" (Est. 1:1).

This introduction to *Esther Rabbah I* makes the familiar points that the compilation wishes to emphasize, the ones that the scriptural book registers through its narrative. That completes the opening composite of the document, a complex but beautifully organized exposition of Esth 1:1 in light of Deut 28:66–68.

But how does the Midrash process work through the sequence of verses of Esther? Let us now turn to a single, protracted example of how *Esther Rabbah I* expounds a verse of the book of Esther. Once more through indentation we identify the primary from the subordinate components of the composite.

Esther Rabbah I X:i.1–11

"Now it came to pass in the days of Ahasuerus, the Ahasuerus who reigned from India to Ethiopia over one hundred and twenty-seven provinces" (Esth 1:1):

1. A. "Now it came to pass in the days of Ahasuerus:"
   B. Said R. Joshua b. Qorhah, "(He was called Ahasuerus) because he blackened the face of the Israelites like the sides of a pot (and the word for blacken and the name Ahasuerus use the same letters)."
   C. R. Levi said, "It is because he gave the Israelites a headache through their fasting and self-affliction (and the word for make the head ache and the name Ahasuerus use the same letters)."
   D. R. Levi said, "It is because he made them drink gall and wormwood (and the word for make drink gall and the name Ahasuerus use the same letters)."
   E. And R. Judah b. R. Simon said, "It is because he wanted to uproot the Israelites at their roots (and the word for uproot and the name Ahasuerus use the same letters)."
   F. R. Tahalipa bar bar Hana said, "It is because he was the brother of the chief, (and the word for brother of the chief or head and the name Ahasuerus use the same letters) the brother of Nebuchadnezzar."

Now, we see, the verse itself is the focus, and the details require attention in their own terms. While we are able to discern large principles that are invoked, here I see no underlying or encompassing program that accounts for the selection of details for exposition or for the character of the exposition. We see that *Esther Rabbah I* contains not only a theological statement but two other kinds of exposition, philological-exegetical and narrative. The latter enriches the story, the former clarifies its details.

   G. But was he really his brother? Is it not the fact that the one was Chaldean and the other Median?
      H. But (what they have in common is that) this one stopped work on the house of the sanctuary, and the other destroyed it. Therefore Scripture treated them as equivalent.
      I. That is in line with the following verse of Scripture: "Even one who is slack in the work is brother to the one who is a destroyer" (Prov. 18:9).
      J. "Even one who is slack in the work:" this refers to Ahasuerus, who stopped work on the house of the sanctuary.
      K. "is brother to the one who is a destroyer:" this is Nebuchadnezzar, who destroyed the house of the sanctuary.

What follows involves a judgment on the principal players of the narrative, which the cited sages set forth by their acute grasp of the details. Thus Ahasuerus is judged by actions that run parallel, his betrayal first of his wife then of his ally. Here the sages impart their own profound mastery of the details to the reading of the story viewed whole.

2. A. Another comment on the phrase, "(in the days of) Ahasuerus, the (Ahasuerus) (Hebrew: he is Ahasuerus who . . .):"
   B. R. Judah and R. Nehemiah:
   C. One of them said, "'The Ahasuerus' who killed his wife on account of his ally is the same Ahasuerus who killed his ally on account of his wife."
   D. The other of them (text: R. Nehemiah) said, "'The Ahasuerus' who stopped the building of the house of the sanctuary is the same Ahasuerus who decreed that it be built."
      E. But is he the one who made that decree? Was it not Cyrus who made that decree? For it is written, "In the first year of Cyrus the king, Cyrus the king made a decree concerning the house of God . . . let the house be built" (Ezra 6:3).
      F. At that time all of his councilors came before him and said to him, "Your father made a decree that it not be rebuilt, and you decree that it be rebuilt? Now can one king nullify the decrees of another king?"
      G. He said to them, "Bring me copies of the state archives."
      H. They brought him copies of the state archives, and therein was written, "Then there was found at Ahmetha in the palace . . . a roll" (Ezra 6:2).
      I. And what was written in it? "Make a decree to cause these men to cease" (Ezra 4:21).
      J. He said to them, "Is it written, 'for all time'? What is written is only, 'until a decree will be made by me'" (Ezra 4:21).
      K. "Who can see that if father were alive, he would not build it?"
      L. Therefore Scripture includes him with the prophets: "And the elders of the Jews built and prospered, through the prophesying of Haggai" (Ezra 6:14). (Cf. Simon, p. 19, n. 5: Therefore it is as if he had himself decreed that it should be built. For that reason the order to rebuild is ascribed to Ahasuerus.)

The next unit also involves collecting data from diverse passages and finding the general rule that links one fact to another and yields a proposition. The rule concerns the implications of the grammatical construction that is cited.

3. A. "(in the days of Ahasuerus), the (Ahasuerus) (Hebrew: he is Ahasuerus who . . .):"
   B. The word "he" appears five times in a pejorative sense, and five times in a positive sense.
      C. The five usages in a pejorative sense are these:
      D. "He (Nimrod) was a mighty hunter before the Lord" (Gen. 10:9).
      E. "He (Esau) is Esau the father of the Edomites" (Gen. 36:43).
      F. "These are (he is) that Dathan and Abiram" (Num. 26:9).
      G. "He is king Ahaz" (2 Chr. 28:22).
      H. "he is Ahasuerus who. . . ."

I. The five usages in a positive sense are these:
J. "Abram, he is Abraham" (1 Chr. 1:27).
K. "These are he, Moses and Aaron" (Ex. 6:27).
L. "These are he, Aaron and Moses" (Ex. 6:26).
M. "And David was he, the youngest" (1 Sam. 17:14).
N. "Has not he, Hezekiah" (2 Chr. 32:12).
O. "He is Ezra, who went up from Babylonia" (Ezra 7:9).
  P. R. Berekhiah in the name of rabbis from there (Babylonia): "We have one that is better than them all: 'He is the Lord our God, his judgments are in all the earth' (Ps. 105:7).
  Q. "For the trait of his mercy is for ever."

The next set moves from a philological observation to a biographical-historical one: who is this Ahasuerus? How is he identified with others known to us? So philology gives way to history.

4. A. "(the) Ahasuerus (who reigned from India to Ethiopia over one hundred and twenty-seven provinces):"
   B. R. Levi and rabbis:
   C. R. Levi said, "Ahasuerus is the same as Artaxerxes. Why is he called Ahasuerus? Because whoever remembers him gets a headache, (and the word for make the head ache and the name Ahasuerus use the same letters)."
   D. And rabbis say, "Artaxerxes is the same as Ahasuerus. Why is his name Artaxerxes? Because he would get mad and then feel sorry (*martiah vehash*, and the letters for those words occur in the name Artaxerxes)."
5. A. "(the) Ahasuerus (who reigned from India to Ethiopia over one hundred and twenty-seven provinces):"
   B. R. Isaac and rabbis:
   C. R. Isaac said, "He is the Ahasuerus in whose times all troubles came: 'There was great mourning among the Jews.'
   D. "He is (a different) Ahasuerus in whose times all blessings came: 'The Jews had gladness and joy, a feast and a holiday' (Est. 8:17)."
   E. Rabbis said, "He is the Ahasuerus before Esther went in to him, and he is the same Ahasuerus after Esther went in to him,
   F. "for he did not have sexual relations with menstruating women." (Simon, p. 20, ns. 7, 8: He was sensual. But thus he became a different person, as it were.)

Now the sages state their opinion of Ahasuerus: he was a negligible figure. He was a weakling. He did not rule his empire, he just reigned within it. That accounts for his acceptance of Haman's proposal.

6. A. "... who reigned (from India to Ethiopia over one hundred and twenty-seven provinces):"

      B. ("Reigned") but up to now had not actually ruled.
7. A. "from India to Ethiopia:"
    B. But is it not the fact that the distance from Hodu to Cush is negligible?
    C. The sense is this: Just as he ruled from Hodu to Kush, so he ruled over one hundred and twenty-seven provinces."
8. A. Along these same lines: "For he had dominion over all the region on this side of the River, from Tiphsah even to Gaza" (1 Kgs. 5:4).
    B. But is it not the fact that the distance from Tiphsah to Gaza is negligible?
    C. The sense is this: Just as he ruled from Tiphsah to Gaza, so he ruled over the whole world.
9. A. Along these same lines: "From the Temple up to Jerusalem, kings shall bring presents to you" (Ps. 68:30):
    B. But is it not the fact that the distance from the Temple to Jerusalem is negligible?
    C. The sense is this: Just as the offerings extend from the Temple to Jerusalem, so there will be a parade of messengers with gifts for the Messiah: "Yes, all kings shall prostrate themselves before him" (Ps. 72:11).
    D. R. Kohen, brother of R. Hiyya b. Abba, said, "Just as the Presence of God is located from the temple to Jerusalem, so will the presence of God fill the world from one end to the other: 'And let the whole earth be filled with his glory, Amen and Amen' (Ps. 72:19)."

Once again, Ahasuerus is diminished: he is compared to the Israelite kings, David and Solomon, who also ruled over large empires. By that standard he does not measure up.

10. A. (the Ahasuerus who reigned from India to Ethiopia) over one hundred and twenty-seven provinces:
    B. R. Eleazar in the name of R. Hanina: "And is it not the fact that there are two hundred fifty-two hyparchies in the world (many more than one hundred twenty-seven? How can he have ruled over the whole world?)
    C. "David ruled them all: 'And the fame of David went out into all lands' (1 Chr. 14:17).
    D. "Solomon ruled them all: 'And Solomon ruled over all the kingdoms' (1 Kgs. 5:1).
    E. "Ahab ruled them all: 'As the Lord your God lives, there is no nation or kingdom where my Lord has not sent to seek you and imposed an oath on the kingdom' (1 Kgs. 18:10).
    F. "Can one impose an oath where one does not rule?
    G. "Further evidence of the same fact: 'Then he numbered the young men of the princes of the provinces, and they were two hundred and thirty-two' (1 Kgs. 20:15)."

H. Where were the rest of them?
I. R. Levi and rabbis:
J. R. Levi said, "They died in the famine in the time of Elijah."
K. Rabbis said, "Ben Hadad came and took them: 'And Ben Hadad, king of Aram, gathered all his army together, and there were thirty-two kings with him, horses and chariots, and he went up and besieged Samaria and fought against it' (1 Kgs. 20:1).
L. We look for twenty, and you mention thirty-two?
M. Some provinces rebelled and he took some men and held them as hostages."
N. R. Berekiah and Rabbis on the verse, "He has caused the arrows of his quiver to enter into my reins" (Lam. 3:5):
O. (Following Simon:) R. Berekiah said, "This means that they took prisoners and hostages."
P. (Following Simon:) Rabbis said, "The prisoners were called *bene ukaifi* because they were curbed with manacles *(arkuf)*. The hostages are called *bene amorai* because they are exchanged *(temurot)* for their fathers, and so it says, 'The hostages *(bene hataarubot)* also' (2 Kgs. 14:14), so called because they were substitutes *(meurabot)* for their fathers." (Simon, p. 22, n. 5: This is a digression introduced because of the reference to hostages.)

(Resuming the discussion left off at G:)

Q. "Nebuchadnezzar ruled them all: 'And wherever the children of men, the beasts of the field and the fowl of heaven dwell, he has given them into your hand' (Dan. 2:38).
R. "Cyrus ruled them all: 'Thus said Cyrus . . . all the kingdoms of the earth has the Lord given me' (Ezra 1:2).
S. "Darius ruled them all: 'Then king Darius wrote to all the peoples' (Dan. 6:26).
T. "Ahasuerus ruled only half of them!"
11. A. Why over only half?
B. R. Huna in the name of R. Aha and rabbis:
C. R. Huna in the name of R. Aha said, "Said to him the Holy One, blessed be he, 'You have divided my kingdom: "He is the God who is in Jerusalem" (Ezra 1:3). As you live, I will divide your kingdom!'"
D. Rabbis say, "Said to him the Holy One, blessed be he, 'You have divided the size of my house: "The height thereof three-score cubits" (Ezra 6:3 [but the first temple was a hundred and twenty cubits high, so 2 Chr. 3:4]). By your life, I will divide your kingdom!'"

Enough of the unit has been presented to show the character of the document as a systematic exegesis of the book of Esther Chapters One and Two. What we see is, the construction is systematic, and the exegesis is dense and close. But through the details a clear viewpoint and proposition on the topic at hand do emerge.

What does *Esther Rabbah I* contribute?

One contribution that stands out is the systematic and successful absorption of the story of Esther into the Rabbinic system and structure. It is the introduction, into the utterly irrational situation faced by the Jews of Mordecai's and Esther's day, of the considerations of divine justice and mercy, the functioning of God's rational plan and program, and all of the rest of Rabbinic rationalism. That effort to encompass the story within the familiar parameters of Rabbinic Judaism and its reading of the Torah and prophets—misfortune because of sin, followed by repentance, provoking God's forgiveness and reconciliation—does not coalesce in well-articulated and fully worked out category-formations. But it does surface, time and again, in our survey of the inchoate statements of the document, when these are allowed to stand, each on its own.

The statement of *Esther Rabbah I* and *Ruth Rabbah*

The Torah governs in an unconventional context. It transforms the gentile into an Israelite, and the sage of the Torah, represented by Mordecai, is able to accomplish the Torah's goals through a woman, a comparable paradox. Gender thus defines the focus for both *Esther Rabbah I* and *Ruth Rabbah*, yielding the opposite of what is anticipated of woman.

As we shall now see, *Ruth Rabbah* has the Messiah born of an outsider, just as *Esther Rabbah I* has salvation come through a woman. Esther and Mordecai, the woman and the sage-Messiah, function in *Esther Rabbah I* in much the same way that Ruth and Boaz, the woman and the sage-Messiah and David's forebears, do in the work of *Ruth Rabbah*. While the sages of *Ruth Rabbah* face their own, distinctive problem of the way the outsider becomes the insider, still, *Ruth Rabbah* and *Esther Rabbah I* deal with the same fundamental fact: the Messiah-sage dictates the future of Israel, because he (never she) realizes the rule of the Torah. In *Esther Rabbah I* many things say one thing: the Torah dictates Israel's fate. Specifically, if you want to know what that fate will be, study the Torah, and if you want to control that fate, follow the model of the sage-Messiah.

10

Ruth in *Ruth Rabbah*

A Gentile Woman Saves Israel through the Torah

Ruth Rabbah, of indeterminate date and venue but possibly of the sixth century C.E., mediates the book of Ruth to Judaism. In reading the story of how Ruth, originally a Moabite, became an Israelite, indeed ancestress of David and hence of the Messiah, *Ruth Rabbah* conveys only one message, expressed in a variety of components. It concerns the outsider who becomes the principal, the origin of Israel's Messiah out of Moab, and how this miracle is accomplished through mastery of the Torah.

The principal points

The main points of the document, deriving from the narrative of Ruth, are these:

(1) Israel's fate depends upon its proper conduct toward its leaders.

(2) The leaders must not be arrogant.

(3) The admission of the outsider depends upon the rules of the Torah. These differentiate among outsiders. Those who know the rules are able to apply them accurately and mercifully.

(4) The proselyte is accepted because the Torah makes it possible to do so, and the condition of acceptance is complete and total submission to the Torah. (Thus Boaz taught Ruth the rules of the Torah, and she obeyed them carefully.)

(5) Those proselytes who are accepted are respected by God and are completely equal to all other Israelites. Those who marry them are masters of the Torah, and their descendants are masters of the Torah. (Thus Boaz in his day and David in his day were the same in this regard.)

(6) What the proselyte therefore accomplishes is to take shelter under the wings of God's presence, and the proselyte who does so stands in the royal line of David, Solomon, and the Messiah.

Over and over again, we see, the point is made that Ruth the Moabitess, perceived by the ignorant as an outsider, enjoyed complete equality with all other Israelites, because she had accepted the yoke of the Torah, married a great sage, and through her descendants would produce the Messiah-sage, David.

What changes a gentile into an Israelite is the Torah

That is the theological principle that animates the Rabbinic system throughout: the Torah is what makes Israel Israel. Here sages invoke the extraordinary power of the Torah to join opposites—Israelite/gentile, Messiah/utter outsider—into a single figure, and to accomplish this union of opposites through a woman. The femininity of Ruth is critical to the whole as much as is her Moabite origin. The two modes of the (from the Israelite perspective) abnormal, outsider as against Israelite, woman as against man, therefore are invoked. Both serve the same purpose, to show how, through the Torah, all things become one. That is the message of the document, and, seen whole, the principal message, to which all other points prove peripheral.

A commentary in the narrowest sense—verse by verse amplification, paraphrase, exposition—this document states in an enormous number of ways that the Torah is what dictates Israel's fate. If you want to know what that fate will be, study the Torah, and if you want to control that fate, follow the model of the sage-Messiah. As usual, therefore, what we find is a recasting of the Deuteronomic-prophetic theology.

The propositions of *Ruth Rabbah*

Three categories contain the topical and propositional messages of the document. These are as follows (with reference to the pertinent passage in parentheses):

Israel and God

Israel's relationship with God encompasses the matter of the covenant, the Torah, and the Land of Israel, all of which bring to concrete and material expression the nature and standing of that relationship. This is a topic treated only casually by our compilers. They make a perfectly standard point. It is that Israel suffers because of sin (I:i). The famine in the time of the judges was because of Israel's rebellion: "My children are rebellious. But as to exterminating them, that is not possible, and to bring them back to Egypt is not possible, and to trade them for some other nation is something I cannot do. But this shall I do for them: lo, I shall torment them with suffering and afflict them with famine in the days when the judges judge" (III:i). This was because they got overconfident (III:ii).

Sometimes God saves Israel on account of its merit, sometimes for his own name's sake (X:i). God's punishment of Israel is always proportionate and appropriate, so LXXIV:i: "Just as in the beginning, Israel gave praise for the redemption: 'This is my God and I will glorify him' (Ex. 15:2), now it is for the substitution (of false gods for God): 'Thus they exchanged their glory for the likeness of an ox that eats grass' (Ps. 106:20). You have nothing so repulsive and disgusting and strange as an ox when it is eating grass. In the beginning they would effect acquisition through the removal of the sandal, as it is said, 'Now this was the custom in former times in Israel concerning redeeming and exchanging: to confirm a transaction, the one drew off his sandal and gave it to the other, and this was the manner of attesting in Israel.' But now it is by means of the rite of cutting off." None of this forms a centerpiece of interest, and all of it complements the principal points of the writing.

Israel and the nations

Israel's relationship with the nations is treated with interest in Israel's history, past, present, and future, and how that cyclical pattern is to be known. This topic is not addressed at all. Only one nation figures in a consequential way, and that is Moab. Under these circumstances we can hardly generalize and say that Moab stands for everybody outside of Israel. That is precisely the opposite of the fact. Moab stands for a problem within Israel, the Messiah from the periphery; and the solution to the problem lies within Israel and not in its relationships to the other, the nations.

Israel on its own

Israel on its own concerns the holy nation's understanding of itself: who is Israel, who is not? Within the same rubric we find consideration of Israel's capacity to naturalize the outsider, so to define itself as to extend its own limits, and other questions of self-definition. And, finally, when Israel considers itself, a principal concern is the nature of leadership, for the leader stands for and embodies the people. Therein lies the paradox of the base-document and the Midrash compilation alike: how can the leader most wanted, the Messiah, come, as a matter of fact, from the excluded people and not from the holy people? Phrased in this way, the question yields the obvious answer: through the Torah as embodied by the sage, anybody can become Israel, and any Israelite can find his way to the center. So the principal message repeats itself on all occasions.

But Israel on its own entails recognition of Israel's sinfulness and rebellion. The sin of Israel, which caused the famine, was that it was judging its own judges. "He further said to the Israelites, 'So God says to Israel, "I have given a share of glory to the judges and I have called them gods, and the Israelites nonetheless humiliate them. Woe to a generation that judges its judges"'" (I:i). The Israelites were slothful in burying Joshua, and that showed disrespect to their leader (II:i). They were slothful about repentance in the time of the judges, and that is what caused the famine; excess of commitment to one's own affairs leads to sin. The Israelites did not honor the prophets (III:iii). The old have to bear with the young, and the young with the old, or Israel will go into exile (IV:i).

The generation that judges its leadership ("judges") will be penalized (V:i). Arrogance to the authority of the Torah is penalized (V:i). Elimelech was punished because he broke the peoples' heart; everyone depended upon him, and he proved undependable (V:iii); so bad leadership will destroy Israel. When the years of drought came, his maid went out into the market place, with her basket in her hand. So the people of the town said, "Is this the one on whom we depended, that he can provide for the whole town with ten years of food? Lo, his maid is standing in the marketplace with her basket in her hand!" The leadership of a community is its glory: "The great man of a town—he is its splendor, he is its glory, he is its praise. When he has turned from there, so too have turned its splendor, glory, and praise" (XI:i.1C).

Who is Israel and how does a gentile become part of Israel?

A distinct but fundamental component of the theory of Israel on its own concerns who is Israel and how one becomes a part of Israel. That theme proves fundamental to our document, so much of which is preoccupied with how Ruth can be the progenitor of the Messiah, deriving as she does not only from gentile but from Moabite stock. Israel's history follows rules that are to be learned in Scripture; nothing is random and all things are connected (IV:ii). The fact that the king of Moab honored God explains why God raised up from Moab "a son who will sit on the throne of the Lord" (VIII:i.3). The proselyte is discouraged but then accepted. Thus XVI:i.2B: "People are to turn a proselyte away. But if he is insistent beyond that point, he is accepted. A person should always push away with the left hand while offering encouragement with the right." Orpah, who left Naomi, was rewarded for the little that she did for her, but she was raped when she left her (XVIII:i.1–3). When Orpah went back to her people, she went back to her gods (XIX:i).

Ruth's intention to convert was absolutely firm, and Naomi laid out all the problems for her, but she acceded to every condition (XX:i)—certainly the most powerful statement in the entirety of *Ruth Rabbah*. The entire passage is cited later in this chapter.

Proselytes are respected by God, so XXII:i: "And when Naomi saw that she was determined to go with her, (she said no more):" Said R. Judah b. R. Simon, "Notice how precious are proselytes before the Omnipresent. Once she had decided to convert, the Scripture treats her as equivalent to Naomi." Boaz, for his part, was equally virtuous and free of sins (XXVI:i). The law provided for the conversion of Ammonite and Moabite women, but not Ammonite and Moabite men, so the acceptance of Ruth the Moabite was fully in accord with the law, and anyone who did not know that fact was an ignoramus (XXVI:i.4, among many passages). An Israelite hero who came from Ruth and Boaz was David, who was a great master of the Torah. Thus, "he was 'Skillful in playing, and a mighty man of war, prudent in affairs, good-looking, and the Lord is with him'" (1 Sam. 16:18): "Skillful in playing," in Scripture; "and a mighty man of valor," in Mishnah; "a man of war," who knows the give and take of the war of the Torah; "prudent in affairs," in good deeds; "good-looking," in Talmud; "prudent in affairs," able to reason deductively; good-looking," enlightened in law; "and the Lord is with him," the law accords with his opinions.

Ruth truly accepted Judaism upon the instruction of Boaz:

Ruth Rabbah XXXIV:i.1

Thus:
- A. "Then Boaz said to Ruth, 'Now listen, my daughter, do not go to glean in another field'":
- B. This is on the strength of the verse, "You shall have no other gods before me" (Ex. 20:3).
- C. "'... or leave this one'":
- D. This is on the strength of the verse, "This is my God and I will glorify him" (Ex. 15:2).
- E. "but keep close to my maidens":
- F. This speaks of the righteous, who are called maidens: "Will you play with him as with a bird, or will you bind him for your maidens" (Job 40:29).

The glosses invest the statement with a vast tapestry of meaning. Boaz speaks to Ruth as a Jew by choice, and the entire exchange is now typological. Note also the typological meanings imputed at XXXV:i.1–5. Ruth had prophetic power (XXXVI:ii). Ruth was rewarded for her sincere conversion by Solomon (XXXVIII:i.1).

Taking shelter under the wings of the Presence of God, which is what the convert does, is the greatest merit accorded to all who do deeds of grace. Thus,

Ruth Rabbah XXXIIII:i.2

- H. "So notice the power of the righteous and the power of righteousness are the power of those who do deeds of grace.
- I. "For they take shelter not in the shadow of the dawn, nor in the shadow of the wings of the earth, not in the shadow of the wings of the sun, nor in the shadow of the wings of the hayyot, nor in the shadow of the wings of the cherubim or the seraphim.
- J. "But under whose wings do they take shelter?

K. "They take shelter under the shadow of the One at whose word the world was created: 'How precious is your loving kindness O God, and the children of men take refuge in the shadow of your wings' (Ps. 36:8)."

The language that Boaz used to Ruth, "Come here," bore with it deeper reference to these: David, Solomon, the throne as held by the Davidic monarchy, and ultimately, the Messiah, e.g., in the following instance.

Ruth Rabbah XL:i.5

A. "The fifth interpretation refers to the Messiah: 'Come here': means, to the throne.
B. "'. . . and eat some bread': this is the bread of the throne.
C. "'. . . and dip your morsel in vinegar': this refers to suffering: 'But he was wounded because of our transgressions' (Is. 53:5).
D. "'So she sat beside the reapers': for the throne is destined to be taken from him for a time: 'For I will gather all nations against Jerusalem to battle and the city shall be taken' (Zech. 14:2).
E. "'. . . and he passed to her parched grain': for he will be restored to the throne: 'And he shall smite the land with the rod of his mouth' (Is. 11:4)."
F. R. Berekhiah in the name of R. Levi: "As was the first redeemer, so is the last redeemer:
G. "Just as the first redeemer was revealed and then hidden from them—"
H. And how long was a hidden? Three months: "And they met Moses and Aaron" (Ex. 5:20),
I. [reverting to G:] "so the last redeemer will be revealed to them and then hidden from them."

Boaz instructed Ruth on how to be a proper Israelite woman:

Ruth Rabbah LII:i.1–3

1. A. "Wash therefore and anoint yourself":
   B. "Wash yourself": from the filth of idolatry that is yours.
   C. ". . . and anoint yourself": this refers to the religious deeds and acts of righteousness [that are required of an Israelite].
2. A. "and put on your best clothes":

This refers to her Sabbath clothing. So did Naomi encompass Ruth within Israel:

3. A. ". . . and go down to the threshing floor":
   B. She said to her, "My merit will go down there with you."

Moab, whence Ruth came, was conceived:

Ruth Rabbah LV:i.1

C. . . . not for the sake of fornication but for the sake of heaven.

Boaz, for his part, was a master of the Torah and when he ate and drank, that formed a typology for his study of the Torah (LVI:i). His was a life of grace, Torah study, and marriage for holy purposes. Whoever trusts in God is exalted, and that refers to Ruth and Boaz; God put it in his heart to bless her (LVII:i). David sang Psalms to thank God for his great-grandmother, Ruth, citing the relevant verse.

Ruth Rabbah LIX:i.5

A. . . ."[At midnight I will rise to give thanks to you] because of your righteous judgments" (Ps. 119:62):
B. [David speaks,] "The acts of judgment that you brought upon the Ammonites and Moabites.
C. "And the righteous deeds that you carried out for my grandfather and my grandmother [Boaz, Ruth, of whom David speaks here].
D. "For had he hastily cursed her but once, where should I have come from?
E. "But you put in his heart the will to bless her: 'And he said, "May you be blessed by the Lord."'"

Because of the merit of the six measures that Boaz gave Ruth, six righteous persons came forth from him, each with six virtues: David, Hezekiah, Josiah, Hananiah-Mishael-Azariah (counted as one), Daniel and the royal Messiah.

God facilitated the union of Ruth and Boaz (LXVIII:i). Boaz's relative was ignorant for not knowing that while a male Moabite was excluded, a female one was acceptable for marriage. The blessing of Boaz was, "May all the children you have come from this righteous woman" (LXXIX:i), and that is precisely the blessing accorded to Isaac and to Elkanah. God made Ruth an ovary, which she had lacked (LXXX:i). Naomi was blessed with blessings, thus:

Ruth Rabbah LXXXI:i.1–2

1. A. "Then the women said to Naomi, 'Blessed be the Lord, who has not left you this day without next of kin; and may his name be renowned in Israel'":
   B. Just as "this day" rules dominion in the firmament, so will your descendants rule and govern Israel forever.
2. A. Said R. Hunia, "On account of the blessings of the women, the line of David was not wholly exterminated in the time of Athaliah."

Propositions particular to *Ruth Rabbah*

The only proposition both important in, and particular to, *Ruth Rabbah* is that proselytes are precious to God. Once they decide to convert, they are equivalent to Israelites (XXII:i.1). Converting to Judaism is "to take shelter under the wings of the Presence of God," and marks a person as one who performs deeds of righteousness and grace. Those who do deeds of righteousness and grace take shelter not in the shadow of the dawn, nor in the shadow of the wings of the earth, not in the shadow of the wings of the sun, nor in the shadow of the wings of the *hayyot*, nor in the shadow of the wings of the cherubim or the seraphim, but only under the shadow of the One at whose word the world was created (XXXVIII:i.2). The convert to Israel is washed of the filth of idolatry and anointed in the religious deeds and acts of righteousness that are required of an Israelite (LII:i.1).

But are these propositions particular to *Ruth Rabbah*?

The logic of the theological system of Rabbinic Judaism demands a negative answer to this question. If the Israelite is Israelite by reason of the Torah, then, simple logic insists, the Torah works its power of sanctification on any human being equally. It is what a person affirms and accepts and accomplishes that marks the person as Israel: affirming the Torah, accepting the dominion of God, accomplishing deeds that fulfill the law of the Torah—these signify that the individual is Israelite and belongs to that unique community, Israel. And since that is the fact, what basis is there for making distinctions within Israel or among Israelites? There is no such basis, the very definition of what is Israel and what are the nations of the world leaves no room for such a distinction. A person is either Israel or not-Israel, and within Israel are (from this perspective) no gradations or distinctions. True, the legal system of the Halakhah, in line with Scripture, recognizes Israel's castes, priests, Levites, Israelites, and the rest. But the same Halakhic system recognizes the possibility that the convert's descendant may become High Priest—and the book of Ruth underscores the same conception in connection with the Messiah. In that setting, the book of Ruth at its most particular turns out to form a generic work of Torah-exposition, pure and simple.

How the data form a system

The whole then coheres in an entirely familiar pattern. God relates to man through the Torah, which distinguishes humanity into two parts: Israel, who accept God's rule, and the nations, who reject that rule. Israel meets God through the Torah. What Israel knows about God is that he is just and merciful. He is just, so he punishes sin, which is rebellion, and he is merciful, so he accepts the repentant sinner. In the end of days God will send a Messiah. The particular statements, tied to specific verses, coalesce into the specified category-formations, which themselves cohere in a simple, systematic statement. And, for reasons amply spelled out in the opening unit of this chapter, that statement matches the encompassing structure and system that the Rabbinic documents yield when they are read within the logic of mythic monotheism. The upshot is simple: knowing the book of Ruth in its scriptural context, we could readily have predicted the character and program of *Ruth Rabbah*. There are no surprises.

A sample passage

The document is comprised of two distinct types of compositions: First, the intersecting-verse/base-verse exposition; second, the verse-by-verse commentary. In the former, a verse of Ruth is juxtaposed with a verse selected from some other book of the Scriptures, and the latter imposes context and meaning on the verse of Ruth. In this way, Scripture is treated as unitary and not divided into books. In the latter, the verses of the book of Ruth are systematically cited and glossed, with the cumulative effect already epitomized above. Here is the first of the two types of compositions:

Ruth Rabbah I:i.1–11

1. A. ("And it came to pass in the days when the judges ruled, there was a famine in the land, and a certain man of Bethlehem in Judah went to sojourn in the country of Moab, he and his wife and his two sons. The name of the man was Elimelech, and the name of his wife Naomi, and the names of his two sons were Mahlon and Chilion; they were Ephrathites from Bethlehem in Judah. They went into the country of Moab and remained there:") "And it came to pass in the days when the judges ruled (judged):"
   B. R. Yohanan commenced discourse by citing (the following verse of Scripture: "Hear, O my people, and I will speak; O Israel, and I will testify against you. [God, your God, I am.])" (Ps. 50:7).
   C. Said R. Yohanan, "People give evidence only in the hearing (of the accused)."
2. A. R. Yudan b. R. Simon said, "In the past, Israel was called by a name just like every other nation, e.g., 'And Sabta and Raamah and Sabteca' (Gen. 10:7).
   B. "But from now on, 'my people,' as in the verse, 'Hear, O my people, and I will speak; O Israel, and I will testify against you.'
   C. "Whence did you gain the merit to be called 'my people'?
   D. "It is from the time that 'I will speak.'
   E. "That is, it is from what you said before me at Sinai: 'All that the Lord has spoken we will do and obey' (Ex. 24:7)."

3. A. Said R. Yohanan, "'Hear, O my people:' concerning the past.
   B. "'and I will speak:' concerning the age to come.
   C. "'Hear, O my people:' in this world.
   D. "'and I will speak:' in the world to come.
   E. "It is so that what to say before the angelic princes of the nations of the world, who are destined to complain before me, saying, 'Lord of the ages, these worship idols and those worship idols, these practice fornication, and those practice fornication, these shed blood and those shed blood, these go down to the Garden of Eden, while those go down to Gehenna! (Unfair!)'
   F. "At that moment the angelic defender of Israel (Michael) remains silent.
   G. "That is the meaning of the verse, 'And at that time shall Michael stand up' (Dan. 12:1)."
4. A. And is there a session (of the court) that is held in heaven?
   B. And did not R. Hanina say, "There is no sitting in heaven: 'I came near to one of the standing ones' (Dan. 7:16).
   C. "and the meaning of the word for 'standing ones' is ones who stood by, as in this verse: 'Above him stood the seraphim' (Is. 6:2); 'And all the host of heaven standing on his right hand and on his left' (2 Chr. 18:18).
   D. "And yet the verse at hand says, 'And at that time shall Michael stand up' (Dan. 12:1)!
   E. "What is the meaning of 'And at that time shall Michael stand up' (Dan. 12:1)?
   F. "He is silenced, as in this usage: 'And shall I wait because they speak not, because they stand still and do not answer any more' (Job 32:16)."
5. A. (Continuing 3.F:) "Said to him the Holy One, blessed be he, 'Do you stand silent and not defend my children? By your life, I shall speak in righteousness and save my children.'"
6. A. And in virtue of what righteousness?
   B. R. Eleazar and R. Yohanan:
   C. One said, "In virtue of the righteousness that you did for my world by accepting my Torah. For had you not accepted my Torah, I should have turned the world back to formlessness and void."
   D. For R. Huna in the name of R. Aha said, "'When the earth and all the inhabitants thereof are dissolved. (I myself establish the pillars of it.)' (Ps. 75:4): the world should already have been dissolved were it not for the Israelites who stood before Mount Sinai. (Supply: For had you not accepted my Torah, I should have turned the world back to formlessness and void.)
   E. "And who founded the world? 'I myself establish the pillars of it.'
   F. "It is in virtue of the 'I' that 'I myself establish the pillars of it.'"
   G. The other said, "It is in virtue of the righteousness that you did in your own behalf by accepting my Torah.

H. "For if you had not, I should have assimilated you among the nations."
7. A. "God, your God, I am:"
   B. R. Yohanan said, "'It's enough for you that I am your patron.'"
   C. R. Simeon b. Laqish said, "'Even though I am your patron, what good does my patronage do for you in judgment?'"
8. A. Taught R. Simeon b. Yohanan (concerning the verse, "God, your God, I am"), "I am God for everybody in the world, but I have assigned my name in particular only to my people, Israel.
   B. "I am called not 'the God of all nations' but 'the God of Israel.'"
9. A. "God, your God, I am:"
   B. R. Yudan interpreted the verse to speak of Moses: "Said the Holy One, blessed be he, to Moses, 'Even though I called you "God" as to Pharaoh, "God, your God, I am" over you.'"
10. A. ("God, your God, I am:")
    B. R. Abba bar Yudan interpreted the verse to speak of Israel: "Even though I called you 'gods,' as it is said, 'I said, You are gods' (Ps. 82:6), nonetheless, 'God, your God, I am "over you."'"
11. A. ("God, your God, I am:")
    B. Rabbis interpreted the verse to speak of the judges: "Even though I called you gods, 'You shall not revile gods' (that is, judges) (Ex. 22:27), 'God, your God, I am' over you."
    C. "He further said to the Israelites, 'I have given a share of glory to the judges and I have called them gods, and the (Israelites) humiliate them.'
    D. "Woe to a generation that judges its judges."
    E. (Supply: "And it came to pass in the days when the judges were judged.")

What joins Sections 1–3? I see no shared proposition, but only a common reference-point, which is the intersecting verse. Section 4 is interpolated to enrich 3G, Section 5 continues Section 3, and so does Section 6. From that point on, we have a sequence of discrete compositions, none of which acknowledges the presence of anything fore or aft. So, overall, the composite is a fine example of the working of fixed associative logic. The interest of the composition as a whole is achieved at Section 11, which (as I read it) wishes to explain why the famine came about. And the answer is that the people were judging the judges. The intersecting verse is beautifully attained in the concluding composition therefore, and it does lead to precisely what the framer of the whole has wanted to say. But the prior twists and turns are hardly required. Section 2, for example, has no bearing upon the issue, and Section 3 scarcely is relevant. Only if we assume that the purpose of Yohanan's exposition at Section 3 is to explain how the Messiah comes about, which is at stake in the book of Ruth, can we suppose that there is any clear connection between Yohanan's exposition and *Ruth Rabbah's*. But that is very far-fetched, and, it follows, Section 3, with Section 4 tacked on, then Sections 5–6, are simply inserted, serving the intersecting verse in its own terms, but the base verse in no way. Sections 7–8 serve no more pertinently than the prior items. Sections 9–11 then form the bridge to our base-verse, and if my interpolation of section 11E is correct, then they do make the desired point.

Second, we take up an exposition of a verse of Ruth in its own terms. We see that the documentary interest presides over the detailed and (formally) atomistic exegesis.

Ruth Rabbah XX:i.1–4

1. A. "But Ruth said, 'Entreat me not to leave you or to return from following you'":
   B. What is the meaning of "entreat me not to leave you"?
   C. This is what she said to her, "Do not sin against me. Do not take your troubles from me." [The words for "entreat" and "troubles" share the same consonants.]
2. A. "... to leave you or to return from following you, for where you go I will go, and where you lodge I will lodge; your people shall be my people, and your God my God":
   B. "Under all circumstances I intend to convert, but it is better that it be through your action and not through that of another."
3. A. When Naomi heard her say this, she began laying out for her the laws that govern proselytes.
   B. She said to her, "My daughter, it is not the way of Israelite women to go to theaters and circuses put on by idolators."
   C. She said to her, "Where you go I will go."
   D. She said to her, "My daughter, it is not the way of Israelite women to live in a house that lacks a mezuzah."
   E. She said to her, "Where you lodge I will lodge."
   F. "... your people shall be my people":
   G. This refers to the penalties and admonitions against sinning.
   H. "... and your God my God":
   I. This refers to the other religious duties.
4. A. Another interpretation of the statement, "for where you go I will go":
   B. to the tent of meeting, Gilgal, Shiloh, Nob, Gibeon, and the eternal house.
   C. "... and where you lodge I will lodge":
   D. "I shall spend the night concerned about the offerings."
   E. "... your people shall be my people":
   F. "so nullifying my idol."
   G. "... and your God my God":
   H. "to pay a full recompense for my action."

The expansion of the story of the Ruth's conversion is accomplished in several ways. First of all, her personal loyalty to Naomi is shown in Sections 1–2 not to be the principal motivation. Section 3 then explains the relevance of each of

Ruth's statements to the duties of the Israelite, and Section 4 restates matters in terms of the holy life of the cult. I simply cannot imagine a more profound revision of the tale, or a more authentic one. When we wish to find out how the oral Torah transforms the written one into what we now call Judaism, but what our sages called "the one whole Torah—oral and written—of our lord Moses at Sinai," we can point to no more appropriate passage than this simple and unadorned composition. And, I think it clear, the interests of what we classify as a commentary have generated the whole. This is how theology comes to expression in exegesis.

Ruth Rabbah XXI:i.1–3

1. A. "where you die I will die:"(Ruth 1:17)
   B. this refers to the four modes of inflicting the death penalty that a court uses: stoning, burning, slaying, and strangulation.
2. A. "and there will I be buried:"
   B. this refers to the two burial grounds that are provided for the use of the court,
   C. one for those who are stoned and burned, the other for the use of those who are slain or strangled.

Sections 1 and 2 fit together as readings in a common way of related components of a verse. But I see no proposition here, rather a cogent exegetical composite.

3. A. "May the Lord do so to me and more also (if even death parts me from you):"
   B. She said to her, "My daughter, whatever you can accomplish in the way of religious duties and acts of righteousness in this world, accomplish.
   C. "Truly in the age to come, 'death parts me from you.'"

Section 3 may be said to relate to Sections 1–2 through the shared base-verse, hence via fixed associative logic. This brief snippet suffices to convey the flavor of the verse-by-verse exegesis of the document.

What does *Ruth Rabbah* contribute?

Ruth Rabbah contributes the recapitulation of the message of the book of Ruth and its "Rabbinization." By "Rabbinization" is meant, the introduction of the generative myths and symbols particular to Rabbinic Judaism, e.g., Torah learned through discipleship, the dual media of transmission of the Torah, and the like. Working forward from the book of Ruth permits us to see how the Rabbinic compilers have imposed upon the narrative the givens of their structure and system. Take for example the symbolic centrality of Torah: its study and performance of its commandments. The book of Ruth knows nothing of the priority of the Torah as the formulation of Israel's being.

For example, the book of Ruth is explicit in linking Ruth to her descendant, David, with a clear statement that she and Boaz are the ancestors of the Messiah through the house of David. But then in Scripture David is not represented as the master of the Torah that, for Judaism, defines what matters about him and his Messianic descendant. Again, the book of Ruth does not articulate concern about the prohibition of marriage to a Moabite, though one may claim that the very siting of Ruth in Moab suffices to raise the issue. But for the Rabbinic sages, Ruth's Moabite affiliation forms one of the keys to the entire transaction, thus Boaz had to have mastered the Torah to know the correct exegesis of the prohibition of Moab (males, not females).

Reading the parts of Scripture together as a single whole

What the compilers of *Ruth Rabbah* have done is read the book of Ruth in that broader context that is defined by the result of seeing Scripture whole and complete. Only when the entirety of the received Scripture is deemed a coherent whole does the concept of "the Torah" encompass all of the scriptural books. Only then does that whole, "the Torah," exceed the sum of the parts. Then the whole, the Torah, with its commandments and its power of regeneration and reconstruction, finds for each of the parts, the individual books, a distinctive task. Each of the biblical books is then assigned its particular place within the structure of that whole that the Torah read whole yields: the comprehensive theology. The exercise carried out in section I of this chapter in retrospect proves more critical than, at the outset, it appeared to have been.

So were we to limit our estimate of the contribution of *Ruth Rabbah* to the "Rabbinization" of the narrative, we should miss the very heart and soul of the matter. The "Rabbinization" that the compilers of *Ruth Rabbah* have done takes on its own dimension. What is involved is finding in the book of Ruth those connections that link the book of Ruth to the other components of the Torah. The matrix then is the encompassing theology, the Torah read whole. The context is the theological system and structure that realize that theology, the particular assignment carried out, for the Torah, by the book of Ruth. And the contents are determined by finding in that book the answers to the questions precipitated for the Rabbinic compilers of the document by their theological task.

The Rabbinic sages work from the Torah, viewed whole, to the hermeneutics required for each of its principal parts, and thence to the exegesis guided and shaped by the generative logic of that hermeneutics. "To rabbinize" is to see matters all together and all at once, complete, in proportion and in balance: systemically and systematically. It is to grasp the whole Torah, not just the components of the Torah one by one: to tell the story not bit by bit but whole and start to finish, as no one before them had done, and as no one after them would again have to do.

11

Song of Songs in *Song of Songs Rabbah*

Reading Holy Israel's Relationship to God within the Symbols of a Love-Song

The Song of Songs[1] finds a place in the Torah because that collection of love-songs when mediated by the Rabbinic Midrash speaks about the relationship between God and Israel. The intent of the compilers of *Song of Songs Rabbah*, which is of indeterminate date but possibly deriving from the sixth century C.E., is to realize that reading. What this means is that the Rabbinic exegetes of the successive verses of Song of Songs turn to everyday experience—the love of husband and wife—for a metaphor of God's love for Israel and Israel's love for God. Then, when Solomon's song says, "O that you would kiss me with the kisses of your mouth! For your love is better than wine," (Song 1:2), the sages think of how God kissed Israel. And they find specific occasions in Scripture's narrative to show precisely when that took place, e.g., at the Sea.

The Rabbinic sages who compiled *Song of Songs Rabbah* read the Song of Songs as a sequence of expressions of urgent love between God and Israel, the holy people. How they convey the intensity of Israel's love of God forms the point of special interest. They do not articulate their message in so many words. They turn language into a repertoire of opaque symbols in the form of words. Specifically, they set forth sequences of words that connote meanings, elicit emotions, stand for events, form the verbal equivalent of pictures or music or dance or poetry. Through the repertoire of these verbal-symbols and their arrangement and rearrangement, the message the authors wish to convey emerges. The message of the document comes not so much from stories of what happened or did not happen, assertions of truth or denials of error, but rather from the repetitious rehearsal of sets of words used as symbols.

To take one instance, we are told that a certain expression of love in the poetry of the Song of Songs is God's speaking to Israel about (1) the Sea, (2) Sinai,

---

[1] Also called in the Christian Bible, "the Song of Solomon" — both titles referring to the opening line, "The Song of Songs, which is Solomon's."

and (3) the world to come; or (1) the first redemption, the one from Egypt; (2) the second redemption, the one from Babylonia; and (3) the third redemption, the one at the end of days. The repertoire of symbols covers Temple and schoolhouse, personal piety and public worship, and other matched pairs and sequences of coherent matters, all of them seen as embedded within the poetry. Here is Scripture's poetry read as metaphor, and the task of the reader is to organize that for which each image of the poem stands. So Israel's holy life is metaphorized through the poetry of love and beloved, Lover and Israel.

What, for example, do the compilers say through their readings of the metaphor of the nut-tree for Israel? First, Israel prospers when it gives scarce resources for the study of the Torah or for carrying out religious duties; second, Israel sins but atones, and Torah is the medium of atonement; third, Israel is identified through carrying out its religious duties, e.g., circumcision; fourth, Israel's leaders had best watch their step; fifth, Israel may be nothing well-balanced but will be in glory in the coming age; sixth, Israel has plenty of room for outsiders but cannot afford to lose a single member. What we have is a repertoire of fundamentals, dealing with Torah and Torah-study, the moral life and atonement, Israel and its holy way of life, Israel and its coming salvation. What this adds up to, then, is not argument for proposition, hence comparison and contrast and rule-making of a philosophical order, but rather a theological structure—comprising well-defined attitudes. Because of the character of *Song of Songs Rabbah*, the topical program of the document is best portrayed through the actual workings of the "another matter" compositions.

Theological Propositions of the eight parashiyyot of *Song of Songs Rabbah*—how they cohere in an inductive reading

The eight chapters of Song of Songs yield eight large composites in *Song of Songs Rabbah*. If we read them topically, we may state the principal theological propositions of the Midrash compilation.

God and man, God and Israel

The general principle is, God enters into an intense relationship of love with Israel, and Israel with God. God's love for Israel responds to Israel's acceptance of the Torah at Sinai and continuing obedience to its commandments. God's relationship to mankind in general does not define the category-formation, God and man. Rather, it is defined by God's relationship to Israel and through Israel to the rest of humanity. The fundamental theological principle is, Israel alone knows God as God has made himself known, which is in the Torah. God wishes to be exalted only by Israel. Israel alone produces martyrs to sanctify his name (XCVII:i.1,4; XCVIII:i.1). Just as in the foregoing, the point is: God embraces Israel for its loyalty to him, extending even to martyrdom. Israel alone accepted the Torah and God's dominion thereby (XCVIII:i.2).

How do God and Israel relate? *Song of Songs Rabbah* leaves no doubt that it is a relationship of lovers. God yearns for Israel. Israel yearns for God. Israel and God are reciprocally responsive and dependent, with Israel God's beloved. God's relationship to Israel and Israel's to God is captured in these pairs: God/nation; father/son; shepherd/flock; guard/vineyard; for me against my enemies, for him against those that spite him; song/song; praise/praise. Therefore Israel can ask what it needs, and God can ask what he needs, which is embodied in the sanctuary (XXXIII:i.1–8).

How does Israel elicit God's love? It is through carrying out their religious duties. In reciting the Shema, studying the Torah in synagogues and houses of study and schools, Israel provokes the response of God's love (CI:i.1). Israel's sexual purity emits a fragrance pleasing to God (akin to the fragrance of the offerings). Israel saves up for God, and God for Israel, religious duties and good deeds matched by what awaits those that take refuge in God (CII:i.1–2, 6–7).

God so loves Israel as to call her his daughter, his sister, and his mother (XLIV:ii.1). God bestows marks of affection upon Israel, when, as at the Sea, Israel relies on God's salvation and consequently sings God's praises, or accepts the Torah, or makes offerings in the tabernacle or in the Temple (II:I.1–7). All these represent occasions at which God and Israel come together in their love. Israel is beautiful in making the offerings, comely in the Holy Things. Righteous Israelite women of the generation of the wilderness did not contribute their jewelry to the golden calf (LXXX:i.1–2).

God and Israel relate through the covenant and the oaths that realize it. God is held captive by his oath to bring his Presence to dwell in Israel, an oath to Jacob and to Moses (XCIV:i.4–7). Through various media of sanctification, God has imposed his will on Israel to carry out his will in the world. God imposed an oath on Israel by the patriarchs and matriarchs who accomplished his will, by the tribal progenitors, by circumcision, by the martyrs in general or those of the generation of repression, by those who carried out God's will in the world and through whom he carried out his will, who poured out blood for the sanctification of God's name (XXIV:i.1–4). All of these represent the ones who are bound by the covenant.

"Israel" means those that love and are loved by God: those that will rise from the grave for eternal life. To express this idea, the Israel of Scripture serves as a metaphor, and "the maidens" who are the beloved supply the imagery for that metaphor.

Song of Songs Rabbah XIX:i.5

C. "So too the entire world was created only on account of the Torah. For twenty-six generations the Holy One, blessed be He, looked down upon his world and saw it full of thorns and brambles, for example, the Generation of Enosh, the generation of the Flood, and the Sodomites.

D. "He planned to render the world useless and to destroy it: 'The Lord sat enthroned at the flood' (Ps. 29:10).

E. "But he found in the world a single red rose, Israel, that was destined to stand before Mount Sinai and to say before the Holy One, blessed be He, 'Whatever the Lord has said we shall do and we shall obey' (Ex. 24:7).

F. "Said the Holy One, blessed be He, [Lev. R.:] 'Israel is worthy that the entire world be saved on its account.'" [Song: "for the sake of the Torah and those who study it...."]

Israel at the Sea, singing the Song, or Israel at Sinai, declaring its obedience to God, Israel when subjugated to the kingdoms, singing its study of Torah, Israel at the tent of meeting, proclaiming song, and the pilgrim festivals, reciting the Hallel-psalms—these represent the interchangeable realizations of moments of God's love for Israel and vice versa (XXXI:ii). Israel yearns for God the way a woman yearns for her husband or the Evil Impulse yearns for wicked people. Even though Israel is faint, it continues to hope for God's salvation and continues to declare his unity (XCIX:i.1–2).

What, then, of Israel in relationship to God, and, concomitantly, how is Israel defined? Israel are those that know God, gentiles are those that reject him and worship idols. Israel is marked by religious duties and good deeds; the righteous are Israel's redemption; Israel will endure both in this world and the world to come; it is easy to tell Israelites from the nations; Israel is made ready for the coming redemption (XIX:i.11). Signals of Israel's coming redemption are Moses and Aaron, circumcision, the entry into the Land, the end of idolatry, the intervention at the Sea, the Song—interchangeably and in no special order (XXIX:i.1–2). The first, and as we now see, the generative native category-formation is, the definition and character of God's and Israel's relationship. It is established by the Torah, God's self-manifestation, and the acceptance of the Torah's commandments by Israel at Sinai. The Torah is how Israel knows God, and those that do not accept the Torah cannot know God as God wishes to be known. The relationship then is defined as covenantal and marked by mutual love and reciprocal acts of dedication.

The upshot is simply stated. God's love for Israel is as strong as death, the jealousy over their idolatry is cruel as the grave. The same contrast is drawn between Isaac's love for Esau and Esau's hatred of Jacob; Jacob's love for Joseph and his brothers' hatred of Joseph; Jonathan's love for David and Saul's hatred of David; a man's love for his wife and the jealousy she provokes in him by speaking with another man; the love of the generation that suffered the repression for God's sake, and the jealousy that God holds for Zion, that is his zeal for Zion (CVIII:ii.1–6). Now to the relationship of God to the gentiles, comparable to the relationship of Israel to the gentiles, and for the same reason.

God and the Nations, Israel and the Nations

The theological proposition of this rubric is, God rejects the nations, by reason of their idolatry, and Israel separates itself from the nations for the same reason. The nations respond by enticing Israel to idolatry and by hating Israel for its rejection of their idolatry and adherence to the Torah of Sinai.

All other category-formations subordinate themselves to the first: God and Man, yielding the key relationship, God and Israel. The starting point is, God makes himself known to Man through the Torah, and the nations reject the Torah and therefore do not know God. That is why they worship idols. Only Israel knows and loves and worships God, as we have just seen. And that brings us to the parallel relationships that form the second principal category-formation, God/the nations and God/Israel. God's relationship with the nations is not comparable to God's relationship with Israel, and the nations' relationship with Israel serves merely as an instrument to carry out God's purpose in regard to Israel. The nations do not concede that the God of Israel is the one and only, the true God; they maintain he is no different from any other god (LXIX:i.1).

What difference distinguishes Israel from the nations? It is "Sinai," which stands for God's giving, and Israel's accepting, the Torah. That is the memorial monument, a witness to the nations of the world. Israel and the nations are there differentiated. The nations are differentiated from Israel by the Torah. The nations of the world fled from God's shade on the day on which the Torah was given, but Israel delighted in his shadow. Israel at Sinai displayed its loyalty to God, by agreeing to carry out the Torah even before knowing what was required by it. Israel is praised solely for its adherence to the Torah and ripened only at Pentecost, when the Torah was given (XX:i.1). At Sinai Israel was cleansed of its sins. The angels crowned each Israelite. There were no bereaved, no injured, among them. Moses then extolled the Israelites for being filled with Torah-teachings, for their modesty and self-restraint (XLVIII:ii, v). As a consequence of Sinai, Israel is further differentiated by the priestly watches and the offerings, then the Sanhedrin, associated with the Temple and priesthood. There follows the Day of Atonement, likewise a medium of atonement for Israel (XLVIII:vi–ix).

Israel's encounter with the nations figures in its relationship with God. God punishes Israel through the gentiles, i.e., the four kingdoms. Even though Israel is enslaved among the nations of the world by arbitrary, discriminatory taxes, nonetheless their heart points upward toward their father in heaven (XIX:i.8). God will ultimately burn away the nations to save Israel (XIX:i.9). The nations cannot stifle the love of God for Israel. All their money cannot purchase a single item of the Torah. Nor can their money atone for the martyrdom of Aqiba and his fellows (CIX:i.1–3). The nations taunt Israel, saying that her God has gone away. But Israel remains steadfast, saying, once she had cleaved to him, she cannot depart from him, and vice versa (LXXVII:i.1). The foxes that spoil the vineyard that is Israel are Esau and his generals, that is to say, Rome. The vineyard hedge is restored by Noah or Daniel or Job (XXXII:ii.1,4–6). In Babylonian exile, Israel wallowed in idolatry, losing the priesthood and the throne. God nonetheless loved Israel even then (LXIII:i.1–2). Israel, not the nations, arises to God in repentance for its act of idolatry with the golden calf, and God forgave Israel, but that generation was not to enter the Land of Israel (LXV:i.1, 3, 4, 10).

Israel has fallen into the dominion of four kingdoms and emerged whole from each. Israel is the nation for whom peace is made. It complements this world and the world to come. Because of Israel's merit good things happen. Had Israel not accepted the Torah, God would have returned the world to formlessness and void. The nations taunt Israel for their condition of subjugation; Israel does good things for God and gets bad things in return. If Israel joins the nations, they will be made governors and generals. But Israel rejects gentile idolatry, and maintains that the nations cannot dance for Israel as did the angels, or as God will for the righteous in the age to come (LXXXIX:i.1–11).

Israel's encounter with God through the Torah

The general principle of this rubric is Israel is Israel by reason of the Torah, and gentiles are gentiles by reason of rejecting the Torah. The Rabbinic sages find a great many occasions and ways of making that statement. The Torah is Israel's ornament, comparable to the spoil at the Sea and the spoil of Egypt. The ornaments of the Torah are the letters and the words, the ruled lines. The tabernacle is Israel's ornament, so too the ark, the pillars before the ark. The Torah, the prophets, the Writings, and the Song of Songs—all represent Israel's ornament. So God beautifies Israel through the Torah (XI:i.1–8). God's Presence takes up residence in the ark. The merit accruing to the Torah and those that study it forms an analogue to the ark. The palanquin is, further, the house of the sanctuary; the world is God's palanquin. The throne of glory also registers. The main point comes at the end. The Temple is God's place on earth, corresponding to his house in heaven (XLIII:i–v).

But the Torah is not the only mark of the covenant of love between God and Israel. The jewels around Israel's neck are the Torahs of Scripture (X:i.1–2). The members of the Sanhedrin, the teachers of Scripture and Mishnah, the children who study the Torah, the rabbis, the disciples and their intellectual accomplishments—all represent the jewels that adorn Israel's neck (X:ii,1–4). It is an ornament when Israel declaims the Torah in public (X:iii.1–2). God meets Israel in synagogue and school house and bestows a blessing through the priests (XXVI:ii.1). Nonetheless, if the Torah is not the only "theological thing," it is the main one. Study of the Torah serves to bring the Holy Spirit upon the disciple. Teaching Torah in public is rewarded by the advent of the Holy Spirit, so that one may produce writings inspired by Heaven (I:iv.8; l I:v.1, 9).

When Israel received the Torah directly from God, the Israelites learned and did not forget; when they asked Moses to serve as intermediary, they forgot their learning; but in the age to come, their learning will be restored (II:ii.1, 13). Israel has no intrinsic merit. It enjoys God's love by reason of the merit of the Torah, and of the religious duties that they would perform: the mezuzah, the recitation of the Shema and the Prayer Said Standing (IX:i.10).

God is embodied in the Torah. The teachings of the Torah, the ruled lines of the scroll, the letters—all are encompassed. Even the simplest matters contain meaning. Disciples of the rabbinic sages likewise represent him. Even teachings of the Torah that deal with matters not to be recited in public are pleasant (LXXI:i.1–8, 21–22). The Sanhedrin leads Israel. Israel is strengthened by the water of the Torah, cleansed by the laws (LXXII:i.1, 3). The Torah embodies God. The tablets of the covenant represent the arms, the words of Torah his ornaments; the details of the Torah the jewels, e.g., the Talmud; the book of Leviticus the body. Study of the Torah drains the strength of the people (LXXIV:i.1–9, see also LXXV:i.1).

God's judgment, Israel's repentance and atonement; God's remorse, Israel's consolation

The general principle of this rubric is the same as the foregoing, expressed in more concrete and specific terms. God brings about Israel's repentance. Israel atones for its sins, God forgives them and consoles Israel.

God sustains Israel with law and lore, with Torah in writing and Torah in memory, with the persons and activities and events represented by fire. Though Israel is sick, it is punishment and brings Israel closer to God; though sick, Israel is loved by God. The entire complex at XXII:i.1–8, diverse though it is, holds together within the notion that God loves Israel, therefore punishes Israel for its sins, bringing about a restoration in Israel's relationship with God. By smiting the children God punishes Israel for failing to keep the Torah (IV:ii.1). Israel makes haste to follow God to the Land, where God's presence dwells, in the sanctuary; when God removes his presence from the Land, Israel mourns, because they wanted to live in God's presence (IV:ii.1, 2, 5).

Israel is thus responsible for its own condition. Israel's fate is settled from within, through its own actions. Thus Jeroboam assigned the task of guarding the two golden calves, but Israel did not keep the watch of the priests and Levites. Ahab angered God and made Israel provide for God's enemies, not the true prophet. Jezebel did the same. Zedekiah did the same, thus Elijah and Jeremiah, respectively. Then the lesson is drawn in so many words at VI:iii.7: Israel did not keep the easy law pertaining to the Land of Israel, so it keeps the more onerous law assigned to the Exile.

There is an antidote to sin. The Torah overcomes the impulse to do evil (LXXXVII:i.9). Sin is a mark of neglect of the Torah. When Israel neglects the Torah and commandments, it lives in a perpetual night. When Israel suffers in the night of the nations' rule (here: Egypt), it then seeks succor through God's messengers (here: Moses) (XXXV:i.3–4; XXXVI:i; XXXVII:i). At XXXVIII:ii.1, the night is Babylon, and Daniel succeeds Moses. When Israel was redeemed the first time, from Egypt, Israelite sinners perished, those who repented were redeemed (XXX:i.1). Repentance is the key to all else. The person who overcomes his inclination to do evil, such as Moses, David, and Ezra, saves his entire generation (XLVIII:i.8).

Israel is punished in this world because of transgression, but in the world to come they will be rewarded (LXXXVII:i.7). God punishes Israel for going after other gods. Nebuchadnezzar administered God's punishment CXII:i–iii. In the exile, Israel learned to obey God after all:

Song of Songs Rabbah CXIII:i.1

> D. "... when sin had brought it about that the house of the sanctuary should be destroyed and Israel was sent into exile to Babylonia, Nebuchadnezzar said to them, 'Do not listen to the Torah of your father in heaven, but rather, "fall down and worship the image that I have made" (Dan. 3:15).'
> E. "The Israelites said to him, 'You big fool! The very reason that the Holy One, blessed be He, has handed us over to you is because we were bowing down to an idol: "She saw ... the images of the Chaldaeans portrayed with vermilion" (Ezek. 23:14), and yet you say to us, "fall down and worship the image that I have made" (Dan. 3:15). Woe to you!'
> F. "It is at that moment that the Holy One, blessed be He, said, 'My vineyard, my very own, is for myself.'"

Consolation and restoration

The general principle of this rubric is, when Israel repents, God forgives them and consoles them for their suffering. He will further restore their condition, meaning, bring them back to the Land. That is in line with the comparison of Adam and Israel, Eden and the Land, the fall and the exile. Then there is this difference: Adam did not know the power of repentance, but the Torah has taught Israel about that power.

The restoration will return Israel to its condition of perfection. The Temple allowed Israel to raise its head among the nations, and now that it is in ruins, Israel is bowed down. God made it a ruin but will beautify it in the world to come (XLVIII:ix.6–10). When Israel is restored to the Land, it will never be moved, and in the age to come when the restoration takes place, that will mark the end of history (V:iv.1, 3). Israel is presently plunged into a valley of troubles, into the depths. But when God draws Israel out of the valley or the depths, Israel will blossom in good deeds and sing a Song of praise (XVIII:iii.1–3).

Israel already knows how redemption takes place, for there was the first redemption, that from Egypt, to signal the model. The second followed the pattern, and the third and final redemption, at the end of days, is therefore known in advance. From Egyptian bondage, the Israelites were freed and redeemed and made prefects over the entire world, which surprised both the nations and Israel. There are other such cases: Joseph, David, Mordecai, and finally the community of Israel. Even though its present situation is dark, God will bring light (LXXXVIII:i.1–5). God will restore his beloved, though soiled in sins, through the purification of prayer, to the Garden of Eden. God should not respond to the nations of the world, with their blaspheming and cursing of God, by destroying the world. He should take note of Israel, who bless and praise God, and preserve the world (CXV:i.1–5, CXV:ii.1–3).

The commandments are the marks of Israel's distinction before God

The general principle of this rubric is, the specific religious duties carried out by Israel distinguish Israel from the nations. They derive from the Torah and realize its promise. *Song of Songs Rabbah* forms long lists of those religious duties, which beautify Israel in God's sight. Israel may suffer in order to carry them out—all the more so winning God's affection for their steadfast loyalty and love.

The panoply of religious deeds, religious obligations of commission, religious obligations of omission, religious duties of the home, in separating priestly ration and tithes, the religious duties of the field, gleanings, forgotten sheaves, the corner of the field, poor person's tithe, and declaring the field ownerless, the taboo against mixed species, providing a linen cloak with woolen show–fringes, the rules governing planting, the taboo on uncircumcised produce, the laws on produce in the fourth year after the planting of an orchard, circumcision, trimming the wound, reciting the Prayer, reciting the Shema, putting a *mezuzah* on the doorposts of your house, wearing phylacteries, building the tabernacle for the Festival of Tabernacles, taking the palm branch and *etrog* (a special species of citrus fruit) on the Festival of Tabernacles—all mark Israel's beauty in God's sight. These cover the field, garments, food, circumcision, recitation of the Prayer and the Shema, the keeping of the festivals, and the like. Then we proceed to the moral beauty of penitent Israel and Israel practicing good deeds, and end with this world and the world to come. The composition invokes the life of piety and faith to characterize what makes Israel beautiful before God (XV:i.1 = XCV:i.1).

Israel, "the daughters of Zion/distinction," is marked by circumcision and show-fringes. They behold God ("the king who created . . .") in his fullness. He makes peace between his works and his creatures: fire and Abraham, the sword and Isaac, the angel and Jacob (XLIV:i.1–4). At XLV:i, once more, a repertoire of virtues, some involving actions, others, restraint, all embodying obedience, characterizes Israel in a portrait of a comprehensive character. Israel is beautified by good deeds and acts of loving kindness, performing religious obligations, both positive and negative. These encompass the priestly tithes and agricultural taboos; the laws of circumcision; reciting the Prayer and the Shema; use of the holy objects; keeping the Festival; repentance, good deeds, in this world and in the world to come. Israel is innocent and beautiful when ascending for the pilgrim festivals, which it observes even without the Temple. Israel is distinguished by not shaving, by circumcising, by show-fringes. It is modest. Israel accepts martyrdom for God's sake. Israel atones for the sin of other nations. Israel is loyal to God. God is loyal to Israel and will restore Israel to its land. Israel brings light to the world. Israel at the Sea, through the Song, attained its full beauty; the least of Israelites is full of religious deeds (XLVII:i.1–3).

God will bring the end through the royal messiah at a time of his own choosing, and his hand is not to be forced

The general principle of this rubric is, redemption is an act of grace and cannot be coerced. When God redeems Israel, it is at his time, not Israel's. He responds then to the righteous people among Israel and to the merit acquired by their deeds. God will further ignore the character of Israel, performing an act of pure grace. And this will be through the royal Messiah (XXV:I.1–4). The nations (the kingdoms) are bound by an oath that they not oppress Israel excessively and so force God to intervene, bringing on the coming of the end of days before God's plan. So too, Israel is subject to an oath not to rebel against the dominion of the kingdoms and force the end. Both parties must leave space for the advent of the royal Messiah to perform his task (XXIV:ii.1, 4, and compare XXIV:iii.2). When the Israelite exiles return to Zion, the nations are going to bring them to the Messiah. God did as much long ago. Israel will be presented to the royal Messiah as gifts (LII:ii.1, 5, 7).

A sample passage

Here is a representative passage of the Midrash compilation. It shows how a sequence of "theological things"—events, religious imperatives, theological doctrines—are joined together in a common list, making a single point.

Song of Songs Rabbah V: i.1–12

1. A. "I am very dark, but comely, [O daughters of Jerusalem, like the tents of Kedar, like the curtains of Solomon]" (Song 1:5):
   B. "I am dark" in my deeds.
   C. "But comely" in the deeds of my forebears.
2. A. "I am very dark, but comely:"
   B. Said the Community of Israel, "'I am dark' in my view, 'but comely' before my Creator."
   C. For it is written, "Are you not as the children of the Ethiopians to Me, O children of Israel, says the Lord" (Amos 9:7):
   D. "as the children of the Ethiopians"—in your sight.
   E. But "to Me, O children of Israel, says the Lord."
3. A. Another interpretation of the verse, "I am very dark:" in Egypt.
   B. "but comely:" in Egypt.
   C. "I am very dark" in Egypt: "But they rebelled against me and would not hearken to me" (Ez. 20:8).
   D. "but comely" in Egypt: with the blood of the Passover offering and circumcision, "And when I passed by you and saw you wallowing in your blood, I said to you, In your blood live" (Ez. 16:6)—in the blood of the Passover. [This verse is recited at the rite of circumcision]

E. "I said to you, In your blood live" Ez. 16:6)—in the blood of the circumcision.
4. A. Another interpretation of the verse, "I am very dark:" at the sea, "They were rebellious at the sea, even the Red Sea" (Ps. 106:7).
   B. "but comely:" at the sea, "This is my God and I will be comely for him" (Ex. 15:2).
5. A. "I am very dark:" at Marah, "And the people murmured against Moses, saying, What shall we drink" Ex. 15:24).
   B. "but comely:" at Marah, "And he cried to the Lord and the Lord showed him a tree, and he cast it into the waters and the waters were made sweet" (Ex. 15:25).
6. A. "I am very dark:" at Rephidim, "And the name of the place was called Massah and Meribah" (Ex. 17:7).
   B. "but comely:" at Rephidim, "And Moses built an altar and called it by the name 'the Lord is my banner'" (Ex. 17:15).
7. A. "I am very dark:" at Horeb, "And they made a calf at Horeb" (Ps. 106:19).
   B. "but comely:" at Horeb, "And they said, All that the Lord has spoken we will do and obey" (Ex. 24:7).
8. A. "I am very dark:" in the wilderness, "How often did they rebel against him in the wilderness" (Ps. 78:40).
   B. "but comely:" in the wilderness at the setting up of the tabernacle, "And on the day that the tabernacle was set up" (Num. 9:15).
9. A. "I am very dark:" in the deed of the spies, "And they spread an evil report of the land" (Num. 13:32).
   B. "but comely:" in the deed of Joshua and Caleb, "Save for Caleb, the son of Jephunneh the Kenizzite" (Num. 32:12).
10. A. "I am very dark:" at Shittim, "And Israel abode at Shittim and the people began to commit harlotry with the daughters of Moab" (Num. 25:1).
    B. "but comely:" at Shittim, "Then arose Phinehas and wrought judgment" (Ps. 106:30).
11. A. "I am very dark:" through Achan, "But the children of Israel committed a trespass concerning the devoted thing" (Josh. 7:1).
    B. "but comely:" through Joshua, "And Joshua said to Achan, My son, give I pray you glory" (Josh. 7:19).
12. A. "I am very dark:" through the kings of Israel.
    B. "but comely:" through the kings of Judah.
    C. If with my dark ones that I had, it was such that "I am comely," all the more so with my prophets.

Song of Songs Rabbah V:ii.5

A. [As to the verse, "I am very dark, but comely," R. Levi b. R. Haita gave three interpretations:

B. "'I am very dark:' all the days of the week.
C. "'but comely:' on the Sabbath.
D. "'I am very dark:' all the days of the year.
E. "'but comely:' on the Day of Atonement.
F. "'I am very dark:' among the Ten Tribes.
G. "'but comely:' in the tribe of Judah and Benjamin.
H. "'I am very dark:' in this world.
I. "'but comely:' in the world to come."

The contrast of dark and comely yields a variety of applications; in all of them the same situation that is the one also is the other, and the rest follows in a wonderfully well-crafted composition. What is the repertoire of items? Dark in deeds but comely in ancestry; dark in my view but comely before God; dark when rebellious, comely when obedient, a point made at Section 3, for Egypt; Section 4, for the sea; Section 5, for Marah; Section 6, for Massah and Meribah; Section 7, for Horeb; Section 8, for the wilderness; Section 9, for the spies in the Land; Section 10, for Shittim; Section 11, for Achan/Joshua and the conquest of the Land; and Section 12, for Israel and Judah. We therefore have worked through the repertoire of events that contained the mixture of rebellion and obedience. The theological substrate of this catalogue is hardly difficult to articulate.

Song of Songs Rabbah XXIII:i.1–4

1. A. "O that his left hand were under my head:"
   B. this refers to the first tablets.
   C. "and that his right hand embraced me:"
   D. this refers to the second tablets.
2. A. Another interpretation of the verse, "O that his left hand were under my head:"
   B. this refers to the show-fringes.
   C. "and that his right hand embraced me:"
   D. this refers to the phylacteries.
3. A. Another interpretation of the verse, "O that his left hand were under my head:"
   B. this refers to the recitation of the *Shema.*
   C. "and that his right hand embraced me:"
   D. this refers to the Prayer.
4. A. Another interpretation of the verse, "O that his left hand were under my head:"
   B. this refers to the tabernacle.
   C. "and that his right hand embraced me:"
   D. this refers to the cloud of the Presence of God in the world to come: "The sun shall no longer be your light by day nor for brightness will the moon give light to you" (Is. 60:19). Then what gives light to you? "The Lord shall be your everlasting light" (Is. 60:20).

Now our repertoire of reference-points is (1) the Ten Commandments; (2) the show-fringes and phylacteries; (3) the Shema and the Prayer; (4) the tabernacle and the cloud of the Presence of God in the world to come. Why we invoke, as our candidates for the metaphor at hand, the Ten Commandments, show-fringes and phylacteries, recitation of the Shema and the Prayer, the tabernacle and the cloud of the Presence of God, and the *mezuzah,* seems to me clear from the very catalogue. These reach their climax in the analogy between the home and the tabernacle, the embrace of God and the Presence of God. So the whole is meant to list those things that draw the Israelite near God and make the Israelite cleave to God, as the base-verse says, hence the right hand and the left stand for the most intimate components of the life of the individual and the home with God.

What does *Song of Songs Rabbah* contribute?

Song of Songs Rabbah, like *Genesis Rabbah* and *Pesiqta deRab Kahana,* also makes a distinctive, and in some ways unique contribution to the larger statement of Rabbinic Judaism. The Scriptural medium uniquely matches the theological message. What the Rabbinic sages can have said *only* in response to Song of Songs is, God's love for Israel, and Israel's love for God, is comparable to the love of woman and man, and God yearns for Israel as much as Israel yearns for God—if that characterization of theological relationships in affective symbols was their intent, as it manifestly was, then only Song of Songs can have served to make that point. What is implicit in other Midrash compilations can have been made explicit only here. So the system as a whole is not only recapitulated. Its principal message attained particularization only here. And in order to say that each concrete detail of the practice of the Torah and the commandments embodies that yearning of God for Israel and Israel for God—in order to formulate and set into the context of relationship those "theological things," events, activities, attitudes alike—only Song of Songs can have served. What is episodic elsewhere is routine here, what is characteristic over all comes to acute expression here.

The unique contribution of *Song of Songs Rabbah* is best captured in the debate on the status of Song of Songs in Scripture. For here we see fully articulated the position of The Rabbinic sages who deemed the love poems to belong in the canon—their physical sanctification as sacred scrolls to be protected by the purity laws. The basic idea is, people will treat as holy what cannot be routinely handled but must be protected:

Mishnah-tractate *Yadayim* 3:5

G. All sacred scriptures impart uncleanness to hands.

H. The Song of Songs and Qohelet impart uncleanness to hands.

I. R. Judah says, "The Song of Songs imparts uncleanness to hands, but as to Qohelet there is dispute."
J. R. Yosé says, "Qohelet does not impart uncleanness to hands, but as to Song of Songs there is dispute."
K. Rabbi Simeon says, "Qohelet is among the lenient rulings of the House of Shammai and strict rulings of the House of Hillel."
L. Said R. Simeon b. Azzai, "I have a tradition from the testimony of the seventy-two elders,
M. "on the day on which they seated R. Eleazar b. Azariah in the session,
N. "that the Song of Songs and Qohelet do impart uncleanness to hands."
O. Said R. Aqiba, "Heaven forbid! No Israelite man ever disputed concerning Song of Songs that it imparts uncleanness to hands.
P. "For the entire age is not so worthy as the day on which the Song of Songs was given to Israel.
Q. "For all the scriptures are holy, but the Song of Songs is holiest of all.
R. "And if they disputed, they disputed only concerning Qohelet."
S. Said R. Yohanan b. Joshua, the son of R. Aqiba's father-in-law, concurring with the opinion of Ben Azzai, "Indeed did they dispute, and indeed did they come to a decision."

The Rabbinic sages judged that the meaning of the love poems was, and can only have been, precisely the sense they imputed to them. On what basis did they reach that conclusion and affirm it? The entirety of Scripture is made to attest to that meaning. Read start to finish, Genesis through Kings in light of Prophecy told the story of God's search for man and election of Israel—and the consequence of God's love for Israel. Reading forward from Scripture, the Rabbinic sages found in Israel's everyday life the embodiments of the love of Israel for God. Devotion to the Torah, practice of the commandments—the whole corpus of sanctification of the material transactions of Israel sustained that reading. Reading the entirety of Scripture into Song of Songs, producing *Song of Songs Rabbah*—that deductive process of working from the whole to the parts permitted no other result. For placing this component of Scripture into the context of the whole of Scripture yielded the conclusion reached here. *Song of Songs Rabbah* contributes the articulation of what is implicit in the canon of Scripture: the reason why Song of Songs belongs. It is, as Aqiba says, holiest of all.

12

Lamentations in *Lamentations Rabbah*

Updating Scripture's Response to the First Temple's Destruction by Showing How an Event Defines a Pattern

The theme of *Lamentations Rabbah*, a systematic verse-by-verse commentary to the book of Lamentations of indeterminate date, is Israel's relationship with God, as embodied in the destruction of the Temple and the loss of Jerusalem, both in 586 B.C.E. and in 70 C.E. The biblical book subject to the Midrash compilation, attributed to Jeremiah, concerns the first event, and *Lamentations Rabbah* takes up the same matter, now extending the inquiry to the later calamities. Its message concerning Israel and God, stated with special reference to the destruction of the Temple in 586 B.C.E and in 70 C.E., as well as to the catastrophe of Bar Kokhba's rebellion, is that the stipulative covenant set forth in the Torah governs that relationship. Therefore nothing is arbitrary, and everything that happens to Israel makes sense and bears meaning. With the covenant to explain events, Israel is not helpless before its fate but through its conduct controls its own destiny.

But that theological proposition does not capture the way in which *Lamentations Rabbah* recasts and renews the book of Lamentations, only the way in which it imparts coherence to that work. What is genuinely fresh is the Rabbinic narrative of how God wept for, and with, Israel, so transforming doctrine into emotion. This it does through narrative. *Lamentations Rabbah* sets forth a vast and highly articulated corpus of narrative writing. The main body of the narratives of the document focuses upon the theological challenge of the exile of ancient Israel to Assyria and Babylonia, the destruction of the Second Temple, and the loss of the war led by Bar Kokhba. A cognate theme addresses Israel's relationships with the nations, and both Israel's and the nations' relationships with God. These relationships are defined by God's loathing of idolatry. And within the framework of theodicy, the theme of human suffering and sense of loss is ever-present, joined to the thesis that nothing is arbitrary and that justice governs.

The covenantal theology

The events conform to rules, and from those rules, a message of comfort is derived. It is that Israel has been punished for her sins, but can repent and thereby atone for them, and, when she does, she will be forgiven and comforted in double measure:

Lamentations Rabbah LVI:i.14

A. When they sinned in double measure, they were smitten in double measure, but they were comforted in double measure.
B. When they sinned in double measure: "Jerusalem has sinned a sin" (Lam. 1:8).
C. ... they were smitten in double measure: "that she has received from the Lord's hand double for all her sins" (Is. 40:2).
D. ... but they were comforted in double measure: "Comfort, comfort my people, says your God. (Speak tenderly to the heart of Jerusalem and cry to her that her warfare is ended, that her iniquity is pardoned, that she has received from the Lord's hand double for all her sins)" (Is. 40:1–2).

The message concerning Israel's relationship to God is that the stipulative covenant still and always governs. Therefore everything that happens to Israel makes sense and bears meaning. Israel is not helpless before its fate but controls its own destiny. This is the one, whole message of our compilation, and it is the only message that is repeated throughout; everything else proves secondary and derivative of the fundamental proposition that the destruction of the Temple in Jerusalem in 70 C.E.—as much as in 586 B.C.E.—proves the enduring validity of the covenant, its rules and its promise of redemption.

God and man, God and Israel

Israel's relationship with God is treated with special reference to the covenant, the Torah, and the land. By reason of the sins of the Israelites, they have gone into exile with the destruction of the Temple. The founders of the family, Abraham, Isaac, and Jacob, also went into exile. Now they cannot be accused of lacking in religious duties, attention to teachings of the Torah and of prophecy, carrying out the requirements of righteousness (philanthropy) and good deeds, and the like. The people are at fault for their own condition (I:i.1–7). Torah-study defines the condition of Israel, e.g., "If you have seen (the inhabitants of) towns uprooted from their places in the land of Israel, know that it is because they did not pay the salary of scribes and teachers" (II.i).

So long as Judah and Benjamin—meaning, in this context, the surviving people, after the northern tribes were taken away by the Assyrians—were at home, God could take comfort at the loss of the ten tribes; once they went into exile, God began to mourn (II:ii). Israel (now meaning not the northern tribes, but the remaining Jews) survived Pharaoh and Sennacherib, but not God's punishment (III:i). After the disaster in Jeremiah's time, Israel emerged from Eden—but could come back (IV:i). God did not play favorites among the tribes; when any of them sinned, he punished them through exile (VI:i). Israel was punished because of the ravaging of words of Torah and prophecy, righteous men, religious duties and good deeds (VII:i). The land of Israel, the Torah, and the Temple are ravaged, to the shame of Israel (Jer. 9:19–21) (VIII:i). The Israelites practiced idolatry, still more did the pagans; God was neglected by the people and was left solitary, so God responded to the people's actions (X:i). If you had achieved the merit (using the theological language at hand), then you would have enjoyed everything, but since you did not have the merit, you enjoyed nothing (XI:i).

The Israelites did not trust God, so they suffered disaster (XIII.i). The Israelites scorned God and brought dishonor upon God among the nations (XV:i). While God was generous with the Israelites in the wilderness, under severe conditions, he was harsh with them in civilization, under pleasant conditions, because they sinned and angered him (XVI:i). With merit one drinks good water in Jerusalem, without merit, bad water in the exile of Babylonia; with merit one sings songs and Psalms in Jerusalem, without, dirges and lamentations in Babylonia. At stake is peoples' merit, not God's grace (XIX:i). The contrast is drawn between redemption and disaster, the giving of the Torah and the destruction of the Temple (XX:i). When the Israelites went into exile among the nations of the world, not one of them could produce a word of Torah from his mouth; God punished Israel for its sins (XXI:i). Idolatry was the cause (XXII:i). The destruction of the Temple was possible only because God had already abandoned it (XXIV:ii). When the Temple was destroyed, God was answerable to the patriarchs for what he had done (XXIV:ii). The Presence of God departed from the Temple by stages (XXV:i).

The Holy One punishes Israel only after bringing testimony against them (XXVII:i). The road that led from the salvation of Hezekiah is the one that brought Israel to the disaster brought about by Nebuchadnezzar. Then the Israelite kings believed, but the pagan king did not believe; and God gave the Israelite kings a reward for their faith, through Hezekiah, and to the pagan king, without his believing and without obeying, were handed over Jerusalem and its Temple (XXX:i). Before the Israelites went into exile, the Holy One, blessed be he, called them "bad." But when they had gone into exile, he began to sing their praises (XXXI:i). The Israelites were sent into exile only after they had defied the Unique One of the world, the Ten Commandments, circumcision, which had been given to the twentieth generation (Abraham), and the Pentateuch (XXXV:ii, iii). When the Temple was destroyed and Israel went into exile, God mourned in the manner that mortals do (XXXV:iv). The prophetic critique of Israel is mitigated by mercy.

Israel stands in an ambiguous relationship with God, both divorced and not divorced (XXXV:vi, vii).

Before God penalizes, he has already prepared the healing for the penalty. As to all the harsh prophecies that Jeremiah issued against the Israelites, Isaiah first of all anticipated each and pronounced healing for it (XXXVI:ii). The Israelites err for weeping frivolously, "but in the end there will be a real weeping for good cause" (XXXVI:iv, v). The ten tribes went into exile, but the Presence of God did not go into exile. Judah and Benjamin went into exile, but the Presence of God did not go into exile. But when the children went into exile, then the Presence of God went into exile (XXXIX:iii). The great men of Israel turned their faces away when they saw people sinning, and God did the same to them (XL:ii). When the Israelites carry out the will of the Holy One, they add strength to the strength of heaven, and when they do not, they weaken the power of the One above (XL:ii). The exile and the redemption will match (XL:ii). In her affliction, Jerusalem remembered her rebellion against God (XLI:i).

When the gentile nations sin, there is no sequel in punishment, but when the Israelites sin, they also are punished (XLII:i). God considered carefully how to bring the evil upon Israel (XLVIII:i). God suffers with Israel and for Israel (L:i), a minor theme in a massive compilation of stories. By observing their religious duties the Israelites became distinguished before God (LIII:i). With every thing with which the Israelites sinned, they were smitten, and with that same thing they will be comforted. When they sinned with the head, they were smitten at the head, but they were comforted through the head (LVI:i). There is an exact match between Israel's triumph and Israel's downfall. Just as these—the people of Jericho—were punished through the destruction effected by priest and prophet (the priests and Joshua at Jericho), so those—the people of Jerusalem in the time of the Babylonian conquest—were subject to priest and prophet (Jeremiah). Just as these who were punished were penalized through the ram's horn and shouting, so Israel will be saved through ram's horn and shouting (LVII:ii).

God's relationship to Israel was complicated by the relationship to Jacob, thus: "Isn't it the fact that the Israelites are angering me only because of the icon of Jacob that is engraved on my throne? Here, take it, it's thrown in your face!" (LVII:ii). God is engaged with Israel's disaster (LIX:ii). The Israelites did not fully explore the limits of the measure of justice, so the measure of justice did not go to extremes against them (LX:i, LXI:i). God's decree against Jerusalem comes from of old (LXIV:i). God forewarned Israel and showed Israel favor, but it did no good (LXIX:i). God did to Israel precisely what he had threatened long ago (LXXIII:i). But God does not rejoice in punishing Israel. The argument between God and Israel is framed in this way. The Community of Israel says that they are the only ones who accepted God; God says, I rejected everybody else for you (LXXIX:ii). Israel accepted its suffering as atonement and asked that the suffering expiate the sin (LXXV:i).

God suffers along with Israel, Israel's loyalty will be recognized and appreciated by God, and, in the meantime, the Israelites will find in the Torah the comfort that they require. The nations will be repaid for their actions toward Israel in the interval. Even though the Holy One, blessed be he, is angry with his servants, the righteous, in this world, in the world to come he goes and has mercy on them (LXXXVI:i). God is good to those that deserve it (LXXXVII:i). God mourns for Israel the way human mourners mourn (LXXXVIII:i). God will never abandon Israel (LXXXIX:i). The Holy Spirit brings about redemption (XCV:i). It is better to be punished by God than favored by a gentile king, thus: "Better was the removing of the ring by Pharaoh (for the sealing of decrees to oppress the Israelites) than the forty years during which Moses prophesied concerning them, because it was through this (oppression) that the redemption came about, while through that (prophesying) the redemption did not come about" (CXXII:i).

The upshot here is that persecution in the end is good for Israel, because it produces repentance more rapidly than prophecy ever did, with the result that the redemption is that much nearer. The enemy will also be punished for its sins, and, further, God's punishment is appropriate and well-placed. People get what they deserve, both Israel and the others. God should protect Israel and not leave them among the nations, but that is not what he has done (CXXIII:i). God blames that generation for its own fate, and the ancestors claim that the only reason the Israelites endure is because of the merit of the ancestors. (CXXIX:i). The redemption of the past tells us about the redemption in the future (CXXX:i). "The earlier generations, because they smelled the stench of only part of the tribulations inflicted by the idolatrous kingdoms, became impatient. But we, who dwell in the midst of the four kingdoms, how much the more (are we impatient)!" (CXXXI:i.1B).

God's redemption is certain, so people who are suffering should be glad, since that is a guarantee of coming redemption; thus (CXL:i.1G),

> For if those who outrage him [Rome] he treats in such a favorable way, those who do his will all the more so! So if the words of the prophet Uriah are carried out, the words of the prophet Zechariah will be carried out, while if the words of the prophet Uriah prove false, then the words of the prophet Zechariah will not be true either.

So Aqiba responds (CXL:i.2J),

> I was laughing with pleasure because the words of Uriah have been carried out, and that means that the words of Zechariah in the future will be carried out.

The Temple will be restored, and Israel will regain its place, as God's throne and consort, respectively (CXLI:i). Punishment and rejection will be followed by forgiveness and reconciliation (CXLII:i). The Jews can accomplish part of the task on their own, even though they throw themselves wholly on God's mercy. The desired age is either like that of Adam, or like that of Moses and Solomon, or like that of Noah and Abel; all three possibilities link the coming redemption to a time of perfection, Eden, or the age prior to idolatry, or the time of Moses and Solomon, the builders of the Tabernacle and the Temple, respectively (CXLIII:i). If there is rejection, then there is no hope, but if there is anger, there is hope, because someone who is angry may in the end be appeased. Whenever there is an allusion to divine anger, that too is a mark of hope (CXLIV:i).

God and the nations, Israel and the nations

Israel's relationship with the nations is treated with interest in Israel's history, past, present, and future, and how that cyclical is to be known. But there is no theory of "the other," or the outsider here; the nations are the enemy; the compilers find nothing of merit to report about them. Israel's difference from the other, for which God is responsible, accounts for the dislike that the nations express toward Israel; Israel's present condition as minority, different and despised on account of the difference, is God's fault and choice. Israel was besieged not only by the Babylonians but also the neighbors, the Ammonites and Moabites (IX:i), and God will punish them too. The public ridicule of Jews' religious rites contrasts with the Jews' own perception of their condition. The exposition of Ps. 69:13 in terms of gentiles' ridicule of Jews' practices—the Jews' poverty, their Sabbath and Seventh Year observance—is followed by a re-exposition of the Jews' practices, now with respect to the ninth of Ab (XVII:i). Even though the nations of the world go into exile, their exile is not really an exile at all. But as for Israel, their exile really is an exile. The nations of the world, who eat the bread and drink the wine of others, do not really experience exile. But the Israelites, who do not eat the bread and drink the wine of others, really do experience exile (XXXVII:i).

The Ammonites and Moabites joined with the enemy and behaved very spitefully (XLIV:i). When the Israelites fled from the destruction of Jerusalem, the nations of the world sent word everywhere to which they fled and shut them out (LV:i). But this was to be blamed on God: "If we had intermarried with them, they would have accepted us." LXIX:i There are ten references to "might" of Israel; when the Israelites sinned, these forms of might were taken away from them and given to the nations of the world. The nations of the world ridicule the Jews for their religious observances (LXXXIII:i). These propositions simply expose, in their own framework, the same proposition as the ones concerning God's relationship to Israel and Israel's relationship to God. The relationship between Israel and the nations forms a subset of that of Israel and God; nothing in the former relationship happens on its own, but all things express, in this mundane context, the rules and effects of the rules that govern in the transcendent one. All we learn about Israel and the nations is that the covenant endures, bearing its own inevitable sanctions and consequences.

Israel on its own

Israel on its own forms a subordinated and trivial theme; whatever messages we do find take on meaning only in the initial framework, that defined by Israel's relationship with God. Israel is never on its own. The bitterness of the ninth of Ab is contrasted with the bitter herbs with which the first redemption is celebrated (XVIII:i). The same contrast is drawn between the giving of the Torah and the destruction of the Temple (XX:i). If Israel had found rest among the nations, she would not have returned to the holy land (XXXVII:ii). The glory of Israel lay in its relationship to God, in the Sanhedrin, in the disciples of sages, in the priestly watches, in the children (XL:i). Israel first suffers, then rejoices; her unfortunate condition marks the fact that Israel stands at the center of things (LIX:iii). Israel has declined through the generations, thus: "In olden times, when people held the Sanhedrin in awe, naughty words were never included in songs. But when the Sanhedrin was abolished, naughty words were inserted in songs. In olden times, when troubles came upon Israel, they stopped rejoicing on that account. Now that both have come to an end (no more singing, no more banquet halls), 'The joy of our hearts has ceased; our dancing has been turned to mourning'" (CXXXVII:i).

A sample passage

The compilation makes extensive use of sustained narrative, of which the following is remarkable. What the narrative shows is that trait that we have found most indicative of Rabbinic Midrash: the capacity to see Scripture whole, to bring to bear the entire message upon any of the parts, and to assemble the parts to establish a governing proposition for the whole. I should offer the following story as one of the many sublime passages of the Rabbinic Midrash, and representative of them all:

Lamentations Rabbah XXIV:ii.1–3

[At issue is the following verse of Scripture—The Valley of Vision Pronouncement. "What can have happened to you that you have gone, all of you, up on the roofs, O you who were full of tumult, you clamorous town, you city so gay? Your slain are not the slain of the sword, nor the dead of battle. Your officers have all departed; they fled far away; your survivors were all taken captive, taken captive without their bows. That is why I say, 'Let me be, I will weep bitterly. Press not to comfort me for the ruin of my poor people.' For my Lord God of Hosts had a day of tumult and din and confusion—Kir raged in the Valley of Vision, and Shoa on the hill; while Elam bore the quiver in troops of mounted men, and Kir bared the shield—and your choicest lowlands were filled with chariots and horsemen; they stormed at Judah's gateway and pressed beyond its screen. You gave thought on that day to the arms in the Forest House, and you took note of the many breaches in the city of David. And you collected the water of the Lower Pool; and you counted the houses of Jerusalem and pulled houses down to fortify the wall; and you constructed a basin between the two walls for the water of the old pool. But you gave no thought to him who planned it, you took no note of him who designed it long before. My Lord God of Hosts summoned on that day weeping and lamenting, to tonsuring and girding with sackcloth. Instead there was rejoicing and merriment, killing of cattle and slaughtering of sheep, eating of meat and drinking of wine: 'Eat and drink for tomorrow we die!' Then the Lord of Hosts revealed himself to my ears: 'This iniquity shall never be forgiven you until you die,' said my Lord God of Hosts" (Isaiah 22:1–14):)]

1. A. Another interpretation of the passage, "My Lord God of Hosts summoned on that day to weeping and lamenting, to tonsuring and girding with sackcloth:"
   B. When the Holy One, blessed be he, considered destroying the house of the sanctuary, he said, "So long as I am within it, the nations of the world cannot lay a hand on it.
   C. "I shall close my eyes to it and take an oath that I shall not become engaged with it until the time of the end."
   D. Then the enemies came and destroyed it.
   E. Forthwith the Holy One, blessed be he, took an oath by his right hand and put it behind him: "He has drawn back his right hand from before the enemy" (Lam. 2:3).
   F. At that moment the enemies entered the sanctuary and burned it up.
   G. When it had burned, the Holy One, blessed be he, said, "I do not have any dwelling on earth any more. I shall take up my presence from there and go up to my earlier dwelling."
   H. That is in line with this verse: "I will go and return to my place, until they acknowledge their guilt and seek my face" (Hos. 5:15).
   I. At that moment the Holy One, blessed be he, wept, saying, "Woe is me! What have I done! I have brought my Presence to dwell below on account of the Israelites, and now that they have sinned, I have gone back to my earlier dwelling. Heaven forfend that I now become a joke to the nations and an object of ridicule among peoples."
   J. At that moment Metatron (an important angelic figure) came, prostrated himself, and said before him, "Lord of the world, let me weep, but don't you weep!"
   K. He said to him, "If you do not let me weep now, I shall retreat to a place in which you have no right to enter, and there I shall weep."
   L. That is in line with this verse: "But if you will not hear it, my soul shall weep in secret for pride" (Jer. 13:17).
2. A. Said the Holy One, blessed be he, to the ministering angels, "Let's go and see what the enemies have done to my house."
   B. Forthwith the Holy One, blessed be he, and the ministering angels went forth, with Jeremiah before them.
   C. When the Holy One, blessed be he, saw the house of the sanctuary, he said, "This is certainly my house, and this is my resting place, and the enemies have come and done whatever they pleased with it!"
   D. At that moment the Holy One, blessed be he, wept, saying "Woe is me for my house! O children of mine—where are you? O priests of mine—where are you? O you who love me—where are you? What shall I do for you? I warned you, but you did not repent."

E. Said the Holy One, blessed be he, to Jeremiah, "Today I am like a man who had an only son, who made a marriage canopy for him, and the son died under his marriage canopy. Should you not feel pain for me and for my son?

F. "Go and call Abraham, Isaac, Jacob, and Moses from their graves, for they know how to weep."

G. (Jeremiah) said before him, "Lord of the world, I don't know where Moses is buried."

H. The Holy One, blessed be he, said to him, "Go and stand at the bank of the Jordan and raise your voice and call him, 'Son of Amram, son of Amram, rise up and see your flock, which the enemy has swallowed up!'"

I. Jeremiah immediately went to the cave of Machpelah and said to the founders of the world (the patriarchs and matriarchs), "Arise, for the time has come for you to be called before the Holy One, blessed be he."

J. They said to him, "Why?"

K. He said to them, "I don't know," because he was afraid that they would say to him, "In your time this has come upon our children!"

L. Jeremiah left them and went to the bank of the Jordan and cried out, "Son of Amram, son of Amram, rise up, for the time has come for you to be called before the Holy One, blessed be he."

M. Moses said to him, "What makes this day so special, that I am called before the Holy One, blessed be he?"

N. He said to them, "I don't know."

O. Moses left him and went to the ministering angels, for he had known them from the time of the giving of the Torah. He said to them, "You who serve on high! Do you know on what account I am summoned before the Holy One, blessed be he?"

P. They said to him, "Son of Amram! Don't you know that the house of the sanctuary has been destroyed, and the Israelites taken away into exile?"

Q. So he cried and wept until he came to the fathers of the world. They too forthwith tore their garments and put their hands on their heads, crying and weeping, up to the gates of the house of the sanctuary.

R. When the Holy One, blessed be he, saw them, forthwith: "My Lord God of Hosts summoned on that day to weeping and lamenting, to tonsuring and girding with sackcloth."

S. Were it not stated explicitly in a verse of Scripture, it would not be possible to make this statement.

T. And they went weeping from this gate to that, like a man whose deceased child lies before him,

U. and the Holy One, blessed be he, wept, lamenting, "Woe for a king who prospers in his youth and not in his old age."

3. A. Said R. Samuel bar Nahman, "When the Temple was destroyed, Abraham came before the Holy One, blessed be he, weeping, pulling

at his beard and tearing his hair, striking his face, tearing his clothes, with ashes on his head, walking about the Temple, weeping and crying, saying before the Holy One, blessed be he,

B. "'How does it happen that I am treated differently from every other nation and language, that I should be brought to such humiliation and shame!'

C. "When the ministering angels saw him, they too (Cohen, p. 43:) composed lamentations, arranging themselves in rows, saying,

D. "'the highways lie waste, the wayfaring man ceases' (Is. 33:8)."

E. "What is the meaning of the statement, 'the highways lie waste'?

F. "Said the ministering angels before the Holy One, blessed be he, 'The highways that you paved to Jerusalem, so that the wayfarers would not cease, how have they become a desolation?'

G. "'the wayfaring man ceases:'

H. "Said the ministering angels before the Holy One, blessed be he, 'How have the ways become deserted, on which the Israelites would come and go for the pilgrim festivals?'

I. "'You have broken the covenant:'

J. "Said the ministering angels before the Holy One, blessed be he, 'Lord of the world, the covenant that was made with their father, Abraham, has been broken, the one through which the world was settled and through which you were made known in the world, that you are the most high God, the one who possesses heaven and earth.'

K. "'He has despised the cities:'

L. "Said the ministering angels before the Holy One, blessed be he, 'You have despised Jerusalem and Zion after you have chosen them!'

M. "Thus Scripture says, 'Have you utterly rejected Judah? Has your soul loathed Zion?' (Jer. 14:19).

N. "'He regards not Enosh:'

O. "Said the ministering angels before the Holy One, blessed be he, 'Even as much as the generation of Enosh, chief of all idol worshippers, you have not valued Israel!'

P. "At that moment the Holy One, blessed be he, responded to the ministering angels, saying to them, 'How does it happen that you are composing lamentations, arranging themselves in rows, on this account?'

Q. "They said to him, 'Lord of the world! It is on account of Abraham, who loved you, who came to your house and lamented and wept. How does it happen that you didn't pay any attention to him?'

R. "He said to them, 'From the day on which my beloved died, going off to his eternal house, he has not come to my house, and now "what is my beloved doing in my house" (Jer. 11:15)?'

S. "Said Abraham before the Holy One, blessed be he, 'Lord of the world! How does it happen that you have sent my children into exile and handed them over to the nations? And they have killed them with all manner of disgusting forms of death! And you have destroyed the house of the sanctuary, the place on which I offered up my son Isaac as a burnt-offering before you!?'

T. "Said to Abraham the Holy One, blessed be he, 'Your children sinned and violated the whole Torah, transgressing the twenty-two letters that are used to write it: "Yes, all Israel have transgressed your Torah" (Dan. 9:11).'

U. "Said Abraham before the Holy One, blessed be he, 'Lord of the world, who will give testimony against the Israelites, that they have violated your Torah?'

V. "He said to him, 'Let the Torah come and give testimony against the Israelites.'

W. "Forthwith the Torah came to give testimony against them.

X. "Said Abraham to her, 'My daughter, have you come to give testimony against the Israelites that they have violated your religious duties? and are you not ashamed on my account? Remember the day on which the Holy One, blessed be he, tried to sell you to all the nations and languages of the world, and no one wanted to accept you, until my children came to Mount Sinai and they accepted you and honored you! And now are you coming to give testimony against them on their day of disaster?'

Y. "When the Torah heard this, she went off to one side and did not testify against them.

Z. "Said the Holy One, blessed be he, to Abraham, 'Then let the twenty-two letters of the alphabet come and give testimony against the Israelites.'

AA. "Forthwith the twenty-two letters of the alphabet came to give testimony against them.

BB. "The *aleph* came to give testimony against the Israelites, that they had violated the Torah.

CC. "Said Abraham to her, 'Aleph, you are the head of all of the letters of the alphabet, and have you now come to give testimony against the Israelites on the day of their disaster?'

DD. "'Remember the day on which the Holy One, blessed be he, revealed himself on Mount Sinai and began his discourse with you: "I (*anokhi*, beginning with aleph) am the Lord your God who brought you out of the Land of Egypt, out of the house of bondage" (Ex. 20:2).

EE. "'But not a single nation or language was willing to take you on, except for my children! And are you now going to give testimony against my children?'

FF. "Forthwith the *aleph* went off to one side and did not testify against them.

GG. "The *beth* came to give testimony against the Israelites.

HH. "Said Abraham to her, 'My daughter, have you come to give testimony against my children, who are meticulous about the Five Books of the

Torah, at the head of which you stand, as it is said, "In the beginning (bereshith) God created . . ." (Gen. 1:1)?'

II. "Forthwith the *beth* went off to one side and did not testify against them.

JJ. "The *gimel* came to give testimony against the Israelites.

KK. "Said Abraham to her, '*Gimel,* have you come to give testimony against my children, that they have violated the Torah? Is there any nation, besides my children, that carries out the religious duty of wearing showfringes, at the head of which you stand, as it is said, "Twisted cords (gedelim) you shall make for yourself" (Dt. 22:12).'

LL. "Forthwith the *gimel* went off to one said and did not testify against them.

MM. "Now when all of the letters of the alphabet in succession then realized that Abraham had silenced them, they were ashamed and stood off and would not testify against Israel.

NN. "Abraham forthwith commenced speaking before the Holy One, blessed be he, saying to him, 'Lord of the world, when I was a hundred years old, you gave me a son. And when he had already reached the age of volition, a boy thirty-seven years of age, you told me, "offer him up as a burnt-offering before me"!

OO. "'And I became harsh to him and had no mercy for him, but I myself tied him up. Are you not going to remember this and have mercy on my children?'

PP. "Isaac forthwith commenced speaking before the Holy One, blessed be he, saying to him, 'Lord of the world, when father said to me, "God will see to the lamb for the offering for himself, my son" (Gen. 22:8), I did not object to what you had said, but I was bound willingly, with all my heart, on the altar, and spread forth my neck under the knife. Are you not going to remember this and have mercy on my children!'

QQ. "Jacob forthwith commenced speaking before the Holy One, blessed be he, saying to him, 'Lord of the world, did I not remain in the house of Laban for twenty years? And when I went forth from his house, the wicked Esau met me and wanted to kill my children, and I gave myself over to death in their behalf. Now my children are handed over to their enemies like sheep for slaughter, after I raised them like fledglings of chickens. I bore on their account the anguish of raising children, for through most of my life I was pained greatly on their account. And now are you not going to remember this and have mercy on my children!'

RR. "Moses forthwith commenced speaking before the Holy One, blessed be he, saying to him, 'Lord of the world, was I not a faithful shepherd for the Israelites for forty years? I ran before them in the desert like a horse. And when the time came for them to enter the land, you issued a decree against me in the wilderness that there my bones would fall.

	And now that they have gone into exile, you have sent to me to mourn and weep for them.'
SS.	"This is in line with the proverb people say: 'When it's good for my master, it's not good for me, but when its bad for him, it's bad for me!'
TT.	"Then Moses said to Jeremiah, 'Go before me, so I may go and bring them in and see who will lay a hand on them.'
UU.	"Said to him Jeremiah, 'It isn't even possible to go along the road, because of the corpses.'
VV.	"He said to him, 'Nonetheless.'
WW.	"Forthwith Moses went along, with Jeremiah leading the way, until they came to the waters of Babylon.
XX.	"They saw Moses and said to one another, 'Here comes the son of Amram from his grave to redeem us from the hand of our oppressors.'
YY.	"An echo went forth and said, 'It is a decree from before me.'
ZZ.	"Then said Moses to them, 'My children, to bring you back is not possible, for the decree has already been issued. But the Omnipresent will bring you back quickly.' Then he left them.
AAA.	"Then they raised up their voices in weeping until the sound rose on high: 'By the rivers of Babylon there we sat down, yes, we wept' (Ps. 137:1).
BBB.	"When Moses came back to the founders of the world (the patriarchs and matriarchs), they said to him, 'What have the enemies done to our children?'
CCC.	"He said to them, 'Some of them he killed, the hands of some of them he bound behind their back, some of them he put in iron chains, some of them he stripped naked, some of them died on the way, and their corpses were left for the vultures of heaven and the hyenas of the earth, some of them were left for the sun, starving and thirsting.'
DDD.	"Then they began to weep and sing dirges: 'Woe for what has happened to our children! How have you become orphans without a father! How have you had to sleep in the hot sun during the summer without clothes and covers! How have you had to walk over rocks and stones without shoes and sandals! How were you burdened with a heavy bundle of sand! How were your hands bound behind your backs! How were you left unable even to swallow the spit in your mouths!'
EEE.	"Moses then said, 'Cursed are you, O sun! Why did you not grow dark when the enemy went into the house of the sanctuary?'
FFF.	"The sun answered him, 'By your life, Moses, faithful shepherd! They would not let me nor did they leave me alone, but beat me with sixty whips of fire, saying, "Go, pour out your light."'
GGG.	"Moses then said, 'Woe for your brilliance, O Temple, how has it become darkened? Woe that its time has come to be destroyed, for the building to be reduced to ruins, for the school children to be killed, for their parents to go into captivity and exile and the sword!'

HHH. "Moses then said, 'O you who have taken the captives! I impose an oath on you by your lives! If you kill, do not kill with a cruel form of death, do not exterminate them utterly, do not kill a son before his father, a daughter before her mother, for the time will come for the Lord of heaven to exact a full reckoning from you!'

III. "The wicked Chaldeans did not do things this way, but they brought a son before his mother and said to the father, 'Go, kill him!' The mother wept, her tears flowing over him, and the father hung his head.

JJJ. "And further Moses said before him, 'Lord of the world! You have written in your Torah, "Whether it is a cow or a ewe, you shall not kill it and its young both in one day" (Lev. 22:28).

KKK. "'But have they not killed any number of children along with their mothers, and yet you remain silent!'

LLL. "Then Rachel, our mother, leapt to the fray and said to the Holy One, blessed be he, 'Lord of the world! It is perfectly self-evident to you that your servant, Jacob, loved me with a mighty love, and worked for me for father for seven years, but when those seven years were fulfilled, and the time came for my wedding to my husband, father planned to substitute my sister for me in the marriage to my husband. Now that matter was very hard for me, for I knew the deceit, and I told my husband and gave him a sign by which he would know the difference between me and my sister, so that my father would not be able to trade me off. But then I regretted it and I bore my passion, and I had mercy for my sister, that she should not be shamed. So in the evening for my husband they substituted my sister for me, and I gave my sister all the signs that I had given to my husband, so that he would think that she was Rachel.

MMM. "'And not only so, but I crawled under the bed on which he was lying with my sister, while she remained silent, and I made all the replies so that he would not discern the voice of my sister.

NNN. "'I paid my sister only kindness, and I was not jealous of her, and I did not allow her to be shamed, and I am a mere mortal, dust and ashes. Now I had no envy of my rival, and I did not place her at risk for shame and humiliation. But you are the King, living and enduring and merciful. How does it happen that you are jealous of idolatry, which is nothing, and so have sent my children into exile, allowed them to be killed by the sword, permitted the enemy to do whatever they wanted to them?!'

OOO. "Forthwith the mercy of the Holy One, blessed be he, welled up, and he said, 'For Rachel I am going to bring the Israelites back to their land.'

PPP. "That is in line with this verse of Scripture: 'Thus said the Lord: A cry is heard in Ramah, wailing, bitter weeping, Rachel weeping for her children. She refuses to be comforted for her children, who are gone. Thus said the Lord, Restrain your voice from weeping, your eyes from shedding tears; for there is a reward for your labor, declares the Lord; they shall return from the enemy's land, and there is hope for your future, declares the Lord: your children shall return to their country' (Jer. 31:15–17)."

The story is unitary and scarcely glossed. Telling the story formed for the compilers a necessary medium for setting forth its theological message. That is because the details of the story embody that message in exemplary, concrete terms, with a consequent power and effect that a mere statement of theological abstractions cannot attain. The Rabbinic sages have no better medium than sustained narrative for expressing their message: *God wept—with Israel, for Israel.* How else than through narrative to portray God as mourning for the destruction, how else to engage the patriarchs, Moses, Jeremiah, and Rachel, in the confrontation with God on what God has brought about, I cannot begin to imagine. Narrative alone can say what the compilers wish to say in response to the book of Lamentations and the events it portrays. What the Midrash compilation accomplishes is the humanization of God in relationship to Israel in response to the calamities brought about within the very covenantal relationship of God and Israel. That is why the narrative forms the sole possible medium for carrying to its climax the theological message of *Lamentations Rabbah*—but not of the book of Lamentations, which contains no hint that God wept.

13

The Calendar of Judaism in *Pesiqta deRab Kahana*

Telling Time by Judaism's Clock

To this point we have followed the way in which Rabbinic Midrash finds truth in the Torah and validates truth through appeal to the Torah. But there is one document that presents its appeal for validation to nature, namely, to the stars. *Pesiqta deRab Kahana* demonstrates that Israel's identification of sacred time on earth corresponds with the movement of the moon and the stars around the earth in heaven. Israel here matches astral paths above. The sacred calendar of synagogue lections signals the astral harmony lived out by earthly Israel, a truly formidable claim that does not fully match the one made by Rabbinic Midrash in general.

A compilation of twenty-eight propositional discourses, *Pesiqta deRab Kahana*[1] innovates because it appeals for its themes and lections to the liturgical calendar, rather than to a Pentateuchal book. It sets forth expositions of verses of Scripture chosen in accord with the requirements of the liturgical calendar, e.g., a verse important in the Passover lection or one pertinent to the 9th of Ab. The other Midrash compilations of the formative age organize their materials around books of Scripture, e.g., *Leviticus Rabbah* around passages of Leviticus, *Sifra* around Leviticus as well. But that is not the case in *Pesiqta deRab Kahana*. That is why we cannot present an account of how *Pesiqta deRab Kahana* treats the book of Leviticus, but rather, how *Pesiqta deRab Kahana* treats the festival of Passover, and so throughout. And only at the end shall we grasp what is truly at stake in this remarkable Midrash compilation.

---

[1] *Pisqa* yields "chapter," so the plural can be rendered, "chapters attributed to R. Kahana."

The logic of coherent discourse

The first shift concerns the logic of coherent discourse: what holds a sentence together with another sentence to form a coherent proposition. *Pesiqta deRab Kahana* abandons the pretense that fixed associative connections derive solely from Scripture. In each exposition, a holy day has told our authorship what topic it wishes to take up—and therefore also what verses of Scripture (if any) prove suitable to that topic and its exposition. These are by seasons, as follows:

Adar-Nisan-Sivan
    Passover-Pentecost: *Pisqaot* 2–12
    (possible exception: *Pisqa* 6)
Tammuz-Ab-Elul
    The Ninth of Ab: *Pisqaot* 13–22
Tishré
    Tishré 1–22: *Pisqaot* 23–28

Only *Pisqa* 1 (possibly also *Pisqa* 6) falls out of synchronic relationship with a long sequence of special occasions in the synagogal lections.

The seasons/the special occasions of the astral year

The twenty-eight parashiyyot of *Pesiqta deRab Kahana* in order follow the synagogal lections from early spring through fall, or, in the Western calendar, from late February or early March through late September or early October, approximately half of the solar year, 27 weeks, and somewhat more than half of the lunar year. On the very surface, the basic building block is the theme of a given lectionary Sabbath—that is, a Sabbath distinguished by a particular lection—and not the theme dictated by a given passage of Scripture, let alone the exposition of the language or proposition of such a scriptural verse. The topical program of the document may be defined very simply: expositions of themes dictated by special Sabbaths or festivals and their lections.

Pisqa/Base-verse	Topic or Occasion
1. *On the day Moses completed* (Num. 7:1)	Torah-lection for the Sabbath of Hanukkah
2. *When you take the census* (Ex. 30:12)	Torah-lection for the Sabbath of Sheqalim first of the four Sabbaths prior to the advent of Nisan, in which Passover falls
3. *Remember Amalek* (Deut. 25:17–19)	Torah-lection for the Sabbath of Zakhor second of the four Sabbaths

		prior to the advent of Nisan, in which Passover falls
4.	*Red heifer* (Num. 19:1ff.)	Torah-lection for the Sabbath of Parah third of the four Sabbaths prior to the advent of Nisan, in which Passover falls
5.	*This month* (Ex. 12:1–2)	Torah-lection for the Sabbath of Hahodesh fourth of the four Sabbaths prior to the advent of Nisan, in which Passover falls
6.	*My offerings* (Num. 28:1–4)	Torah-lection for the New Moon which falls on a weekday
7.	*It came to pass at midnight* (Ex. 12:29–32)	Torah-lection for the first day of Passover
8.	*The first sheaf* (Lev. 23:11)	Torah-lection for the second day of Passover on which the first sheaves of barley were harvested and waved as an offering
9.	*When a bull or sheep or goat is born* (Lev. 22:26)	Lection for Passover
10.	*You shall set aside a tithe* (Deut. 14:22)	Torah-lection for Sabbath during Passover in the Land of Israel or for the eighth day of Passover outside of the Land of Israel
11.	*When Pharaoh let the people go* (Ex. 13:17–18)	Torah-lection for the Seventh Day of Passover
12.	*In the third month* (Ex. 19:1ff.)	Torah-lection for Pentecost
13.	*The words of Jeremiah* (Jer. 1:1–3)	Prophetic lection for the first of three Sabbaths prior to the Ninth of Ab
14.	*Hear* (Jer. 2:4–6)	Prophetic lection for the second of three Sabbaths prior to the Ninth of Ab
15.	*How lonely sits the city* (Lam. 1:1–2)	Prophetic lection for the third of three Sabbaths prior to the Ninth of Ab
16.	*Comfort* (Is. 40:1–2)	Prophetic lection for the first of three Sabbaths following the Ninth of Ab
17.	*But Zion said* (Is. 49:14–16)	Prophetic lection for the second of three Sabbaths following the Ninth of Ab

18. *O afflicted one, storm tossed* (Is. 54:11–14)	Prophetic lection for the third of three Sabbaths following the Ninth of Ab
19. *I even I am he who comforts you* (Is. 51:12–15)	Prophetic lection for the fourth of three Sabbaths following the Ninth of Ab
20. *Sing aloud, O barren woman* (Is. 54:1ff.)	Prophetic lection for the fifth of three Sabbaths following the Ninth of Ab
21. *Arise, Shine* (Is. 60:1–3)	Prophetic lection for the sixth of three Sabbaths following the Ninth of Ab
22. *I will greatly rejoice in the Lord* (Is. 61:10–11)	Prophetic lection for the seventh of three Sabbaths following the Ninth of Ab
23. *The New Year*	No base verse indicated. The theme is God's justice and judgment.
24. *Return O Israel to the Lord your God* (Hos. 14:1–3)	Prophetic lection for the Sabbath of Repentance between New Year and Day of Atonement
25. *Selihot*	No base verse indicated. The theme is God's forgiveness.
26. *After the death of the two sons of Aaron* (Lev. 16:1ff.)	Torah-lection for the Day of Atonement
27. *And you shall take on the first day* (Lev. 23:39–43)	Torah-lection for the first day of the Festival of Tabernacles
28. *On the eighth day* (Num. 29:35–39)	Torah-lection for the Eighth Day of Solemn Assembly[2]

This catalogue draws our attention to three eccentric *Pisqaot*, distinguished by their failure to build discourse upon the base verse. These are Section 4, which may fairly claim that its topic, the red cow, occurs in exact verbal formulation in the verses it cites; Section 23, the New Year, and Section 25, *Selihot*. The last-named may or may not take an integral place in the structure of the whole. But the middle item, the New Year, on the very surface is essential to a structure that clearly wishes to follow the line of holy days onward through the Sabbath of Repentance, the Day of Atonement, the Festival of Tabernacles, and the Eighth Day of Solemn Assembly.

These synagogal discourses, read in their entirety, form a coherent statement of three, now familiar, propositions:

---

[2] Neusner, *Pesiqta deRab Kahana*, xli–iv.

God loves Israel

That love is unconditional, and Israel's response to God must be obedience to the religious duties that God has assigned, which will produce merit. Israel's obedience to God is what will save Israel. That means doing the religious duties as required by the Torah, which is the mark of God's love for—and regeneration of—Israel. The tabernacle symbolizes the union of Israel and God. When Israel does what God asks above, Israel will prosper down below. If Israel remembers Amalek down below, God will remember Amalek up above and will wipe him out. A mark of Israel's loyalty to God is remembering Amalek. God does not require the animals that are sacrificed, since man could never match God's appetite, if that were the issue, but the savor pleases God (as a mark of Israel's loyalty and obedience). The first sheaf returns to God God's fair share of the gifts that God bestows on Israel, and those who give it benefit, while those who hold it back suffer. Observing religious duties, typified by the rites of The Festival, Tabernacles, brings a great reward of that merit that ultimately leads to redemption. God's ways are just, righteous and merciful, as shown by God's concern that the offspring remain with the mother for seven days. God's love for Israel is so intense that he wants to hold them back for an extra day after The Festival in order to spend more time with them, because, unlike the nations of the world, Israel knows how to please God. This is a mark of God's love for Israel.

God is reasonable and when Israel has been punished, it is in accord with God's rules

God forgives penitent Israel and is abundant in mercy. Laughter is vain because it is mixed with grief. A wise person will not expect too much joy. But when people suffer, there ordinarily is a good reason for it. That is only one sign that God is reasonable and that God never did anything lawless and wrong to Israel or made unreasonable demands, and there was, therefore, no reason for Israel to lose confidence in God or to abandon him. God punished Israel to be sure. But this was done with reason. Nothing happened to Israel of which God did not give fair warning in advance, and Israel's failure to heed the prophets brought about her fall. And God will forgive a faithful Israel. Even though the Israelites sinned by making the golden calf, God forgave them and raised them up. On the New Year, God executes justice, but the justice is tempered with mercy. The rites of the New Year bring about divine judgment and also forgiveness because of the merit of the fathers. Israel must repent and return to the Lord, who is merciful and will forgive them for their sins. The penitential season of the New Year and Day of Atonement is the right time for confession and penitence, and God is sure to accept penitence. By exercising his power of mercy, the already-merciful God grows still stronger in mercy.

God will save Israel personally at a time and circumstance of his own choosing

Israel may know what the future redemption will be like, because of the redemption from Egypt. The paradox of the red cow, that what imparts uncleanness, namely touching the ashes of the red cow, produces cleanness, is part of God's ineffable wisdom, which man cannot fathom. Only God can know the precise moment of Israel's redemption. That is something man cannot find out on his own. But God will certainly fulfill the predictions of the prophets about Israel's coming redemption. The Exodus from Egypt is the paradigm of the coming redemption. Israel has lost Eden—but can come home, and, with God's help, will. God's unique power is shown through Israel's unique suffering. In God's own time, he will redeem Israel.

To develop this point, the authorship proceeds to further facts, worked out in its propositional discourses. The lunar calendar, particular to Israel, marks Israel as favored by God, for the new moon signals the coming of Israel's redemption, and the particular new moon that will mark the actual event is that of Nisan. When God chooses to redeem Israel, Israel's enemies will have no power to stop him, because God will force Israel's enemies to serve Israel, because of Israel's purity and loyalty to God. Israel's enemies are punished, and what they propose to do to Israel, God does to them. Both directly and through the prophets, God is the source of true comfort, which he will bring to Israel.

Israel thinks that God has forsaken them. But it is Israel who forsook God. God's love has never failed, and will never fail. Even though he has been angry, his mercy still is near and God has the power and will to save Israel. God has designated the godly for himself and has already promised to redeem them. He will assuredly do so. God personally is the one who will comfort Israel. While Israel says there is no comfort, in fact, God will comfort Israel. Zion/Israel is like a barren woman, but Zion will bring forth children, and Israel will be comforted. Both God and Israel will bring light to Zion, which will give light to the world. The rebuilding of Zion will be a source of joy for the entire world, not for Israel alone. God will rejoice in Israel, Israel in God, like bride and groom.

Astral Israel: the theology of *Pesiqta deRab Kahana*

Pesiqta deRab Kahana's compilers thus register standard points. What we have here is a new way of conveying a familiar theological proposition. But what is new makes all the difference. Consider the unfolding message imposed by *Pesiqta deRab Kahana* upon the lectionary cycle and essentially distinct from it. From Hanukkah through Pentecost, Israel in nature's time celebrates its meeting with God in the Temple. Then follow the days of desiccation and death, three weeks of mourning, when Israel's rebellion against God brings about God's abandonment of the Temple. With Israel's rebellion fully requited in the disaster, there succeed the seven Sabbaths of consolation for the penitent, corporate Israel. Then, correspondingly, come the Days of Awe, the individual Israelite's time to recapitulate in his own being the main lines of corporate Israel's story of sin, punishment, suffering and atonement and the rest. The Days of Awe, the New Year and the Day of Atonement, marked by repentance for sin, atonement, and prayer for forgiveness, then correspond to the days from the seventeenth of Tammuz to the ninth of Ab and the weeks following. At the end follows the climactic moment, the Festival par excellence, Tabernacles, with the promise of renewal.

That program, laid out in the lectionary cycle superimposed on the Pentateuchal one, presents the main points of Rabbinic theology in its doctrine that builds on the correspondence of Adam and Israel, Eden and the Land. And this rabbinization of the liturgical experience does not match the way in which the Pentateuchal lections, whether annual or triennial, organize the sacred calendar of synagogue worship. A curious disjuncture imposes itself on the two distinct sequences, (1) the narrative-historical sequence of the Pentateuch, (2) the paradigmatic of the lunar cycle.

The Pentateuchal lectionary cycle recapitulates the narrative sequence from Adam to the border of the promised land. By extension through Joshua, Judges, Samuel, and Kings, the narrative (if not the lectionary) cycle ends where it began: loss of Eden, loss of Jerusalem. By contrast, the lectionary program of *Pesiqta deRab Kahana* hardly works through the same narrative in the same sequence at all. There is no beginning, middle, and end, constructed in a teleological sequence out of the narrative history of Israel. Now, the events of the natural year, signified in the movement of the lunar months correlated with the solar seasons, built around the first full moon after the vernal and autumnal equinoxes in particular, do match certain moments in Israel's life. But these are not in the temporal order so paramount in the lectionary narrative from Genesis through Numbers plus Deuteronomy. They follow their own order and sequence. The occasions of nature matched by moments in Israel's pattern of conduct and its consequence thus are removed from the narrative framework, e.g., of Genesis through Kings. Events are no longer unique, linear, sequential—teleological. They now are formed into moments of an exemplary character, out of time altogether, out of phase with the Pentateuchal-narrative setting. Thought is no longer teleological but rather paradigmatic.

No wonder, then, that *Pesiqta deRab Kahana* starts where it does, with the rededication of the Temple signified by Hanukkah. In the repertoire of events gathered in the document, that is the only logical starting point; the alternative, the end point, is impossible. That is then followed by the leap to the four Sabbaths preparatory to Passover, with the rest in sequence! With the preparations for the celebration of Israel's beginning in the Exodus and at Sinai marking the starting point, the rest of the natural year lays itself out against the main lines of the liturgical year. There is then this cycle:

(1) the preparation of the Temple, dedication, then purification;

(2) the beginnings at Passover-Pentecost;

(3) the catastrophe of Tammuz-Ab, the season of death, then the consolation quick to follow, and at the end;

(4) the recapitulation of the same cycle in Elul and Tishré—sin, punishment, atonement, consolation and renewal, as the life-cycle of nature and the rhythm of Israelite existence correspond and signify, each, the reliability and renewal of the other.

The unique theological perspective of *Pesiqta deRab Kahana*

Change the order and the entire construction collapses into gibberish. What is unique in the document's theology thus emerges when we see the total message in lectionary context. Pesiqta's "text" is nature, not Scripture—the passage of the seasons, on the one side, and the sequence of lunar months, on the other, as these correlate and are correlated with exemplary occasions in Israel's existence. The *Pisqaot* follow the sequence of nature's year, as I have already stressed. Internally, the individual *Pisqa* finds coherence in the unfolding of the message that pertains to that occasion in nature and history. So *Pesiqta deRab Kahana* does not organize its discourse around Scripture at all. The base-verses all are selected utterly out of the context of the books of Scripture in which they occur.

Chosen for a focus are those passages of Scripture that speak to liturgical occasions set by the passage of the moon and the solar seasons in the heavens. The sequence and sense of coherence then derive solely from the lunar-solar calendar. *Pesiqta deRab Kahana* therefore forms an exercise in correlating Israel's affairs on earth with the movement of the heavenly bodies. Israel's history, linear and sequential, is no longer pertinent. Now exemplary moments, chosen out of time and not arranged in temporal sequence, define matters. Hence the natural, seasonal passage of the moon in the heavens signals paradigmatic moments in Israel's life on earth. Israel on earth responds—and corresponds—to the heavenly bodies above. It would claim more than the document establishes to describe *Pesiqta deRab Kahana* as an exercise in astral religion—but not by much.

The parts and the whole

The parts count only as part of the whole. Seen one by one, they find counterparts in other documents, if not verbatim then in proposition or implication. It is only as part of a whole possessing its own logic of coherent discourse that we grasp its logic and understand the documentary program and message. When we look back over the theological compositions and composites, we discern the sequential unfolding of the document's themes. These form a continuous statement, with a beginning, middle, and end: beginning with the dedication of the Temple/tabernacle, ending with the climactic moments of Tabernacles (including the Eighth Day of Solemn Assembly). They therefore turn out to conform to a required, logical order. By "required" I mean that if we change the sequence of themes in any detail, situating one theme somewhere other than in its present location the entire document falls to pieces. Its logic and cogency then derive from the lunar calendar, which signals moments in Israel's encounter with God through the natural life of the Land and its seasons, rainy, then dry, then rainy, spring, summer, autumn.

Two cycles of time joined

In their present sequence and only in that sequence, the purposeful ordering of the document's theological propositions emerge. And these represent a decision by the authorship of the document. They bring into relationship two cycles of time: historical-narrative and natural-paradigmatic.

First, the historical-narrative cycle, built on teleology, recapitulates the cycle of synagogue lections of the Pentateuch, the one that sets into sequence the events of humanity's history from creation, through the fall, past the flood, to the formation of Israel as a family and its reformation as a kingdom of priests and a holy people. It is the story of Israel's recapitulation of Adam's experience, with its calamity but, in the case of repentant Israel, also with the promise of a different ending.

Second, the natural-paradigmatic cycle, highlighted among the Rabbinic Midrash compilations only here, is the cycle of the seasons, as these flow in sequence from the dedication of the Temple through its rites on distinguished occasions defined by the movement of heavenly bodies, the moon correlated with the solar seasons. It is nature's logic, heaven's logic—a different mode of organizing time altogether, one in which the paradigm of Israel's existence is recast. It is transformed from a linear sequence of one-time historical events into a pattern of recurrent moments in nature. These heavenly occasions capture points of intersection between Israel and God, corresponding to the unfolding of the seasons—hence, in the language used earlier, "natural-paradigmatic."

The details correspond. And why not? For both cycles focus upon the same entity, Israel in relationship to God. But the one, the established lectionary cycle from Genesis through Deuteronomy, tells a story, and the other, the supererogatory lectionary cycle of particular Sabbaths and special occasions, celebrates events in the heavens and their corresponding moments in Israel's eternal existence. The narrative-teleological cycle conveys its messages through the story that it tells. By the natural-paradigmatic cycle these messages are abstracted from that story and set forth as propositions of a general character.

The upshot may be simply stated. In bypassing the Pentateuchal cycle altogether, the authorship of *Pesiqta deRab Kahana* has adopted an intellectual structure of its own. It is one that is different from the unfolding of Israel's life in time through a sequence of one-time, particular events: the day this happened, the time that remarkable, unique event took place. Sequence is everything, story nothing. The sequence invokes that logic to which I have already made reference: the logic of Israel's moral, covenanted existence, its life with God.

Cosmos and history

Pesiqta deRab Kahana builds upon its own cosmic sense of world order. It makes its own judgment on the meaning of the cyclical sequence of the movement of the heavenly bodies. It defines in its own way the encounter of Israel and God, in earth and in heaven, always in correspondence. This is, then, a different way of framing Israel's and God's relationship from the established one that begins with Genesis and concludes with Deuteronomy, the familiar comparison of Adam and Israel, Eden and the Land.

The theology of astral Israel and the reading of Scripture

The theology of astral Israel bears its consequences for the reading of Scripture. Now the times and the seasons embody heaven's account of Israel on earth. Scripture is not the only voice of God, nature's time and sequence speaks for him as well. And, it follows, if Scripture is no longer the sole supernatural message, then Israel in time no longer follows a simple, linear sequence. Rather we have a perspective on matters formed from Heaven's view: this season responds to Israel's conduct in that circumstance, this event in the heavens correlates with that activity of Israel on earth.

The account bears a cyclicality that the Pentateuchal narrative does not possess. Thus the document viewed whole imposes upon the cycle of narrative—the story of Israel in time—that other cycle, the cycle of nature. One may characterize the resulting cycle as a competing, or at least, as a correlative, mode of recapitulating Israel's record from its beginnings to now. Annually Israel dedicates the Temple, prepares it for the pilgrims, celebrates the advent of freedom and receives the Torah. Annually Israel rebels against the Torah and sins, is punished through the loss of the Temple. Annually Israel atones and repents, and God consoles and forgives. And annually Israelites recapitulate that same cycle of sin and atonement, consolation and forgiveness, so that, year by year, the rains follow the Festival of Tabernacles in a renewal of nature's—and Israel's—cycle.

What has happened to the scriptural story, which is linear, sequential, and historical, not cyclical, episodic, and exemplary? *Pesiqta deRab Kahana* takes over and reshapes *the results* of Israel's continuous narrative from Creation to destruction and the hope of restoration and incorporates the linear into the paradigmatic structure. The narrative tells of Adam's loss of Eden, then—with Genesis through Kings in hand—Israel's loss of the Land. The consequences to be drawn from that story—that sin leads to punishment, but repentance leads to restoration and renewal—define the paradigm discerned in the very movement of the moon and the solar seasons by *Pesiqta deRab Kahana*. At issue then is how to break the cycle signified by the natural year. Israel has the power, any time, any year, to disrupt that cycle and inaugurate the end of history and nature as then known. So when I say that *Pesiqta deRab Kahana* has folded the results of Israel's narrative into a pattern yielded by the very givens of the natural world and its times and seasons, I refer to the recapitulation, in reference to the natural year, of the consequences to be drawn from the comparison of Israel and Adam, the Land and Eden, that the scriptural account, read continuously, has yielded.

Then the continuous, linear, one-directional narrative is folded into the cycle of nature's time, marked by seasons and events in heaven, with their counterpart, which is the celebration of nature at the altar of the Temple through offerings that signify particular events in the unfolding of the natural year. These, further, are correlated with paradigmatic moments in Israel's year. So the story of the Temple on earth recapitulates in Israel's setting the story of the passage of the seasons, but with this proviso: the seasons follow the course that they do because they signal the unfolding existence of Israel, with special reference to its Temple altar, where God and Israel meet. Because Israel repeats its conduct, nature recapitulates its cycles. But there will come a new heaven and a new earth, when Israel completes the work badly begun by Adam.

The absolute, fixed order of the document once more

Now we see the basis of the claim that the tight logic of the document was such that changing the position of a single exposition or *Pisqa* will have ruined the entire construction. A moment of reflection on the articulated plan of the whole shows that for a construction with its focus on the Temple, nexus of heaven and earth, the sole possible starting point was Hanukkah: today the Temple commences. Then what could have followed? The only logical continuation is with the four Sabbaths prior to the advent of Nisan, with Passover following two weeks later. These Sabbaths then prepare the way for the pilgrim festival, Passover-Pentecost. From the climactic season, Passover-Pentecost, with the end of the rains, follows the long dry season, marked by the Temple's destruction.

Then comes Israel's repentance. That is in two correlated phases, corporate and individual. First is the corporate with the ninth of Ab, then the individual with the penitential season of Elul followed by the New Year, the day of remembrance, and the Day of Atonement. Thus is realized the time of renewal marked by judgment of the year gone by and renewal of life in the year to come. Once the natural year, celebrated in Temple rite, defines the heart of the matter, then the matter is set. That is why, within the logic of the natural year embodied in the Temple rites, there is no other sufficient sequence, no other starting point that is able to realize the governing program of the document viewed whole.

Here—as mediated by the theology of *Pesiqta deRab Kahana*—is where Israel encounters that reading of the Torah other than the one beginning with Creation and ending at the border of the Land of Israel in the weekly lectionary cycle encompassing Genesis through Deuteronomy. The document's authorship has undertaken to expound the Torah in the sequence of the natural year in such a way as annually to tell the tale of Israel's conduct embodied in the passage of the seasons, celebrated in the realization of the Temple, where God and Israel meet. The plan is therefore to show how what happens to the Temple in all times signifies the relationship of God and corporate Israel and recapitulates the relationship of God and the individual Israelite.

Then came the liturgical lections of the synagogue's special occasions. They recount the story encompassing the Festival cycle and related, special Sabbaths. Autonomous of the sequence of Sabbath lections that begins with Genesis and concludes with Deuteronomy, it makes its own selections of appropriate occasions and their inexorable themes. In its context, its statement is unique.

Nature and renewal

Through its lectionary cycle, *Pesiqta deRab Kahana* makes Israel's progress through the year of nature into an annual journey of renewal. So while *Pesiqta deRab Kahana* participates in the common theology of Rabbinic Judaism, it affords a rare theological moment within that same Judaism. That is the moment at which theology becomes natural, by which I mean, an interpretation, a realization, of nature. Here theology as intellectual proposition gives way to theology as the explanation of realized experience, both corporate and individual, of nature in all its majesty. No wonder, then, that the issue of the end of days, the resolution of linear time in its Messianic climax, plays so negligible a role in the document. Cyclicality in nature has taken over and assigned a marginal position to those critical components of the historical-Messianic view of Israel's existence, the end of days and the advent of the Messiah. Here, consolation means restoration, and the Temple is the focus. Then nature takes over and the movements of the heavenly bodies become determinative. And moreover Israel makes all the difference. In the unfolding of the natural year within the theology of *Pesiqta deRab Kahana*, Israel lives out its theology of repentance and restoration in the inexorable passage of the times and the seasons. All that history can contribute is the unique event that can be transformed into a paradigmatic moment, part of a recurrent pattern.

Does *Pesiqta deRab Kahana* form a theological statement?

Pesiqta deRab Kahana does form a theological statement. It is this: Israel on earth embodies the course of the moon and the solar seasons in heaven, and when Israel mends its way, all of astral nature will respond. All else forms a commentary and is made up of details.

The synagogue through the paramount Torah-cycle calls Israel to rehearse, week by week, the chapters of Israel's formative life: Genesis for the foundation of Israel, Exodus through Numbers, then Deuteronomy, for the definition of Israel. Then, on a given week, Israel once more recapitulates through its paradigmatic and definitive narrative the earthly story of itself. This week the world was made, that week recalls the Flood, the next the call to Abraham, and so throughout. So through the lectionary cycle, annually or triennially, the past is made present, the present resituated in the past, historical time, marked by unique, one-time events, is recapitulated, the past both recognized and renewed. In that context, we recall, *Pesiqta deRab Kahana* has made a remarkable choice to impose upon the story of Israel's formation and definition another dimension, another layer of being: the cosmic. It is now Israel in the context—indeed, in control—of natural time, marked by the stars and the seasons. The Sabbaths of Joseph's story, for example, that in the annual lectionary cycle come in Kislev in accord with the annual cycle of lections, embody in *Pesiqta deRab Kahana* also the occasion of the rededication of the Temple. But these do not intersect. While an exegetical initiative may link the one with the other (reading Scripture to underscore the Temple in the patrimony of Benjamin, for instance, joining the two distinct themes), that is a mere serendipity.

In fact, *Pesiqta deRab Kahana* invokes a distinct layer of Israelite being. Our review of the theological components of the document identifies that layer of being: it concerns Israel's celebration in the Temple, its loss of the Temple, and its hope for forgiveness and restoration of the Temple. It is no wonder that ten of the twenty-eight *Pisqaot* concern themselves with the destruction and consequent consolation. Nor is it surprising that the following sequence of heavenly events—those of Elul and Tishré—recapitulates the pattern of Tammuz-Ab! The one concerns corporate Israel, the other Israel as Israelite, one by one, all before God but judged as individuals. So what *Pesiqta deRab Kahana* contributes to Israel's encounter with God in the Torah is the matter of the coming consolation and redemption. That is now portrayed as heaven's promise. This survey shows that *Pesiqta deRab Kahana* makes a theological statement that is, in its own terms, entirely cogent.

On eschatological matters *Pesiqta deRab Kahana* has its own points of interest, even while concurring with the main propositions given here. The document wishes to underscore that what God is going to do he has already done; that what will happen in the ultimate redemption is already prefigured in this world's experience. What will happen at the end of time has already happened at the beginning, and the advent of the end of time will mark the restoration of the condition of Eden. These propositions do not fit tightly with the framing of matters in more general terms. For the correspondence of end to beginning, while part of the repertoire of the governing theology, hardly limits the eschatological doctrine of that theology. But it is the main point of *Pesiqta deRab Kahana*. So the theological structure of *Pesiqta deRab Kahana* is asymmetrical with that of the Aggadic documents viewed systematically; but it coheres. Where *Pesiqta deRab Kahana* intersects, it conforms in conception with the encompassing system. But the proportions and the emphases are its own.

Pesiqta deRab Kahana's theology in the context of the Rabbinic system and structure

Pesiqta deRab Kahana takes an essential role in the larger theological program of Rabbinic Judaism. This it does by superimposing, upon the Pentateuchal story of Israel's beginning, the narrative of the ending—destruction but also atonement, forgiveness, renewal, for both corporate Israel and the Israelite. The reliable heavens then guarantee what is to come about, the seasons in their sequence embody the promise of the coming redemption: consolation and restoration following repentance, atonement, and forgiveness. The summer drought, the advent of the early rains—these now are made, in the very heart of synagogue liturgy, to signify the existential reality of Israel in its encounter with God.

What makes *Pesiqta deRab Kahana's* revision of the lectionary encounter powerful and persuasive ought not to be missed. It is its emphasis upon the correspondence of the cycle of nature with the exemplary moments of Israel's existence, the whole abstracted from linear history. The dedication and celebration in the Temple, loss of the Temple, atonement and renewal and restoration correspond to nature's cycle. Then, after the season of desiccation and death, the renewal signified by the winter rains, comes the climax of Passover-Pentecost. Then the sequence concludes with the advent of the summer's drought, followed by the renewal once more.

We should not miss the radical change represented by this reading of the cycle of nature that defines the rhythm of the Israelite year. While the lunar-solar calendar conventionally interpreted knows two climactic moments, the first full moon after the vernal equinox, then the same after the autumnal equinox, for Passover and Pentecost, respectively, *Pesiqta deRab Kahana* has constructed a single, continuous cyclical sequence, as I have explained. Events of nature, the unfolding of the lunar year, and events of history, the unfolding of Israel's life in historical time, are formed into a single, unitary construction. That is, furthermore, transformed into a paradigm of the life of not only corporate Israel but also the individual Israelite. Nature, Israel, the Israelite—all now are given their moment in the lectionary life of the synagogue.

The main point of *Pesiqta deRab Kahana*

Implicit in every *Pisqa*, then is the intent to highlight Israel as the counterpart, on earth, to the heavenly bodies. And, as I stress, the unfolding of Israelite existence on earth, the patterns of its relationship with God—these correspond down here to the movement of the moon and sun in the heavens above. But though taken with that correlation, we should not miss the point: the stars in their courses respond to Israel's conduct. The cycle of time as told by *Pesiqta deRab Kahana* treats Israel not as a principal player in world history on earth alone, as does the Pentateuchal cycle as framed by the Rabbinic masters. Rather, Israel now represents a cosmic presence, a heavenly actor on the natural stage of the Temple, along with the moon in relationship to the sun and the passage of the natural seasons.

That is why *Pesiqta deRab Kahana* is unique among the Midrash compilations of the formative age of Rabbinic Judaism. No other Midrash compilation organizes itself around that conception of Israel in relationship with heaven that governs here. No Midrash compilation viewed whole but *Pesiqta deRab Kahana* proposes that what happens to Israel on earth correlates with the movement of the heavenly bodies, the moon and the sun in particular. It is the Midrash in the formative canon of Rabbinic Judaism that endows Israel with astral setting and dimensions, raising Israel from earth to heaven. That is what I mean by "astral Israel."

Astral Israel is not subject to astral influence

Discerning in its activities the recurrent pattern of the skies, *Pesiqta deRab Kahana* substitutes theology for astrology. Then, along with the Bavli's famous composite, "Israel is not subject to planetary influences" (Bavli Shabbat 152b–153a) it forms a kind of anti-astrology, one might say. That is because the message throughout, normative for Rabbinic Judaism, is that Israel makes choices and bears responsibility for those choices. So it relates to the movement of the moon and the sun through the seven levels of heaven signified by the fixed stars. But this is not in the way in which others are subject to the same heavenly movements. Israel drives its own chariot through the skies, the nations are but passengers on a chariot they do not drive.

Israel is *sui generis,* because God alone, and not determinism in any form, dictates what happens to Israel and to Israelites. What happens to Israel is the realization solely of God's will. Gentiles, by contrast, live within the ordinary rules of nature that pertain to all but Israel and so are subject to astrology, having rejected a position in God's dominion and chosen not to live under his rules, beyond nature's. God does not choose to overrule the stars because gentiles do not accept his dominion in the Torah, and that is why they are ruled by impersonal forces of physics. At stake in the logic of an orderly world subject in every detail to the rationality of justice, then, is the working of God's just will. Where God chooses to govern and is so chosen, there the stars affect nothing. So we see once more the working of the doctrine of Israel and the Torah, the gentiles and idolatry. While recognizing the scientific standing of astrology, most sages represented in the Oral Torah nevertheless concurred that when it comes to Israel, God rules, not the stars.

Since the Bavli sets forth systematic topical expositions, not merely random opinion, and organizes those composites in such a way as to indicate the thrust and direction of opinion, I choose for the authoritative statement on astrology the Bavli's one sustained statement on the subject. That systematic statement is so organized as to yield only a single conclusion. Specifically, I focus upon the single most systematic composite on the subject, which is so framed as to demonstrate that astrology does not apply to Israel, the other message that complements and completes that of *Pesiqta deRab Kahana:*

Bavli tractate *Šabbat* 24:4 III.9–12
Folios 156a–b

9. A. It has been stated:
   B. R. Hanina says, "One's star is what makes one smart, one's star is what gives wealth, and Israel is subject to the stars."
   C. R. Yohanan said, "Israel is not subject to the stars."

Clearly, two opinions competed. Two characteristics mark the normative one in a dispute: (1) whose opinion is explored, whose neglected; and (2) whose opinion is complemented with sustaining authorities' views, whose not. In the following, Yohanan's position is analyzed, Hanina's ignored:

   D. And R. Yohanan is consistent with views expressed elsewhere, for said R. Yohanan, "How on the basis of Scripture do we know that Israel is not subject to the stars? As it is said, 'Thus says the Lord, Do not learn the way of the gentiles, nor be dismayed at the signs of the heavens, for the nations are dismayed at them' (Jer. 10:2). They are dismayed, but the Israelites are not dismayed."

Now begins a long sequence of systematic demonstrations that Israel is not subject to astrology. We begin with exegetical-scriptural proof:

10. A. And so Rab takes the view that Israel is not subject to the stars, for said R. Judah said Rab, "How on the basis of Scripture do we know that Israel is not subject to the stars? As it is said, 'And he brought him forth outside' (Gen. 15:5). Said Abraham before the Holy One, blessed be He, 'Lord of the world, "Someone born in my household is my heir" (Gen. 15:3).' He said to him, 'Not at all. "But he who will come forth out of your own loins" (Gen. 1:4).' He said before him, 'Lord of the world, I have closely examined my star, and I have seen that I am destined to have no children.' He said to him, 'Abandon this astrology of yours—Israel is not subject to astrology. Now what's your calculation? [156B] Is it that Jupiter stands in the west [and that is your constellation]? I'll turn it back and set it up in the East.' And so it is written, 'Who has raised up Jupiter from the east? He has summoned it for his sake' (Isa. 41:2)."

Scripture, as always, supplies the initial demonstration. Wherever possible, the patriarchs will be asked to show that, even at the very beginning of Israel, the underlying principle applied. At the next stage, we are given exemplary cases that show us how and why sages maintain that Israel is not subject to astrology. The first case pits astrological judgment against divine intervention; the latter sets aside the testimony of the stars.

Not only so, but a specific reason is adduced to account for the special favor shown the man, which is the man's own supererogatory act of generosity, to which Heaven responds with a supererogatory miracle:

> B. It is also the position of Samuel that Israel is not subject to the stars.
> C. For Samuel and Ablat were in session, and some people going along to a lake. Said Ablat to Samuel, "That man is going but won't come back, a snake will bite him and he'll die."
> D. Said to him Samuel, "Yeah, well, if he's an Israelite, he will go and come back."
> E. While they were in session, he went and came back. Ablat got up and took of the man's knapsack and found in it a snake cut up and lying in two pieces.

So there must be a reason, and the reason has to do with an act of generosity or some other source of *zekhut* (merit). The man acted in a way that the law could not require, but that God could, and did, much appreciate:

> F. Said Samuel to the man, "What did you do [today in particular]?"
> G. He said to him, "Every day we tossed our bread into one pot and ate, but today one of us had no bread, and he was shamed. I said to him, 'I will go and collect the bread.' When I came to him, I made as if to go and collect the bread, so he shouldn't be ashamed."
> H. He said to him, "You have carried out a religious duty."
> I. Samuel went forth and expounded, "'But charity delivers from death' (Prov. 10:2)—not [merely] from a grotesque death, but from death itself."

In the next case astrology is set aside by a sheer accident, which, we shall see in a moment, sages identify as a medium of God's will. Here the astrologers ("Chaldeans") make a flat prediction, and an accident overturns their prognostication; once more, the supererogatory act of generosity accounts for God's personal intervention:

> 11. A. It is also the position of R. Aqiba that Israel is not subject to the stars.
> B. For R. Aqiba had a daughter. Chaldeans [astrologers] told him, "On the day that she goes into the bridal canopy, a snake will bite her and she'll die."
> C. This worried him a lot. On that day she took a brooch and stuck it into the wall, and by chance it sank into the eye of a snake. The next day when she took it out, the snake came trailing along after it.
> D. Her father said to her, "What did you do [today in particular]?"
> E. She said to him, "In the evening a poor man came to the door, and everyone was busy with the banquet so no one could take care of him, so I took some of what was given to me and gave it to him."

F. He said to her, "You have carried out a religious duty."
G. R. Aqiba went forth and expounded, "'But charity delivers from death' (Prov. 10:2)—not from a grotesque death, but from death itself."

If piety on the part of an Israelite overcomes astrology, a lapse in piety for even a moment subjects the man to the influence of the stars. Here keeping one's head covered serves as a sign of fear of Heaven, and the rest follows:

12. A. It is also the position of R. Nahman bar Isaac that Israel is not subject to the stars.
B. For to the mother of R. Nahman bar Isaac the Chaldean said, "Your son will be a thief." She didn't let him go bareheaded, saying, "Keep your head covered, so fear of Heaven may be upon you, and pray for mercy."
C. He didn't know why she said that to him. One day he was in session, studying under a palm tree. His head covering fell off. He lifted his eyes and saw the palm tree, and was overcome by temptation; he climbed up and bit off a cluster of dates with his teeth.

The proof therefore is positive and negative, and the composite leaves no doubt as to the position taken by the Oral Torah, even in the face of dissenting opinion.

If determinism in the form of astrology conflicts with the logic inherent in the theology of a just God, freely acting in a rational way, then what appears to come about by sheer accident—what others may deem sheer chaos—coheres with that logic. Chance or accident reveal God's intent and plan; there is no such thing as sheer chance and pure accident. Sages regard what happens by chance as an act of Heavenly intervention, an event in the dominion of the kingdom of Heaven. In the Oral Torah, casting of lots and other forms of chance yield God's decision. How the lot falls then reflects how God wants things, since God commands and fate conforms. Nothing takes place by chance, so by allowing the dice to fall where they will, man discovers God's wishes. We do not however have a single instance in which sheer chance serves to explain an event in the life of Israel or the gentiles in relationship to Israel. That position, explaining events in private life rather than in public affairs, is formulated more in Halakhic than in aggadic terms. The fact that the identification of chance with God's determinate will forms the premise of entire bodies of the law proves the normative standing of that conviction. The Midrash compilation, *Pesiqta deRab Kahana,* with its Aggadah then makes the affirmative statement that complements and completes the negative one of the Bavli and its Halakhah.

14

The Sages in *The Fathers according to Rabbi Nathan*

In ca. 250 Mishnah-tractate ʾ*Abot,* The Fathers, delivered its message through aphorisms assigned to named sages on the chain of tradition beginning with Moses at Sinai. A few centuries later—the date is indeterminate but it is possibly ca. 500–600—ʾ*Abot deRabbi Natan, The Fathers according to Rabbi Nathan,* a vast secondary expansion of that same tractate, endowed those anonymous names with flesh-and-blood lives. *The Fathers according to Rabbi Nathan* recast the earlier tractate, The Fathers, by adding a sizable number of narratives. While not a compilation of Midrash exegeses, the narratives of *The Fathers according to Rabbi Nathan* belong in any presentation of the Aggadic corpus of formative Rabbinic Judaism. It is a principal theological document of the canon.

The principal doctrinal development in *The Fathers according to Rabbi Nathan* concerns teleology. The earlier document speaks only of the individual, who prepares in this world for the life of the world to come. The teleology of the system outlined by The Fathers calls for the individual to prepare for judgment before God and promises eternal life. *The Fathers according to Rabbi Nathan* for its part is consistent and one-sided when it addresses not so much the individual as the nation, and promises not the life of the world to come for the private person but the age to come for corporate, holy Israel. That is in contrast to this age, which belongs to the (undifferentiated) nations. In this shift of mythic categories the framers of *The Fathers according to Rabbi Nathan* redefine the teleology of Rabbinic Judaism and focus it upon historical and social categories, rather than those that emerge from the life and death of the individual—a striking shift indeed.

The narrative repertoire of *The Fathers according to Rabbi Nathan*

Given a saying of an aphoristic character, whether or not that saying is drawn from The Fathers, the authorship of *The Fathers according to Rabbi Nathan* will do one of the following:

(1) present a secondary expansion, including an example, of the wise saying at hand;

(2) cite a proof-text of Scripture in that same connection;

(3) provide a parable to illustrate the wise saying (as often as not instead of the proof-text);

(4) add a sizable composition of extraneous materials that intersect with the foregoing, either by amplifying the proof-text without regard to the wise saying served by the proof-text, or by enriching discourse on a topic introduced in connection with the base-saying;

(5) tack on a protracted story of a sage and what he said and did, which story may or may not exemplify the teaching of the associated aphorism.

These procedures generally follow a fixed order. Where the authorship of the later document has chosen to cite and amplify sayings in the earlier one, that exercise—*The Fathers according to Rabbi Nathan* amplifying The Fathers—comes first. There may be additional amplification, and what initially appears to augment often turns out to be quite new and so belongs to the second of our two categories: expansions in the form of proof-texts drawn from Scripture, parables, or other sorts of stories, sometimes involving named sages, that illustrate the same point; or sequences of unadorned sayings, not in The Fathers, that make the same point. These come later in a sequence of discourses in *The Fathers according to Rabbi Nathan*. Any appendix of secondary materials on a theme introduced in the primary discourse occurs will be inserted directly after the point at which said theme occurs. Only afterward will the exposition of the saying in The Fathers proceed to a further point. This general order, which is quite logical for a commentary to a received text, predominates throughout.

The sage-story

The compilers made use of the story about the sage to convey powerful propositions lacking all precedent in The Fathers. They made the shift from a document that articulated propositions principally through aphorisms, to one that made points through narrative and particularly through sage-stories. Three traits define the sage-story in *The Fathers according to Rabbi Nathan*.

(1) The story about a sage has a beginning, middle, and end, and rests not only on verbal exchanges ("he said to him . . . , he said to him . . ."), but on (described) action.

(2) The story about a sage unfolds from a point of tension and conflict to a clear resolution and remission of the conflict.

(3) The story about a sage rarely invokes a verse of Scripture and never serves to prove a proposition concerning the meaning of a verse of Scripture.

What about Scripture-stories?

The traits of stories about scriptural figures and themes prove quite the opposite:

(1) In the story about a scriptural hero there is no beginning, middle, and end, and little action. The burden of the narrative is carried by "he said to him . . . , he said to him. . . ." Described action is rare and plays only a slight role in the unfolding of the narrative. Often the narrative consists of little more than a setting for a saying, and the point of the narrative is conveyed not through what is told but through the cited saying.

(2) The story about a scriptural hero is worked out as a tableau, with description of the components of the stationary tableau placed at the center. There is little movement, no point of tension that is resolved.

(3) The story about a scriptural hero always invokes verses from Scripture and makes the imputation of meaning to those verses the center of interest.

So *The Fathers according to Rabbi Nathan* systematically enriches The Fathers with a variety of narratives, each with its own conventions. When the narrators wish to talk about sages, they invoked one set of narrative conventions, deemed appropriate to that topic, and when they turned to make up stories about scriptural heroes and topics, they appealed to quite different narrative conventions.

Topical program

The topical program of *The Fathers according to Rabbi Nathan* in particular emerges only in identifying topics treated in the successor-compilation but not in The Fathers.

There are three points of emphasis in The Fathers lacking all counterpart in restatement and development in *The Fathers according to Rabbi Nathan*. First, the study of the Torah alone does not suffice. One has also to make an honest living through work. In what is particular to *The Fathers according to Rabbi Nathan* we find not that point but its opposite: one should study the Torah and other things will take care of themselves—a claim of a more supernatural character than the one in The Fathers.

A second point of clear interest in the earlier document to which, in the later one, we find no response tells sages to accommodate their wishes to those of the community at large, to accept the importance of the government, to work in community, to practice self-abnegation and restraint in favor of the wishes of others. The sage here is less a supernatural figure than a political leader, eager to conciliate and reconcile the other.

The third and most important, indicative shift in the later document imparts to the teleological question an eschatological answer altogether lacking in the earlier one. The ahistorical teleology of The Fathers gives way to the highly eschatological approach of *The Fathers according to Rabbi Nathan*.

To explain: if we were to ask the authorship of ʾ*Abot* to spell out their teleology, they would draw our attention to their numerous sayings about this life's being a time of preparation for the life of the world to come, on the one side, and to judgment and eternal life, on the other. The focus is on the individual and how he or she lives in this world and prepares for the next. The category is the Israelite, not all Israel, and, commonly in the two documents before us when we speak of the individual, we also tend to find the language of "this world" and "the world to come": ʿ*olam hazzeh*, ʿ*olam habba*. The sequence of sayings about this world and the next form a stunning contrast to the ones about this *age* and the next age: ʿ*olam hazzeh*, *le'atid labo*. In general, though not invariably, the shift in language draws in its wake a shift in social category, from Israelite to Israel, from individual to social entity of group, nation, or people. The word "ʿolam" bears two meanings, "world," and "age." In context, when we find the word bearing the sense of "world," the category under discussion is the private person, and where the required sense, in English, is "age," then—as a rough rule of thumb—what is promised is for the nation.

From "this world and the world to come" to "this age and the age to come"

We can tell that the definitive category is social, therefore national, when at stake is the fate not of the private person but of holy Israel. The concern then is what will happen to the nation in time to come, meaning the coming age, not the coming resurrection. The systemic teleology shifts its focus to the holy people, and, alongside, to the national history of the holy people—now and in the age to come. So in the movement from *this world* and *the world to come* to *this age* and *the age to come* (often expressed as the coming future, *le'atid labo*) we note an accompanying categorical shift in the definitive context: from individual and private life of home and family, to society and historical, public life. That shift then characterizes the teleological movement, as much as the categorical change. And, as we see, it is contained both in general and in detail in the differences we have noticed between The Fathers and *The Fathers according to Rabbi Nathan*.

The national-eschatological interest of the later document, with its focus on living only in the Land of Israel, on the one side, and its contrast between this age, possessed by the gentiles, and the age to come, in which redeemed Israel will enjoy a paramount position, which has no counterpart in the earlier composition, emerges not only in sayings but also in stories about the critical issue, the destruction of Jerusalem and the loss of the Temple, along with the concomitant matter, associated with the former stories, about repentance and how it is achieved at this time.

Yet a further point of development lies in the notion that study of the Torah combined with various virtues, e.g., good deeds and fear of sin, suffices, with a concomitant assurance that making a living no longer matters. Here too the new medium of the later document—the stories about sages—bears the new message. For that conviction emerges not only explicitly, e.g., in the sayings of Hananiah about the power of Torah-study to take away many sources of suffering, Judah b. Ilai's that one should treat words of the Torah as the principal, earning a living as trivial, and so on, but also implicitly in the detail that both Aqiba and Eliezer began poor but through their mastery of Torah ended rich.

The message of the sage-story

The stories about sages make points that correspond to positions taken in statements of viewpoints peculiar to *The Fathers according to Rabbi Nathan*. The Fathers presents an ideal of the sage as model for the everyday life of the individual, who must study the Torah and also work, and through the good life prepare now for life after death, while *The Fathers according to Rabbi Nathan* has a different conception of the sage, of the value and meaning of the study of the Torah, and of the center of interest—and also has selected a new medium for the expression of its distinctive conception:

(1) The sage is now—in *The Fathers according to Rabbi Nathan*—not a judge and teacher alone but also a supernatural figure.

(2) Study of the Torah in preference to making a living promises freedom from the conditions of natural life.

(3) Israel as the holy people seen as a supernatural social entity takes center-stage.

In *The Fathers according to Rabbi Nathan* these innovative points are conveyed not only in sayings but in stories about sages.

The result is that the medium not only carries a new message but also forms a component of that new message. The sage as a supernatural figure now presents Torah-teachings through what he does, not only through what he says. Therefore telling stories about what sages did and the circumstances in which they made their sayings forms part of the Torah, in a way in which, in the earlier document, it clearly did not. The interest in stories about sages proves therefore not merely literary or formal; it is more than a new way of conveying an old message. Stories about the sages are told because sages stand for a message that can emerge only in stories and not in sayings alone. So we turn to a close reading of the stories themselves to review that message and find out why through stories in particular the message now emerges. For what we see is nothing short of a new mode of revelation, that is, of conveying and imparting God's will in the Torah.

Story, history, and biography

Sages conceived of the social entity, Israel, as an extended family, children of a single progenitor, Abraham, with his son and grandson, Isaac and Jacob. Consequently, when they told stories, they centered on family history—and, by extension, on the biography of the Rabbinic sage as critical to family history. The sage in the system of *The Fathers according to Rabbi Nathan* constituted the supernatural father, who replaced the natural one; events in the life of the sage constituted happenings in the history of the family-nation, Israel. So history blended with family, and family with Torah-study. That leads directly to what is most remarkable in the sage-story. The national, salvific history of the nation-family, Israel, took place in such events as the origins of the sage, i.e., his beginnings in Torah-study; the sagacity of the sage, the counterpart to what we should call social history; the doings of the sage in great turnings in the family's history, including, especially, the destruction of the Temple, now perceived as final and decisive; and the death of the sage, while engaged in Torah-study. And these define the four classifications of story in this document: the story about the beginnings of the sage, his sagacity, his great deeds, and his death.

Sagacity and history

The sage plays a public, not solely a private role. The sage as supernatural father forms the critical element in the history of the family, Israel. That history of course is defined by the encounter with Rome in particular. Rome will be represented by its persona, its family hero, counterpart to Abraham or Jacob or Moses, just as is Israel, and that can only be the emperor.

We take up the important story about the destruction of the Temple. That protracted story finds its setting in an exegesis of the saying in The Fathers that the world stands on deeds of loving kindness. These then are found by the exegete at Hos. 6:6, and the intrusion of that verse carries in its wake a narrative—not a story but a narrative-setting for a saying—about Yohanan ben Zakkai and his disciple, Joshua, in the ruins of the Temple. Only at the end of the matter do we find the major historical story of the destruction.

The Fathers according to Rabbi Nathan (Text A) IV:v.1–3

1. A. . . . on deeds of loving kindness: how so?
   B. Lo, Scripture says, For I desire mercy and not sacrifice, (and the knowledge of God rather than burnt offerings) (Hos. 6:6).
   C. To begin with the world was created only on account of loving kindness.
   D. For so it is said, For I have said, the world is built with loving kindness, in the very heavens you establish your faithfulness (Ps. 89:3).

2. A. One time (after the destruction of the Temple) Rabban Yohanan ben Zakkai was going forth from Jerusalem, with R. Joshua following after him. He saw the house of the sanctuary lying in ruins.
   B. R. Joshua said, "Woe is us for this place which lies in ruins, the place in which the sins of Israel used to come to atonement."
   C. He said to him, "My son, do not be distressed. We have another mode of atonement, which is like (atonement through sacrifice), and what is that? It is deeds of loving kindness.
   D. "For so it is said, For I desire mercy and not sacrifice, (and the knowledge of God rather than burnt offerings) (Hos. 6:6)."
3. A. So we find in the case of Daniel, that most desirable man, that he carried out deeds of loving kindness.
   B. And what are the deeds of loving kindness that Daniel did?
   C. If you say that he offering whole offerings and sacrifices, do people offer sacrifices in Babylonia?
   D. And has it not in fact been said, Take heed that you not offer your whole offerings in any place which you see but in the place which the Lord will select in the territory of one of the tribes. There you will offer up your whole offerings (Deut. 12:13–14).
   E. When then were the deeds of loving kindness that Daniel did?
   F. He would adorn the bride and make her happy, join a cortege for the deceased, give a penny to a pauper, pray three times every day,
   G. and his prayer was received with favor,
   H. for it is said, And when Daniel knew that the writing was signed, he went into his house—his windows were open in his upper chamber toward Jerusalem—and he kneeled upon his knees three times a day and prayed and gave thanks before his God as he did aforetime (Dan. 6:11).

This entire construction serves as a prologue to what will now follow, an account of the destruction of the Temple, which forms the background to IV:vi.1. We have not a story but a narrative that forms a setting for a saying, so IV:v.2. From "one time...," we are given the occasion on which the colloquy of B and C, took place. Still, there is a narrative side to matters that emerges from the implicit movement from B to C. But classifying the passage as a story seems to me not justified. The autonomy of the sage-story is shown once more, for the story that follows, utterly independent of the preceding, exhibits all of the indicative traits we have defined and demonstrates that the introductory materials have simply provided a proper setting for the stunning account before us.

The Fathers according to Rabbi Nathan (Text A) IV:vi.1–4

1. A. Now when Vespasian came to destroy Jerusalem, he said to (the inhabitants of the city,) "Idiots! why do you want to destroy this city and burn the house of the sanctuary? For what do I want of you, ex-

cept that you send me a bow or an arrow (as marks of submission to my rule), and I shall go on my way."

B. They said to him, "Just as we sallied out against the first two who came before you and killed them, so shall we sally out and kill you."

C. When Rabban Yohanan ben Zakkai heard, he proclaimed to the men of Jerusalem, saying to them, "My sons, why do you want to destroy this city and burn the house of the sanctuary? For what does he want of you, except that you send him a bow or an arrow, and he will go on his way."

D. They said to him, "Just as we sallied out against the first two who came before him and killed them, so shall we sally out and kill him."

E. Vespasian had stationed men near the walls of the city, and whatever they heard, they would write on an arrow and shoot out over the wall. (They reported) that Rabban Yohanan ben Zakkai was a loyalist of Caesar's.

F. After Rabban Yohanan ben Zakkai had spoken to them one day, a second, and a third, and the people did not accept his counsel, he sent and called his disciples, R. Eliezer and R. Joshua, saying to them, "My sons, go and get me out of here. Make me an ark and I shall go to sleep in it."

G. R. Eliezer took the head and R. Joshua the feet, and toward sunset they carried him until they came to the gates of Jerusalem.

H. The gate keepers said to them, "Who is this?"

I. They said to him, "It is a corpse. Do you not know that a corpse is not kept overnight in Jerusalem."

J. They said to them, "If it is a corpse, take him out," so they took him out and brought him out at sunset, until they came to Vespasian.

K. They opened the ark and he stood before him.

L. He said to him, "Are you Rabban Yohanan ben Zakkai? Indicate what I should give you."

M. He said to him, "I ask from you only Yavneh, to which I shall go, and where I shall teach my disciples, establish prayer (Goldin: a prayer house), and carry out all of the religious duties."

N. He said to him, "Go and do whatever you want."

O. He said to him, "Would you mind if I said something to you."

P. He said to him, "Go ahead."

Q. He said to him, "Lo, you are going to be made sovereign."

R. He said to him, "How do you know?"

S. He said to him, "It is a tradition of ours that the house of the sanctuary will be given over not into the power of a commoner but of a king, for it is said, And he shall cut down the thickets of the forest with iron, and Lebanon (which refers to the Temple) shall fall by a mighty one (Is. 10:34)."

T. People say that not a day, two or three passed before a delegation came to him from his city indicating that the (former) Caesar had died and they had voted for him to ascend the throne.

U. They brought him a catapult and drew it up against the wall of Jerusalem.
V. They brought him cedar beams and put them into the catapult, and he struck them against the wall until a breach had been made in it. They brought the head of a pig and put it into the catapult and tossed it toward the limbs that were on the Temple altar.
W. At that moment Jerusalem was captured.
X. Rabban Yohanan ben Zakkai was in session and with trembling was looking outward, in the way that Eli had sat and waited: Lo, Eli sat upon his seat by the wayside watching, for his heart trembled for the ark of God (1 Sam. 4:13).
Y. When Rabban Yohanan ben Zakkai heard that Jerusalem had been destroyed and the house of the sanctuary burned in flames, he tore his garments, and his disciples tore their garments, and they wept and cried and mourned.

2. A. Scripture says, Open your doors, O Lebanon, that the fire may devour your cedars (Zech. 11:1).
B. That verse refers to the high priests who were in the sanctuary (on the day it was burned).
C. They took their keys in their hands and threw them upward, saying before the Holy One, blessed be he, "Lord of the world, here are your keys which you entrusted to us, for we have not been faithful custodians to carry out the work of the king and to receive support from the table of the king."

3. A. Abraham, Isaac, and Jacob, and the twelve tribes were weeping, crying, and mourning.

4. A. Scripture says, Wail, O cypress tree, for the cedar is fallen, because the glorious ones are spoiled, wail, O you oaks of Bashan, for the strong forest is come down (Zech. 11:2).
B. Wail, O cypress tree, for the cedar is fallen refers to the house of the sanctuary.
C. . . . because the glorious ones are spoiled refers to Abraham, Isaac, and Jacob, and the twelve tribes (who were weeping, crying, and mourning).
D. . . . wail, O you oaks of Bashan refers to Moses, Aaron, and Miriam.
E. . . . for the strong forest is come down refers to the house of the sanctuary.
F. Hark the wailing of the shepherds, for their glory is spoiled (Zech. 11:3) refers to David and Solomon his son.
G. Hark the roaring of young lions, for the thickets of the Jordan are spoiled (Zech. 11:3) speaks of Elijah and Elisha.

The story unfolds in a smooth way from beginning to end. It serves, overall, as an account of the power of the Torah to lead Israel through historical crises.

Specifically, the story-teller at three points places the sage into the scale against the emperor: (1) the comparison of Vespasian and the Jewish troops and Yohanan and the Jewish troops; (2) Vespasian and Yohanan in their direct encounter; then at the end, (3) with the destruction itself, Israel embodied by the sage against Rome realized in Vespasian. Then the Torah makes the difference, for, in the end, Israel will outweigh Rome. The story's themes all form part of the larger topic of Torah-learning. The centerpiece is Yohanan's knowledge that the Temple is going to be destroyed. This he acquired in two ways. First of all, his observation of the conduct of the Israelite army led him to that conclusion. But, second and more important, his knowledge of the Torah told him the deeper meaning of the event, which was in two parts. The one side had Rome get a new emperor. The other, and counterpart, side had Israel get its program for the period beyond the destruction.

The opening unit of the story, (IV:vi.1A–T) seems to me seamless. I can point to no element that could have been omitted without seriously damaging the integrity of the story. I see no intrusions of any kind. If that is a correct judgment, then the climax must come only at S, confirmed by T and what follows. That is to say, it is the power of the sage to know the future because of his knowledge of the Torah. Establishing a place for the teaching of disciples and the performance of other holy duties forms a substrate of the same central theme. And yet, deeper still, lies the theme of the counterpart and opposite: Israel and Rome, sage and emperor. That motif occurs, to begin with at A and C, which have Vespasian and Yohanan say precisely the same thing, with one difference. Vespasian calls the Jewish army "idiots," and Yohanan calls the troops "my sons." Otherwise the statements are the same. And the replies, B and D, are also the same. So the first episode sets the emperor and the sage up as opposites and counterparts.

The second episode has the people unwilling to listen to the sage—the emperor has no role here—leading the sage to conclude that it is time to "make an ark and go to sleep in it." If I had to choose a point of reference, it would be not the sleep of death—then Yohanan would have wanted a bier—but the ark of Noah. Yohanan then forms the counterpart, in the story-teller's choice of the word at hand, to Noah, who will save the world beyond the coming deluge. I would then see F–G as a chapter in a complete story. E, on the one side, and H–J, on the other, link that cogent chapter to the larger context. E prepares us to understand why Vespasian recognizes Yohanan, an important detail added precisely where it had to come, and H–J form the necessary bridge to what is coming.

The next component of the unitary story again places Vespasian in the balance against Yohanan. Now Yohanan tells Vespasian what is going to happen. Each party rises to power as a direct outcome of the destruction of the Temple: sage vs. emperor, one in the scale against the other. The colloquy with Vespasian, L–S, form the only part of the story to rely upon a narrative consisting of "he said to him . . . he said to him. . . ." The point, of course, is clear as already stated. Then comes the necessary denouement, in two parts. First, the Temple actually was destroyed. We are told how in T–W. Second, Yohanan responded in mourning, X–Y.

Here too we have that same counterpart and opposite: Rome, then Israel, with Israel represented by the sage, Rome by the emperor. What follows of course is not narrative, let alone story. IV:vi.2 provides an exegesis in A–B, followed by a colloquy. IV:vi.3 is a singleton, and IV:vi.4 joins the destruction of the Temple to the history of Israel and its heroes, all of whom wept as did Yohanan. But I do not see in the inclusion of IV:vi.4 an attempt to compare Yohanan to the named heroes. This is virtually certain, since the story itself at IV:vi.1X invokes the figure of Eli, who is noteworthy for his omission in IV:vi.4.

The Propositions of Sage-Stories: These are the propositions that emerge in the stories about the education, virtue, great deeds, and death of sages in *The Fathers according to Rabbi Nathan*:

(1) VI:v.1 — Great Torah-authorities began their study of the Torah in their mature years.

(2) VI:v.1 — Patience and persistence in the study of the Torah will guarantee progress in learning.

(3) VI:v.1 — Words of the Torah will wear down the heart and produce repentance. It follows that the purpose of study of the Torah is to purify the heart and produce repentance.

(4) VI:v.1 — Study of the Torah requires systematic analytical inquiry, explanation of detail in terms of a whole, not merely repetition of what is written down. Aqiba is the model of the analytical mode.

(5) VI:v.2 — This is not a story, and its point is already made by the story at hand: patience and persistence wear down the rock.

(6) VI:v.3 — This is not a story and it contains no point.

(7) VI:v.4–6 — People should study even though they are poor. Wives who make it possible for their husbands to study the Torah will be richly rewarded.

(8) VI:vi.1–3 — One may begin study of the Torah in mature years.

(9) VI:vi.1–3 — A person who gains a bad odor because of devotion to study of the Torah will become famous in the study of the Torah.

(10) VI:vi.4 — One who cuts his ties to his family because of devotion to study of the Torah will in the end win out over his siblings and inherit his family's property. More generally: sacrifice in the study of the Torah produces a reward.

Stories on a common theme yield a single message: people may begin study of the Torah at any point in life, and, if they work hard, they will achieve success, riches and fame. If they cut off their ties from their family, they will end up inheriting their family's estate, and if their wives tolerate their long absences and support them and their family, their wives will share in their success, riches, and fame. It follows that the stories on the common theme of the origins of great masters, as preserved in *The Fathers according to Rabbi Nathan,* address the question of the breakup of the families of mature men who choose to study the Torah and respond by promising success, riches, and fame, for those who in mature years do convert to study of the Torah. The lesson of the origins of the great masters is to give up home and family in favor of the Torah. To conclude: does the subject-matter—sages—generate its own narrative literary conventions, that differ from those that guide writers of stories about scriptural figures? Do we find propositions emerging from stories about sages? The answers to both questions decidedly favor the affirmative. The distinctive narrative conventions make one cogent and critical point.

The next set of stories yields these propositions on how the knowledge of the Torah affects the personality and character of the sage, and so they make their own, cogent point:

(1) XV:iv.1   One should be patient even when put to the test. Extraordinary patience is the mark of the great sage.

(2) XV:v.1   The Oral Torah comes down from the ancestors and has to be accepted in good faith, since it is only by tradition that the Torah, written or oral, is to be received and understood.

(3) XV:v.2   The great sage is patient, and through patience and reason wins people to the Torah. The sage who is impatient drives people away from the Torah and deprives them of eternal life.

(4) XII:xiii.1 One who reads the Torah but does not serve as a disciple of the sages does not understand the requirements of the Torah and makes errors which will cost him his life.

(5) XLI:ii.1 If one does not spend his time studying the Torah, he is punished by sickness.

(6) XLI:iii.1 A sage must treat other people with unfailing respect: one should always be as soft as a reed and not as tough as a cedar.

We may state the point of these stories in a simple sentence. The sage learns through study of the Torah, which is accomplished solely by service of the master, to be patient and affable and forebearing.

The stories before us follow diverse patterns, but overall the literary conventions we outlined earlier apply here as well: the story about a sage has a beginning, middle, and end, and the story about a sage also rests not only on verbal exchanges ("he said to him . . . , he said to him . . ."), but on (described or implicit) action; the story about a sage unfolds from a point of tension and conflict to a clear resolution and remission of the conflict; the story about a sage rarely invokes a verse of Scripture. These traits assuredly characterize the stories we have reviewed. That means that where a distinct subject comes into view, the narrator of stories about sages will nonetheless follow a fixed set of everywhere-applicable narrative conventions. The point of differentiation among stories derives from the contrast between the topic, sage, Scripture and its heroes, and other topics. Stories are told in different ways for each topical category.

The stories narrated in *The Fathers according to Rabbi Nathan* establish the following propositions:

(1) IV:vi.1   The sage had the foresight that would have prevented the destruction of the Temple. All that was required was to give the gentile monarch a sign of submission.

(2) IV:vi.1   The sage had the foresight to know that Vespasian would be made emperor. This he learned through his deep knowledge of the Torah.

(3) VI:iv.1   The sage had the foresight to plan even before the destruction of Jerusalem for the life of Israel afterward. That life would involve study of the Torah by master and disciples, the saying of prayer, and the fulfillment of religious duties.

(4) VI:iv.1   Israel and Rome weigh in the balance against one another, the emperor and the sage.

(5) XVII:iii.1   The destruction of the Temple placed Israel under the rule of despicable nations.

(6) VI:ix.1   Divine grace will produce a miracle for someone who takes risks in behalf of the community at large. This is not a Torah-study story and it is not told about a sage.

(7) VI:x.2–3   This story is not told about a sage, but it makes a point cogent with sages-stories. The rich man had foresight and showed generosity, but the zealots ruined things.

These propositions yield a simple point: through knowledge of the Torah the sage leads Israel to the age to come, when Israel will supplant Rome. The leadership of zealots on the battlefield led to the destruction of the Temple, the senseless destruction of the food supply of Jerusalem, the calamity that had overtaken Israel. The leadership of the sages, armed with foresight and backed by God, will show the right way. The fresh topic—the sages and history—does not require the invention of modes of narrative different from those that served to deal with the sages' origins, on the one side, and their personality and sagacity, on the other.

The lessons imparted by the stories of the next group are these:

(1) XIV:iv.1   The oral Torah is the true source of comfort.

(2) XXV:ii.1   When a sage dies, he appears before an incorruptible judge, and, moreover, he does not know for sure what his fate will be.

(3) XXV:iii.1–iv.5 The sage dies in full command of his faculties, giving rulings on questions of the Torah, teaching disciples, assured of knowledge of the future by reason of his mastery of the Torah. The sage at death completes his place in a chain of tradition, having learned from his teachers and handed on to his students knowledge of the Torah. But the tradition progressively diminishes, as the failure of each generation to acquire mastery of the Torah equivalent to that of its predecessor exacts a cost through neglect and forgetfulness of the Torah. The disciples therefore have to bear a heavy burden of guilt for neglect of the Torah that they should acquire from their master, just as he bears that same burden of guilt for not learning what he should have learned from his.

(4) XXXVIII:v.2 Sages suffer the death penalty for the sin of pride.

(5) XXXVIII:v.2 Sages are martyred but know that, in due course, God will punish those who have sinned against them.

These death-scenes yield a variety of lessons as noted, since they present nuanced, and not merely conventional, portraits, with a measure of action and not merely set-piece speeches. If I had to single out the main point sages wished through the topic at hand to underline, it is God's perfect justice. This emerges at Lessons 2, 4, and 5, but cannot be excluded even from the story of Eliezer's death in Lesson 3. The historical events represented by sages' deaths, therefore, are so portrayed as to bring that comfort that is contained within the conviction of divine vengeance for injustice and divine faithfulness in exacting justice on sinners and evil-doers, Israelite and gentile alike. For if the sage is punished for mere pride, there can be no limit to the matter—just as Yohanan b. Zakkai says.

The unique medium of *The Fathers according to Rabbi Nathan*

As in *Lamentations Rabbah,* so here too, people told stories because narrative formed the best possible medium for their message. These are the messages I discern in the four types of sage-stories:

First, the sage begins life when he begins Torah-study. And the sages whose origins are found noteworthy both began in mature years, not in childhood (despite the repeated emphasis of The Fathers upon the unique value of beginning Torah-study in childhood). The proposition implicit in origins-stories then is that any male may start his Torah-study at any point in life and hope for true distinction in the Torah-community. While told each in its own terms and subject to differentiation from the other, the stories make essentially the same point, which is that one can begin Torah-study in mature years and progress to the top. When one does so, one also goes from poverty to wealth through public recognition of one's mastery of the Torah, and a range of parallel propositions along the same lines. The supernatural relationship, which has superseded the natural ones to wife and father, generates glory and honor, riches and fame, for the sage, and, through reflection, for the natural family as well.

Second, patience and forebearance, necessary traits of the sage, serve to win people to the Torah and so to give them their share in eternal life. Sagacity attained through discipleship leads to eternal life. Learning not joined to discipleship yields death. The patience of the sage certifies his successful discipleship, his authentic learning of the Torah. The deeper issue—the traits of personality and character that Torah-learning is supposed to instill—is worked out through the stories before us. And that is the important point: it is specifically through telling stories about sages, not merely formulating abstract statements of their ideal, that the authorship of *The Fathers according to Rabbi Nathan* delivers the message at hand.

Third, all sage-stories in *The Fathers according to Rabbi Nathan* that deal not with the lives and deeds of sages concern the one large historical question facing Israel: its history in this world and destiny in the world to come. History finds its definition in a single event: the encounter with Rome, involving two aspects, first, the destruction of the Temple and the sages' role in dealing with that matter; second, the (associated, consequent) repression of Torah-sages and their study. Israel's history in this world works itself out in the encounter with Rome, Israel's counterpart and opposite, and that history in the world coming soon will see a reversal of roles.

Finally, the death-stories are told under the auspices of the Torah and serve to show the supernatural power of the Torah to transform even the moment of death into an occasion of Torah-learning. The two points, start and finish, defined and delineated the middle. How a sage coped with the death of a loved one had to draw into alignment with how a sage studied the Torah; the Torah obviously provided the model of the correct confrontation in historical time. How a sage died—the death-scene, with its quiet lessons—likewise presented a model for others. The encounter with death took narrative shape in the account of how the sage accepted comfort.

It follows that a particular kind of story in *The Fathers according to Rabbi Nathan,* the sage-story, served a particular purpose, conveying a message that that authorship found best expressed in that medium. That is what distinguishes the Aggadic contribution of *The Fathers according to Rabbi Nathan.*

15

The Theology of Rabbinic Midrash

Theology, hermeneutics, and exegesis

The Midrash compilations differ from one another in topic, logic, and rhetoric. But all of them participate in a common theological system, and a shared structure of category-formations. These animate and sustain the entire Rabbinic canon of the formative age. The surveys in the core of the book, from Chapter Three through Chapter Fourteen, have yielded ample evidence for that judgment, which now requires exposition in its own, comprehensive theological framework.

What, exactly, do I mean by "theology"? A suitable definition is given by Ingolf Dalferth:

> Theology rationally reflects on questions arising in pre-theological religious experience and the discourse of faith; and it is the rationality of its reflective labor in the process of faith seeking understanding which inseparably links it with philosophy. For philosophy is essentially concerned with argument and the attempt to solve conceptual problems, and conceptual problems face theology in all areas of its reflective labors.[1]

In general terms theology thinks philosophically about religion. Religion supplies the data, theology orders the data into propositions that can be generalized, tested against further data, and shown to be harmonious and cogent throughout. In Rabbinic Judaism the Torah supplies the data, the facts of God's presence and activity among men. The sages adduce from those data generalizations, rules that may apply to other data. They form a coherent system of such generalizations about God and his self-manifestation in the Torah. Theology is a generalizing science.

Each document we have examined turns out to share with all the others a corpus of theological ideas that cohere. When the Rabbinic sages read any passage of Scripture, they brought to bear a body of cogent theological narratives and of

---

[1] Ingolf U. Dalferth, *Theology and Philosophy* (Oxford: Basil Blackwell Ltd., 1988), p. vii.

coherent ideas, organized in governing category-formations. That is shown by a simple fact. The Rabbinic Midrash compilations prove purposeful. They do not express chaotic, inchoate religious attitudes, incoherent notions about this and that. Rather, the Rabbinic Midrash translates a particular theological conception into a hermeneutic. That hermeneutic repeatedly comes to concrete expression in details of the reading of passage after passage of Scripture. The upshot is readily stated: (1) A theology realized in a (2) hermeneutic generates (3) exegesis, thus provoking (4) that particular and determinate reading that characterizes a Midrash exegesis.

The Midrashic exercise of generalization and systematization

Scripture, in the Rabbinic Midrash exegesis, is read whole at each of its parts. Scripture gives the particular fact, Midrash in its theological formation then embodies the fact in its larger context of comparable Scripture facts. Midrash treats the fact as a case that in the scriptural context yields a general rule. One example of Midrash exegesis as the transformation of a datum into a case to yield a rule is simply stated. God saved Israel at the Sea by doing certain things; when God saves Israel at the end of days, he will do those same things. The initial fact or *act* of salvation then is generalized into the *procedure* of salvation. Precisely what God did at the Sea he will do in the end of days. That yields the theological model of salvation, indicating what is to be looked for and expected. To show that that is so, numerous other instances of generalization and organization will be provided the reader. In the Rabbinic Midrash, then, the Rabbinic sages transform cases into rules, as in the Mishnah and the Talmuds they turn laws into jurisprudence and jurisprudence into social policy. Here, then, the religious information established by Scripture is translated into theological knowledge bearing broad implications for all eternity.

The upshot is simple. The Rabbinic Midrash shows the way in which the Rabbinic sages turned Scripture's theological facts—things that God said or did—into generalizations that further bring into being and encompass new theological facts. In this context, Scripture represents the counterpart of the facts of nature for the domain of holy Israel. Nature's facts generate propositions, syllogisms that are capable of yielding theories governing a broad range of further facts. For the Rabbinic sages, Scripture's facts work in a comparable way, and the Midrash embodies that working. To summarize: the Rabbinic Midrash turns the facts of Scripture into rules capable of encompassing further facts, forming data into a capacious structure, a working system—theology.

Theology deriving from the realization of the encounter with God in Scripture

Rabbinic Midrash takes place in the encounter, in the Torah, between God and Israel. It also spells out, on the foundations of the revealed record of the

Torah (in its broad sense encompassing the Prophets and Writings), the character and implications of that encounter. The categorical structure of every document of the Rabbinic Midrash encompasses the components, God and man; the Torah; Israel and the nations. The working-system of the Torah finds its dynamic in the struggle between God's plan for creation—to create a perfect world of justice—and man's will. That dialectic embodies in a single paradigm the events contained in the sequences of rebellion–sin–punishment–repentance–atonement and exile and return; or the disruption of world order and the restoration of world order. None of these categories and propositions is new; all repeatedly occur in the Midrash compilations we have encountered.

Let me set forth a somewhat more elaborate synopsis of the same story in these few, still-simple propositions by which I mean to define the four principles of the theology that animate the Rabbinic Midrash (1) compilations, (2) process, and (3) exegeses (to revert to our starting point in the Preface):

(1) God formed creation in accord with a plan, which the Torah reveals. Those who possess the Torah—Israel—know God and those who do not—the gentiles—reject him in favor of idols. What happens to each of the two sectors of humanity, respectively, responds to their relationship with God. Israel in the present age is subordinate to the nations, because God has designated the gentiles as the medium for penalizing Israel's rebellion, meaning through Israel's subordination and exile to provoke Israel to repent.

(2) The perfection of creation, realized in the rule of exact justice, is signified by the timelessness of the world of human affairs, their conformity to a few enduring paradigms that transcend change. No present, past, or future marks time, but only the recapitulation of those patterns.

The third proposition is what imparts energy to the Midrash process in particular:

(3) Israel's condition, public and personal, marks flaws in creation. What disrupts perfection is the sole power capable of standing on its own against God's power, and that is man's will. What man controls and God cannot coerce is man's capacity to form intention and therefore choose either arrogantly to defy, or humbly to love, God. Because man defies God, the sin that results from man's rebellion flaws creation and disrupts world order. The paradigm of the rebellion of Adam in Eden governs, the act of arrogant rebellion leading to exile from Eden thus accounting for the condition of humanity. But, as in the original transaction of alienation and consequent exile, God retains the power to encourage repentance through punishing man's arrogance. In mercy, moreover, God exercises the power to respond to repentance with forgiveness, that is, a change of attitude evoking a counterpart change. Since, commanding his own will, man also has the power to initiate the process of reconciliation with God, through repentance, an act of humility, man may restore the perfection of that order that through arrogance he has marred.

(4) God ultimately will restore that perfection that embodied his plan for creation. In the work of restoration death that comes about by reason of sin will die, the dead will be raised and judged for their deeds in this life, and most of them, having been justified, will go on to eternal life in the world to come. In the paradigm of man restored to Eden is realized in Israel's return to the Land of Israel. In that world or age to come, however, that sector of humanity that through the Torah knows God will encompass all of humanity.

The universalizing method of paradigmatic thinking about matters of Scriptural narrative yields a universalistic message concerning the destiny of humanity.

The message that Scripture yields through Rabbinic Midrash exegesis involves the comparison of Adam and Israel, each having possessed paradise—the Garden of Eden and the Land of Israel, respectively—and each having lost it. The last things are to be known from the first. In the just plan of creation humanity was meant to live in Eden, and Israel in the Land of Israel in time without end. Humanity sinned and lost Eden. Israel sinned and lost the Land. So the sages state, had Israel not sinned, Scripture would have closed with the book of Joshua: the people settled in the Land. Then, at the other end of time, the eschatological restoration of humanity to Eden, Israel to the Land, will bring about that long and tragically-postponed perfection of the world order, sealing the demonstration of the justice of God's plan for creation. Risen from the dead, having atoned through death, humanity will be judged in accord with his deeds. Israel for its part, when it repents and conforms its will to God's, recovers its Eden. So the consequences of rebellion and sin having been overcome, the struggle of humanity's will and God's word having been resolved, God's original plan will be realized at the last. The simple, global logic of the system, with its focus on the world order of justice established by God but disrupted by humanity, leads inexorably to this eschatology of restoration: the restoration of balance, order, proportion—eternity for all who worship the one true God.

Components of that system surface hither and yon, and to see how the Midrash compilations participate in the system, we do well to consider how that is the case. To do so, I take six propositions central to the theological system and structure just now sketched out and show how various Midrash compilations set forth those propositions. That exposition of fundamental points of a single theological system and structure comes to expression without regard to its documentary venue. When we differentiate one document from another, or from all others, we cannot point to a theological emphasis or preference that distinguishes one from another or from all others. A single system surfaces hither and yon, indifferent to documentary lines. In my presentation of the twelve documents of the Rabbinic Midrash I repeatedly pointed to that fact. Now I wish in a more general exercise to instantiate it, doing so six times.

My simple point is, the theological expositions we are about to consider could have appeared in any document of Rabbinic Midrash; they fit into any compilation, whatever its particular topical program or even its distinctive doctrinal position, e.g., *Sifra* on the Mishnah's category-formations. I readily concede that six other, equally fundamental, propositions could have served with the same effect of illustrating the theological cogency of the Rabbinic Midrash. To disprove the proposition at hand, I must identify six other presentations in a systematic manner of propositions that contradict the system and structure outlined above. That I cannot do. I do not believe anybody can.

I claim there is none in the whole of the Rabbinic Midrash. That is to say, my six propositions yield six contrary ones. In the Rabbinic Midrash, can I find at any point equivalently systematic constructions that argue for the contrary view? No, I cannot. If I were to frame a null hypothesis, it would look something like this. Rabbinic Midrash does not rest upon a coherent theological foundation. That is shown by the fact that in the Rabbinic Midrash compilations, I can adduce evidence of equal probative value for the proposition that, e.g., the dead are raised by the Messiah in preparation for judgment, and the dead are not raised (by anybody) and are not judged.

Now we shall test that null hypothesis. I do it by presenting a denial of the six propositions we are about to survey in the Midrash compilations. Were I to find in the dozen documents counterpart demonstrations of the opposite of these propositions, it would disprove my claim that these propositions animate the Midrash compilations uniformly: (1) God will resurrect the dead and judge all for eternal life; (2) God will undertake the restoration of humanity to Eden in the form of Israel to Zion; (3) Scripture yields exile and return as the paramount motif of the Scriptural narrative; (4) the redemption from Egypt prefigures the redemption for the world to come; (5) Israel is destined for life in the world to come; (6) gentiles/idolaters will be denied the world to come. Now I state as fact: no proposition contrary to those I shall now present is entertained in a comparably systematic manner, or in any way at all, in any Midrash compilation. That proves that the system now instantiated in affirmative terms prevails and characterizes the entirety of the Rabbinic Midrash compilations.

First: the resurrection of the dead and judgment unto life eternal

Paradigmatic thinking in monotheism necessarily generates the conviction of resurrection. This is stated explicitly. The certainty of resurrection derives from a simple fact of restorationist theology: God has already shown that he can do it, so *Genesis Rabbah* LXXVII:i.1: "You find that everything that the Holy One, blessed be he, is destined to do in the age to come he has already gone ahead and done through the righteous in this world. The Holy One, blessed be he, will raise the dead, and Elijah raised the dead." Sages deem urgent the task of reading outward and forward from Scripture, and at the critical conclusion of their theological system the Oral Torah focuses upon Scripture's evidence, the regularization of Scripture's facts.

Among the components of that doctrine, that resurrection of the dead is a doctrine set forth by the written Torah and demonstrable within the framework of the Torah occupies a principal place in the Oral Torah's exposition of the topic.

That proposition is demonstrated over and over again. Evidence from the Torah concerning the resurrection of the dead is ubiquitous:

Sifré to Deuteronomy CCCVI:xxviii.3

A. And so did R. Simai say, "There is no passage [in the Torah] which does not contain [clear evidence concerning] the resurrection of the dead, but we have not got the power of exegesis [sufficient to find the pertinent indication].
B. "For it is said, 'He will call to the heaven above and to the earth, that he may judge his people' (Ps. 50:4).
C. "'He will call to the heaven above': this refers to the soul.
D. "'and to the earth': this refers to the body.
E. "'that he may judge his people': who judges with him?
F. "And how on the basis of Scripture do we know that Scripture speaks only of the resurrection of the dead?
G. "As it is said, 'Come from the four winds, O breath, and breathe upon these slain, that they may live' (Ez. 37:9)."

Further proofs of the same proposition are abundant, with the following instances representative of the larger corpus. First, we note the recurrent formula, "how on the basis of the Torah do we know . . . ?" Then we are given a sequence of cases, each one of them, as noted earlier, deriving from an individual, none of them appealing to the eternity of the collectivity of Israel.

How does one stand in judgment, meaning, go through the process of divine review of one's life and actions and emerge in the world to come, restored to the Land that is Eden? Proper conduct and study of Torah lead to standing in judgment and consequent the life of the world to come, and not keeping the one and studying the other deny entry into that life. What is striking is the appeal to Eden for just this message about reentry into the Land.

Leviticus Rabbah XXXV:vi:1–3

1. A. Said R. Abba b. Eliashib, "[The reference at Lev. 26:3 to statutes is to] statutes that bring a person into the life of the world to come.
   B. "That is in line with the following verse of Scripture: 'And he who is left in Zion and remains in Jerusalem will be called holy, everyone who has been recorded for life in Jerusalem' [Is. 4:3]—for he is devoted to [study of] Torah, which is called the tree of life."

Now comes the reference to Eden:

2. A. It has been taught in the name of R. Eliezer, "A sword and a scroll wrapped together were handed down from heaven, as if to say to

them, 'If you keep what is written in this [scroll], you will be saved from the sword,
- B. "'and if not, in the end [the sword] will kill you.'
- C. "Whence is that proposition to be inferred? 'He drove out the man, and at the east of the Garden of Eden he placed the cherubim, and a flaming sword which turned every way, to guard the way to the tree of life' [Gen. 3:4].
- D. "The [first] reference to 'the way' refers to the rules of proper conduct, and the second reference, '[the way to] the tree of life' refers to the Torah."

The same message is given in a different framework:

3. A. It was taught in the name of R. Simeon b. Yohai, "A loaf and a rod wrapped together were given from heaven.
   B. "It was as if to say to them, 'If you keep the Torah, lo, here is bread to eat, and if not, lo, here is a staff with which to be smitten.'
   C. "Whence is that proposition to be inferred? 'If you are willing and obedient, you shall eat the good of the land; but if you refuse and rebel, you shall be devoured by the sword'" (Is. 15:19–20).

The world to come, involving resurrection and judgment, will be attained through the Torah, which teaches proper conduct. That simple doctrine yields the proposition here.

Second: the restoration of humanity to Eden

How, exactly, do the sages envisage restoration? Predictably, because they think paradigmatically and not in historical (let alone cyclical) sequences, the sages find models of the end-time in beginnings. That is why in this context they cluster, and systematically review, the two principal ones, liberation, restoration. First is the account of Israel's liberation from Egypt, the initial act of redemption, which will be recapitulated in the end. Second, comes the story of Adam and Eden for their picture of the world to come, the return of Adam to Eden, now in the form of Israel to Zion.

Whatever model serves out of Scripture, the restorationist eschatology is stated in so many words in the following, which appeals to the rhetoric of return, restoration and renewal:

Lamentations Rabbah CXLIII:i.1–4

1. A. "Restore us to yourself, O Lord, that we may be restored!:"
   B. Said the Community of Israel before the Holy One, blessed be He, "Lord of the world, it all depends on you: 'Restore us to yourself, O Lord.'"

- C. Said to them the Holy One, blessed be He, "It all depends on you: 'Return to me and I will return to you, says the Lord of hosts' (Mal. 3:7)."
- D. Said the Community of Israel before the Holy One, blessed be He, "Lord of the world, it all depends on you: 'Restore us, O God of our salvation' (Ps. 85:5)."
- E. Thus it says, "Restore us to yourself, O Lord, that we may be restored!"

Israel insists that restoration depends on God, but God repays the compliment, and the exchange then is equal: God restores Israel when Israel returns to God, just as we learned when we examined the category of repentance and atonement.

Now we see a sequence of models of redemption. First, as anticipated, comes the explicit comparison of Adam's Eden with the coming restoration, part of a sequence of recapitulated paradigms:

2. A. "Renew our days as of old:"
   B. As in the days of the first Adam: "So he drove out the man and he placed at the east of the garden of Eden the cherubim" (Gen. 3:24). [The word for "east" and the word for "of old" using the same letters, the sense, is this: "Renew our days like those of him in connection with whom *kedem* is stated." After being driven out, Adam repented of his sin.]

The restoration involves the Temple offerings as well, which later on are defined in particular; this is here too "as in the days of old:"

3. A. Another interpretation of the phrase, "Renew our days as of old:"
   B. That is in line with this verse: "Then shall the offering of Judah and Jerusalem be pleasant to the Lord as in the days of old and as in ancient years" (Mal. 3:4).

But the restoration is multi-dimensional, since it involves, also, the figures of Moses and Solomon:

- C. "as in the days of old:" this refers to Moses: "Then his people remembered the days of old, the days of Moses" (Is. 63:11).
- D. "and as in ancient years:" this refers to the time of Solomon.

Noah and Abel, for reasons that are specified, now are introduced; they are necessary for the reason given at the end:

4. A. [Another interpretation of the phrase, "Renew our days as of old:"]
   B. Rabbi says, "'as in the days of old' refers to the time of Noah: 'For this is as the waters of Noah unto me' (Is. 54:9).

C. "'and as in ancient years' refers to the time of Abel, prior to whose time there was no idolatry in the world."

Noah represents the moment at which God made his peace with humanity, even in humanity's flawed condition. Of intense interest for my analysis, within the restorationist pattern, Abel stands for the time before idolatry, so explicitly excluding idolaters from the world to come. While Noah, representing all of humanity, and Abel, standing even for antediluvian humanity, make their appearance, the upshot remains exclusionary. The restoration to perfection involves the exclusion of imperfection, and so idolaters cannot enter the new Eden. But, later on, we shall see other, inclusionary dimensions that logically complete the doctrine of the gentiles in the world to come.

Third: exile and return

The pattern that is adumbrated in these statements encompasses not only restoration, but the recapitulation of the paradigm of oppression, repentance, and reconciliation. For restoration cannot stand by itself but must be placed into that context in which the restoration takes on heavy weight. So not only Adam and Eden, but the entire past of suffering but finally of salvation, is reviewed in the same context. Many salvations, not only one, are recorded for Israel, all of them conforming to a single pattern, which imparts its definition upon the final act of salvation as well, the one that comes with personal resurrection and all-Israel's entry into the world to come. So the paradigm of trouble but salvation for Israel works itself out, and it gives reassurance that God will redeem Israel in the future, as he did in the past; a pattern governs throughout. Indeed, the surest evidence of the coming redemption is the oppression that now takes place.

This point is stated in a variety of ways, taking an important place in the set of doctrines set forth around the theme of the world to come. Here is the simplest statement of why suffering and oppression present cause for renewed hope:

Lamentations Rabbah CXXII:i.1

A. "The punishment of your iniquity, O daughter of Zion, is accomplished, he will keep you in exile no longer"

Now comes the point that the very condition of Israel, its life in exile, serves as guarantee of the redemption that God is going to bring about. That relationship of complementarity—oppression, redemption—is why the act of oppression, now realized, validates the hope for the Messiah to signal the advent of the redemption fulfilled in the world to come. The theology not only accommodates the dissonant fact of Israel's subjugation but finds reassurance in it, as is stated in so many words:

B. R. Helbo in the name of R. Yohanan said, "Better was the removing of the ring by Pharaoh [for the sealing of decrees to oppress the Israelites] than the forty years during which Moses prophesied concerning them, because it was through this [oppression] that the redemption came about, while through that [prophesying] the redemption did not come about."

C. R. Simeon b. Laqish said, "Better was the removing of the ring by Ahasueros decreeing persecution of Israel in Media than the sixty myriads of prophets who prophesied in the days of Elijah, because it was through this [oppression] that the redemption came about, while through that [prophesying] the redemption did not come about."

D. Rabbis said, "Better was the Book of Lamentations than the forty years in which Jeremiah prophesied over them, because in it the Israelites received full settlement of their iniquities on the day the temple was destroyed.

E. "That is in line with the following verse: 'The punishment of your iniquity, O daughter of Zion, is accomplished.'"

In narrative form the statement sets forth the proposition that Israel's future is already clear from its present. Here the prophets provide the key to interpreting the one and anticipating the other. Just as the prophetic prediction of the ruin of Jerusalem has been realized, so the same prophets' promises of ultimate salvation will also come about. That yields a certainty about what is going to happen. The whole then forms a coherent pattern, one that reveals what will happen through what has happened.

If we deal with "last things," for the Oral Torah, "last" does not define a temporal category, or even an ordinal one in the exact sense. By "last things," the sages' theology means the model of things that apply at the last, from now on, for eternity. By that, the sages mean to say the last, the final realization or recapitulation of the ever-present and enduring paradigm(s), creation and Exodus, for instance, as we just noticed. Thus, I cannot sufficiently stress, a paradigm organizes and classifies relationships, treats concrete events as merely exemplary. So the actualities of this one's conduct with, and attitude toward, that One are restated in generalizations, laws or rules. "Love God" defines a relationship, and actions and attitudes that express that relationship then may be exemplified by incidents that show what happens when Israel loves God, or what happens when Israel does not love God. These further may be captured, many cases by a single pattern.

Fourth: redemption from Egypt, redemption for the world to come

In concrete terms that means intense interest will focus on the way in which the redemption of Israel from Egypt compares with the advent of the world to come. This point is made explicitly. The fall of the oppressor at the start of Israel's history and the fall of the nations at the end, character of the redemption of that time and of the coming time, will be matched by the fall of the other at the end and the traits of the redemption that is coming. To see how this is made concrete is to enter into the theological workshop of the sages. No passage more clearly exposes the character of their thought—both its method and its message—than the one that requires them to select paradigmatic moments out of the detritus of history:

Pesiqta deRab Kahana VII:xi.2–3

2. A. R. Levi, son-in-law of R. Zechariah, in the name of R. Berekhiah said, "As at the news concerning Egypt, so they shall be startled at the fall of the adversary (Is. 23:5)."
   B. Said R. Eliezer, "Whenever the name of Tyre is written in Scripture, if it is written out [with all of the letters], then it refers to the province of Tyre. Where it is written without all of its letters [and so appears identical to the word for enemy], the reference of Scripture is to Rome. [So the sense of the verse is that Rome will receive its appropriate reward.]"

Now the fall of Egypt is matched by the fall of Rome, which, we surely should anticipate, is a precondition for the advent of the world to come, at which point, at a minimum, the subjugation of Israel to the pagan empire ceases:

3. A. R. Levi in the name of R. Hama bar Hanina: "He who exacted vengeance from the former [oppressor] will exact vengeance from the latter."

Now the first redemption, from Egypt, is shown to match point by point the final redemption, from Edom/Rome. Each detail finds its counterpart in an amazing selection of consequential facts, properly aligned—ten in all:

   B. "Just as, in Egypt, it was with blood, so with Edom [=Rome] it will be the same: 'I will show wonders in the heavens and in the earth, blood, and fire, and pillars of smoke' (Job 3:3).
   C. "Just as, in Egypt, it was with frogs, so with Edom it will be the same: 'The sound of an uproar from the city, an uproar because of the palace, an uproar of the Lord who renders recompense to his enemies' (Is. 66:6).
   D. "Just as, in Egypt, it was with lice, so with Edom it will be the same: 'The streams of Bosrah will be turned into pitch, and the dust thereof into brimstone, and the land thereof shall become burning pitch (Is. 34:9). Smite the dust of the earth that it may become lice' (Ex. 8:12).
   E. "Just as, in Egypt, it was with swarms of wild beasts, so with Edom it will be the same: 'The pelican and the bittern shall possess it' (Is. 34:11).

F. "Just as, in Egypt, it was with pestilence, so with Edom it will be the same: 'I will plead against Gog with pestilence and with blood' (Ez. 38:22).
G. "Just as, in Egypt, it was with boils, so with Edom it will be the same: 'This shall be the plague wherewith the Lord will smite all the peoples that have warred against Jerusalem: their flesh shall consume away while they stand upon their feet' (Zech. 14:12).
H. "Just as, in Egypt, it was with great stones, so with Edom it will be the same: 'I will cause to rain upon Gog . . . an overflowing shower and great hailstones' (Ez. 38:22).
I. "Just as, in Egypt, it was with locusts, so with Edom it will be the same: 'And you, son of man, thus says the Lord God: Speak to birds of every sort . . . the flesh of the mighty shall you eat . . . blood shall you drink . . . you shall eat fat until you are full and drink blood until you are drunk' (Ez. 39:17–19).
J. "Just as, in Egypt, it was with darkness, so with Edom it will be the same: 'He shall stretch over Edom the line of chaos and the plummet of emptiness' (Is. 34:11).
K. "Just as, in Egypt, he took out their greatest figure and killed him, so with Edom it will be the same: 'A great slaughter in the land of Edom, among them to come down shall be the wild oxen' (Is. 34:6–7)."

Merely juxtaposing "Egypt" and "Edom" suffices to establish that we shall compare the one and the other, and the paradigm of redemption emerges. The known, Egypt, bears the distinguishing trait of marking Israel's initial redemption; then the unknown can be illuminated. Therefore, say "Edom" (=Rome) and no one can miss the point. The stakes are sufficiently identified through the combination of the native categories, and all the rest spells out what is clear at the very outset. I do not think the method of paradigmatic thinking finds more lucid expression than in this articulate statement that the redemption that is coming replicates the redemption that is past in a world that conforms to enduring paradigms. And that must encompass, also, the return to Eden that we have many times considered.

Fifth: life in the world to come

This brings us to the actualities of the world to come, what people are supposed to be doing then. What is going to happen in the age to come? Israel will eat and drink, sing and dance, and enjoy God, who will be lord of the dance. What about the restored Temple? The war of Gog and Magog having concluded, the dead having been returned to the Land and raised, the next stage in the restoration of world order requires the reconstruction of the Temple, where, as we recall, God and humanity, Heaven and earth, meet.

Genesis Rabbah XCVIII:ii.7

A. "Then Jacob called his sons and said, 'Gather yourselves together, that I may tell you what shall befall you in days to come:'"

B. R. Simon said, "He showed them the fall of Gog, in line with this usage: 'It shall be in the end of days ... when I shall be sanctified through you, O Gog' (Ez. 38:16). 'Behold, it shall come upon Edom' (Is. 34:5)."

C. R. Judah said, "He showed them the building of the house of the sanctuary: 'And it shall come to pass in the end of days that the mountain of the Lord's house shall be established' (Is. 2:2)."

D. Rabbis say, "He came to reveal the time of the end to them, but it was hidden from him."

So in the now-familiar sequence of restoration, (1) final war, (2) advent of the Messiah and the resurrection and judgment, and (3) the age to come, next in sequence must be (4) the restoration of Israel to the Land, and (5) rebuilding the Temple, destroyed by reason of Israel's sin.

But what purpose would now be fulfilled by the restoration of the Temple cult—the priesthood to the altar, the Levites to the platform, and all Israel to their courtyards, men's and women's respectively? Since the bulk of offerings in the Temple set forth by Moses in the written Torah had focused upon atonement for sin and guilt, what purpose would the Temple, and its surrogate, the synagogue, now serve? There is only a single one. In the age to come, responding to redemption, all offerings but the thanksgiving offering, appropriately, will cease, all prayers but thanksgiving prayers will cease. So it stands to reason:

Leviticus Rabbah IX:vii.1

A. R. Phineas and R. Levi and R. Yohanan in the name of R. Menahem of Gallia: "In time to come all offerings will come to an end, but the thanksgiving offering will not come to an end.

B. "All forms of prayer will come to an end, but the thanksgiving prayer will not come to an end.

C. "That is in line with that which is written, 'The voice of joy and the voice of gladness, the voice of the bridegroom and the voice of the bride,

D. "'the voice of them that say, "Give thanks to the Lord of hosts"' [Jer. 33:11]. This refers to the thanksgiving prayer.

E. "'Who bring a thanksgiving offering to the house of the Lord' [Jer. 33:11]. This refers to the offering of thanksgiving sacrifice.

F. "And so did David say, 'Your vows are incumbent upon me, O God [I will render thanksgivings to you]' [Ps. 56:13].

G. "'I shall render thanksgiving to you' is not written here, but rather, 'I shall render thanksgivings [plural] to you' [Ps. 56:13].

H. "The reference [of the plural usage], then, is to both the thanksgiving prayer and the thanksgiving offering."

Predicting the character of the Temple offerings in the future presents no difficulty when we recall that at that time, judgment will have taken place, sin removed, and atonement completed. So much of the work of the cult will have been accomplished, leaving only the one thing that remains: to give thanks. And it is not to be missed that the offering that will go forward is the offering that gentiles as much as Israelites may present, yet another mark of the eschatological universalism that characterizes the Judaic monotheism.

Sixth: gentiles and the world to come

So much for individuals and the community, for Israelites and for all Israel. What of gentiles, meaning, idolaters? As we realize full well, gentiles with their idolatry simply will cease to exist; some will perish, just as Israelites will perish, just as the Generation of the Flood, the Generation of the Dispersion, the Men of Sodom, and certain Israelites will perish. But a great many will give up idolatry and thereby become part of Israel. The gentiles as such are not subject to redemption; they have no choice at the advent of the world to come but to accept God or become extinct. But that is not the precise formulation that the system as I see it will set forth. Rather, the correct language is not, the gentiles will cease to exist, but rather, the category, "gentiles with their idolatry," will cease to function. Idolatry having come to an end, God having been recognized by all mankind, everyone will enter the category, "Israel."

Predictably, the sages seek analogies and patterns to work out in concrete terms the result of their compelling logic. In the present matter, the future of gentiles is worked out by analogy to Holy Things—the opposite, and the counterpart in context, of gentiles. Some can be redeemed, some not.

Mekhilta attributed to R. Ishmael LXVII:i.31

B. As to Holy Things, there are those that are subject to redemption and there are those that are not subject to redemption;

C. as to things that may not be eaten, there are those that are subject to redemption and there are those that are not subject to redemption;

D. as to things that may not be used for any sort of benefit, there are those that are subject to redemption and there are those that are not subject to redemption;

E. as to fields and vineyards, there are those that are subject to redemption and there are those that are not subject to redemption;

F. as to bondmen and bondwomen, there are those that are subject to redemption and there are those that are not subject to redemption;

G. as to those subject to the death penalty by a court, there are those that are subject to redemption and there are those that are not subject to redemption;

Now, the paradigm having established the possibilities, we come to the critical point.

    H. so in the age to come, there are those that are subject to redemption and there are those that are not subject to redemption.

The nations cannot be redeemed. That is by definition: their idolatry in the end does them in:

    I. The nations of the world are not subject to redemption: "No man can by any means redeem his brother nor give to God a ransom for him, for too costly is the redemption of their soul" (Ps. 49:8–9).
    J. Precious are the Israelites, for the ransom of whose lives the Holy One, blessed be he, has given the nations of the world:
    K. "I have given Egypt as your ransom" (Is. 43:4).
    L. Why so?
    M. "Since you are precious in my sight and honorable, and I have loved you, therefore I will give men for you and peoples for your life" (Is. 43:3–4).

Once more the past forms a presence in the immediate age, as much as the present participates in the past. Here the future of the gentiles realizes their present. They are idolaters—that is why to begin with they are classified as gentiles—and therefore they will not be redeemed, meaning, they will not stand in judgment or enjoy the eternal life of the world to come.

What of gentiles in general, apart from those self-selected by their conduct toward Israel for eternal Gehenna? In the age to come gentiles will renounce idolatry and accept the one God. There simply will be no more gentiles, everyone will serve God and come under the wings of his Presence, within Israel.

Mekhilta attributed to R. Ishmael XXXIII:i.1

    A. "Who is like you, O Lord, among gods? [Who is like you, majestic in holiness, terrible in glorious deeds, doing wonders?]:"
    B. When the Israelites saw that Pharaoh and his host had perished at the Red Sea, the dominion of the Egyptians was over, and judgments were executed on their idolatry, they all opened their mouths and said, "Who is like you, O Lord, among gods? [Who is like you, majestic in holiness, terrible in glorious deeds, doing wonders?]"

Now the nations participate in praising the one, true God of all creation:

    C. And not the Israelites alone said the song, but also the nations of the world said the song.
    D. When the nations of the world saw that Pharaoh and his host had perished at the Red Sea, the dominion of the Egyptians was over, and judgments were executed on their idolatry, they all renounced their idolatry and opened their mouths and confessed their faith in the

Lord and said, "Who is like you, O Lord, among gods? [Who is like you, majestic in holiness, terrible in glorious deeds, doing wonders?]"

Once more the selected paradigm finds the future in the past, the pattern that governs in the quality of the relationship:

> E. So too you find that the age to come the nations of the world will renounce their idolatry: "O Lord, my strength and my stronghold and my refuge, in the day of affliction to you the nations shall come . . . shall a man make himself gods" (Jer. 16:19–20); "In that day a man shall cast away his idols of silver . . . to go into the clefts of the rocks" (Is. 2:20–21). "And the idols shall utterly perish" (Is. 20:18).

The final step in the unfolding of creation according to plan will be the redemption of the nations of the world, their renunciation of idolatry and acceptance of God's rule. That will bring to perfect closure the drama that began with Adam. The nations' response to Israel's Exodus and redemption from Egypt prefigures what is to come about at the end.

The gentiles' rejection of the Torah as portrayed in Rabbinic Midrash chooses as its setting not the last judgment but the first encounter, that is, the giving of the Torah itself. In the timeless world constructed by the Oral Torah, what happens at the outset exemplifies how things always happen, and what happens at the end embodies what has always taken place. The basic thesis is identical—the gentiles cannot accept the Torah because to do so they would have to deny their very character. But the exposition retains its interest because it takes its own course.

Of special interest, the Torah is embodied in some of the ten commandments—not to murder, not to commit adultery, not to steal. The gentiles are rejected for not keeping the seven commandments assigned to the children of Noah. The upshot is that the reason that the gentiles rejected the Torah is that the Torah prohibits deeds that the gentiles do by their very nature. Israel ultimately is changed by the Torah, so that Israel exhibits traits imparted by their encounter with the Torah. So too with the gentiles, by their nature they are what they are; the Torah has not changed their nature. Once more a single standard applies to both components of humanity, but with opposite effect:

Sifré to Deuteronomy CCCXLIII:iv.1–2

> 1. A. Another teaching concerning the phrase, "He said, 'The Lord came from Sinai'":
>   B. When the Omnipresent appeared to give the Torah to Israel, it was not to Israel alone that he revealed himself but to every nation.
>   C. First of all he came to the children of Esau. He said to them, "Will you accept the Torah?"
>   D. They said to him, "What is written in it?"
>   E. He said to them, "'You shall not murder' (Ex. 20:13)."

F. They said to him, "The very being of 'those men' [namely, us] and of their father is to murder, for it is said, 'But the hands are the hands of Esau"' (Gen. 27:22). 'By your sword you shall live' (Gen. 27:40)."

At this point we cover new ground: other classes of gentiles that reject the Torah. Now the Torah's own narrative takes over, replacing the known facts of world politics, such as the earlier account sets forth, and instead supplying evidence out of Scripture as to the character of the gentile group under discussion:

G. So he went to the children of Ammon and Moab and said to them, "Will you accept the Torah?"
H. They said to him, "What is written in it?"
I. He said to them, "'You shall not commit adultery' (Ex. 20:13)."
J. They said to him, "The very essence of fornication belongs to them [us], for it is said, 'Thus were both the daughters of Lot with child by their fathers' (Gen. 19:36)."
K. So he went to the children of Ishmael and said to them, "Will you accept the Torah?"
L. They said to him, "What is written in it?"
M. He said to them, "'You shall not steal' (Ex. 20:13)."
N. They said to him, "The very essence of their [our] father is thievery, as it is said, 'And he shall be a wild ass of a man' (Gen. 16:12)."
O. And so it went. He went to every nation, asking them, "Will you accept the Torah?"
P. For so it is said, "All the kings of the earth shall give you thanks, O Lord, for they have heard the words of your mouth" (Ps. 138:4).
Q. Might one suppose that they listened and accepted the Torah?
R. Scripture says, "And I will execute vengeance in anger and fury upon the nations, because they did not listen" (Mic. 5:14).

At this point we turn back to the obligations that God has imposed upon the gentiles; these obligations have no bearing upon the acceptance of the Torah; they form part of the ground of being, the condition of existence, of the gentiles. Yet even here, the gentiles do not accept God's authority in matters of natural law:

S. And it is not enough for them that they did not listen, but even the seven religious duties that the children of Noah indeed accepted upon themselves they could not uphold before breaking them.
T. When the Holy One, blessed be He, saw that that is how things were, he gave them to Israel.

Now comes another parable, involving not a king but a common person:

2. A. The matter may be compared to the case of a person who sent his ass and dog to the threshing floor and loaded up a *letekh* of grain on his

ass and three *seahs* of grain on his dog. The ass went along, while the dog panted.

B. He took a seah of grain off the dog and put it on the ass, so with the second, so with the third.

C. Thus was Israel: they accepted the Torah, complete with all its secondary amplifications and minor details, even the seven religious duties that the children of Noah could not uphold without breaking them did the Israelites come along and accept.

D. That is why it is said, "The Lord came from Sinai; he shone upon them from Seir."

In the conclusion we see how the Judaic version of monotheism forms a complete system, making provision for all humanity within the framework of the revealed Torah.

Theology, hermeneutics, and exegesis

The theology of the Rabbinic Midrash tells a simple, sublime story:

(1) God created a perfect, just world and in it made man in his image, equal to God in the power of will.

(2) Man in his arrogance sinned and was expelled from the perfect world and given over to death. God gave man the Torah to purify his heart of sin.

(3) Man, educated by the Torah, in humility can repent, accepting God's will of his own free will. When he does, man will be restored to Eden and eternal life.

In our terms, we should call it a story with a beginning, middle, and end. In sages' framework, we realize, the story embodies an enduring and timeless paradigm of humanity in the encounter with God: man's powerful will and God's powerful word in conflict, and the resolution thereof.

The Rabbinic sages claimed in their Midrash exegesis fully to spell out the message of the written Torah, as they do explicitly in nearly every document and on nearly every page of the Midrash compilations. So too did others outside of their circles. The sages' reading of Scripture recovers, in proportion and accurate stress and balance, the main lines of Scripture's principal story, the one about creation, the fall of man and God's salvation of man through Israel and the Torah, when the Torah succeeds in teaching Israel to repent. If, as Brevard Childs states, "The evangelists read from the New [Testament] backward to the Old,"[2] we may say very simply, *the sages through Midrash exegesis read from the entire written Torah forward to the oral one.*

---

[2] *Biblical Theology of the Old and New Testaments*, p. 720.

Index of Scripture and Ancient Sources

HEBREW BIBLE

Genesis
1:1   170
1:4   189
2:15   42
2:16   42
2:18   113
3:4   213
3:9   42
3:11   42
3:12   113
3:23   42
3:24   42, 214
4:4   76
5:1   62
7:1   76
9:6   58
10:7   139
10:9   126
13:16   44
14:1   33
15:3   189
15:5   189
16:12   53, 223
19:36   53, 223
21:12   76
22:8   170
26:29   115
26:33   115
27:22   53, 223
27:40   53
29:1   36
29:6–7   40
29:40   39
36:43   126
39:10–13   26
41:14   26
49:15   53

Exodus
5:14   95
5:20   136
6:26   127
6:27   127
8:12   217
8:16   26
12:1–2   176
12:1–13:16   47
12:1–23:19   47
12:22   25
12:29–32   176
13–17   47
13:17–18   176
14–31   47
14:13   122
15:1–21   47
15:2   133, 135, 155
15:3   51
15:22–17:7   47
15:24   155
15:25   155
16:3   112
17:7   155
17:8–18:27   47
17:15   155
19:1ff.   176
19:1–20:26   47
20:2   55, 169
20:3   54, 55, 135
20:11   24
20:13   53, 222, 223
20:19   39
21:1–22:23   47
22:24–23:19   47
22:27   141
24:7   53, 139, 148, 155
24:10   51, 52
25:17   114
27:20   42
30:12   175
30:17   93
31:12–13   47
34:4   96
34:28   24
35:1–3   47
40:34   93

Leviticus
9:24   93
10:1   93
10:2   93
10:4   93
11:1–8   82
11:4   80, 81
11:4–8   79
11:5   81, 82
11:6   81, 82
11:7   80, 81, 82
18:2   54
19:1–4   70
19:2   69
19:4   57
19:13   65, 66
19:17–18   70
22:26   176
22:27   76
22:28   172

23:11   176
23:17   94
23:39   25
23:39–40   23
23:39–43   177
24:2   42
25:45   123
26:3   212

Numbers
1:51   12
7:1   175
7:1–6   92, 95, 96
7:9   96
7:10   98
7:12   93
9:15   155
12:2   114
13:32   155
19   93
19:1ff.   176
21:5   113
21:17   36
25:1   113, 155
26:9   126
28:1–4   176
29:35–39   177
32:12   155

Deuteronomy
1:1   20, 109, 112, 113, 114
4:16   57
4:17   57
4:18   57
5:19   59
9:9   24
10:17   99
12–26   102
12:13–14   198
14:2   76
14:7   79, 82
14:8   79
14:22   176
16:21   57
17:16   122
22:12   170
24:15   66
25:17–19   175
28:49   122
28:66–68   119
28:69   123
29:1   123
31:9   20, 109
32:15   20, 109

32:17   56
32:39   52
33:2   52, 53

Joshua
7:1   155
7:19   155

Ruth
1:17   143

1 Samuel
4:13   200
6:3   96
16:18   135
17:14   127

2 Samuel
6:7   96
6:8   97
7:18   3
23:1   21, 22, 110
23:2   22, 110
23:6   110

1 Kings
5:1   128
5:2   3
5:4   128
6:38   28
8:66   36
18:10   128
20:1   129
20:15   128

2 Kings
14:14   129

1 Chronicles
1:27   127
14:17   128
15:11–15   97
24:4–6   96
24:19   97

2 Chronicles
3:4   129
18:18   140
28:22   126
32:12   127
32:23   4
33:13   4

Ezra
1:2   81, 129
1:3   129
4:21   126
6:2   126
6:3   126, 129
6:14   126
7:9   127
8:17   127

Nehemiah
9:7   76

Esther
1:1   119, 124
2:19   81
3:14   121
7:4   124
8:7   123

Job
3:3   217
21:10–12   48
32:16   140
38:14   44
40:29   135

Psalms
20:7   3
29:10   148
30:2   80
35:6   27
36:8   136
43:3–4   221
43:4   221
49:8–9   221
50:4   212
50:7   139
56:13   219
68:30   128
69:13   164
72:11   128
72:19   128
73:25   81
75:4   140
75:11   81
78:40   155
78:70   76
80:14   80
82:6   141
85:5   214
89:3   197
93:1   80
96:10   80

99:1   80
105:7   127
106:7   113, 155
106:19   155
106:20   133
106:23   76
106:30   155
115:1   80
119:62   137
137:1   171
138:4   223
147:8   79
147:12   80

Proverbs
8:10   23, 25
9:5   23, 25
9:8   111
10:2   191
18:9   125
22:29   26, 27, 28

Qoheleth (Ecclesiastes)
1:1   22, 110
1:5–7   22, 110
3:15   75

Song of Songs
1:2   145
1:5   154
5:15   59
8:7   24

Isaiah
2:2   219
2:20–21   222
4:3   212
5:1   4
6:2   140
8:2   12
10:34   198
11:4   5, 136
15:19–20   213
20:18   222
22:1–14   166
23:5   217
29:15   27
31:1   122
33:8   168
34:5   219
34:6–7   218
34:9   217
34:11   217, 218
35:5   44

37:3   4
37:19   55
38:21   4
40:1–2   176
40:2   160
41:2   189
41:4   52
43:10   45, 59
44:6   52
45:19   52
46:4   52
46:7   56
47:6   81
49:14–16   176
51:12–15   177
53:5   4, 136
54:1ff.   177
54:9   76, 214
54:11–14   177
55:2   23, 25
60:1–3   177
60:19   156
60:20   156
61:10–11   177
63:11   214
66:6   217
66:20   95

Jeremiah
1:1–3   176
2:4–6   176
2:7   42
7:9   58
9:19–21   161
10:2   189
11:15   168
13:17   166
14:19   168
15:1   42
16:19–20   222
26:18   12
30:4   21, 109, 110
30:5–7   21, 110
30:20   23
31:15–16   40
31:15–17   173
33:11   219
42:16   122
51:64   21, 109

Lamentations
1:1   42
1:1–2   176
2:3   166

3:5   129

Ezekiel
16:6   154, 155
16:32   58
20:8   154
21:14   79, 80
23:14   152
37:9   212
38:16   219
38:22   218
39:17–19   218

Daniel
2:38   129
2:49   81
3:15   152
4:37   80
6:11   198
6:26   129
7:9   52
7:10   52
7:16   140
9:11   42, 169
12:1   140

Hosea
3:1   58
4:2   58
5:15   166
6:6   197, 198
6:7   41
9:15   42
14:1–3   177

Amos
1:1   21, 109
4:1   21, 109
9:7   154

Obadiah
1:21   82

Micah
5:14   223

Habbakuk
3:6   53

Zechariah
8:4   12
8:5   12
11:1   200
11:2   200

11:3   200
14:2   5, 136
14:12   218

Malachi
3:4   214
3:7   214

MISHNAH

ʾAbot
1:1   64

Baba Meṣiʿa
9:11A   66
9:11B   66
9:12A   65
9:12F   65
9:12G–H   65

Taʿanit
4:6   9
4:7   10

Yadayim
3:5   157

TOSEFTA

Baba Meṣiʿa
10:2E   65

BAVLI

Šabbat
152b–153a   188
156a–b   189

MIDRASH

Esther Rabbah I
I:i.1–11   119
I:i.8   117
II:i.1   117
III:i.1   118
III:i.2   118
III:i.4   118
III:i.5–7   118
V:i.1   117
VIII:i.1   117

IX:i.1   118
IX:i.3   118
X:i.1–11   124
XI:i.1   118
XX:i.1   118
XXIII:ii.16   117
XXXVI:ii.4   117

Fathers According to Rabbi Nathan
IV:v.1–3   197
IV:v.2   198
IV:vi.1   198, 201, 204
IV:vi.1–4   198
IV:vi.2   202
IV:vi.3   202
IV:vi.4   202
VI:iv.1   204
VI:v.1   202
VI:v.2   202
VI:v.3   202
VI:v.4–6   202
VI:vi.1–3   202
VI:vi.4   202
VI:ix.1   204
VI:x.2–3   204
XII:xiii.1   203
XIV:iv.1   204
XV:iv.1   203
XV:v.1   203
XV:v.2   203
XVII:iii.1   204
XXV:ii.1   204
XXV:iii.1–iv.5   205
XXXVIII:v.2   205
XLI:ii.1   203
XLI:iii.1   203

Genesis Rabbah
I:ii   43
II:i   44
II:ii   43
V:i   43
VI:v   44
VIII:ii   44
XII:ix   41
XIX:vii   41
XIX:ix.2   41
XX:i   43
XX:vii   43
XXI:ii   42
XXIV:v   41
XXIV:vii   40
XXIV:ix   41

XXVIII:v   41
XXXIV:i   41
XXXIV:ii–iv   40
XXXIV:x   41
XXXIV:xiii   43
XXXIX:i   43
XXXIX:iii   43
XXXIX:v   43
XXXIX:ix   43
XLI:i   43
XLI:ix.1   44
XLII:iv.4   33
XLIV:i   43
XLVIII:vi   44
XLIX:ix   41
LII:xi   42
LIII:ix   43
LXIII:vi   43
LXV:i   80
LXIX:v   43
LXIX:vii   43
LXX:viii.2–7   35
LXX:ix.1   39
LXXV:iv   43
LXXV:ix   43
LXXVII:i.1   211
LXXVIII:xii   44
XCVIII:ii.7   219

Lamentations Rabbah
I:i.1–7   160
II:i   160
II:ii   161
III:i   161
IV:i   161
VI:i   161
VII:i   161
VIII:i   161
IX:i   164
X:i   161
XI:i   161
XIII:i   161
XV:i   161
XVI:i   161
XVII:i   164
XVIII:i   164
XIX:i   161
XX:i   161, 164
XXII:i   161
XXIV:i   161
XXIV:ii   161
XXIV:ii.1–3   165
XXV:i   161
XXVII:i   161

XXX:i   161
XXXI:i   161
XXXV:ii 161
XXXV:iii 161
XXXV:iv 161
XXXV:vi 162
XXXV:vii 162
XXXVI:ii 162
XXXVI:iv 162
XXXVI:v 162
XXXVII:i 164
XXXVII:ii 165
XXXIX:iii 162
XL:i   165
XL:ii 162
XLI:i 162
XLII:i 162
XLIV:i 164
XLVIII:i 162
L:i   162
LIII:i 162
LV:i 164
LVI:i 162
LVI:i.14 160
LVII:ii 162
LIX:ii 162
LIX:iii 165
LX:i 162
LXI:i 162
LXIV:i 162
LXIX:i 162, 164
LXXV:i 162
LXXIX:ii 162
LXXXIII:i 164
LXXXVI:i 163
LXXXVII:i 163
LXXXIX:i 163
XCV:i 163
CXXII:i 163
CXXII:i.1 215
CXXIII:i 163
CXXIX:i 163
CXXX:i 163
CXXXI:i.1B 163
CXXXVII:i 165
CXL:i.1–2 11
CXL:i.1G 163
CXL:i.2J 163
CXLI:i 163
CXLII:i 163
CXLIII:i 163
CXLIII:i.1–4 213
CXLIV:i 163

Leviticus Rabbah
IX:vii.1 219
XIII:v.9–13 79
XXVII:v.1–2 75
XXXV:vi.1–3 212

Mekhilta attributed to R. Ishmael
XXVII:ii.1 47
XXVII:ii.4–7 47
XXVII:ii.9–17 47
XXXIII:i.1 221
LI:i.1 51
LI:i.4–5 51
LI:i.8–10 51
LII:ii.1 56
LIV:iii.1–6 58
LXII:i.1–7 54
LXII:i.10 54
LXVII:i.31 220

Pesiqta deRab Kahana
VII:xi.2–3 217

Ruth Rabbah
I:i 134
I:i.1–11 139
II:i 134
III:i 133
III:ii 133
III:iii 134
IV:i 134
IV:ii 134
V:i 134
V:iii 134
VIII:i.3 134
X:i 133
XI:i.1C 134
XVI:i.2B 134
XVIII:i.1–3 134
XIX:i 134
XX:i 134
XX:i.1–4 142
XXI:i.1–3 143
XXII:i 134
XXII:i.1 138
XXVI:i 134
XXVI:i.4 135
XXXIV:i.1 135
XXXIV:i.2 135
XXXV:i.1–5 135
XXXVI:ii 135
XXXVIII:i.1 135
XXXVIII:i.2 138

XL:i.1–5 3
XL:i.5 136
LII:i.1 138
LII:i.1–3 136
LV:i.1 137
LVI:i 137
LVII:i 137
LIX:i.5 137
LXVIII:i 137
LXXIV:i 133
LXXIX:i 137
LXXX:i 137
LXXXI:i.1–2 137

Sifra
VII:v.1–2 68
CXCIX:ii.1–7 65

Sifré to Deuteronomy
I:i.1–5 20, 109
I:ii.1–2 111
I:iii.1 112
I:iii.2 112
I:iv.1–x.4 112
I:vii.2–3 113
I:vii.4 113
I:viii.1 113
I:ix.1 114
I:ix.2 114
I:x.4 115
CCCVI:xxviii.3 212
CCCXLIII:iv.1–2 222

Sifré to Numbers
I:x.1 99
I:x.2–3 99
I:xi.1 99
VIII:viii.1–2 101
XI:i.1–10 100
XVIII:i.1 101
XLI:ii.2 100
XLI:ii.4 100
XLII:i.2 99
XLIV:i.1–ii.3 92
XLV:i.1–ii.4 94
XLVI:i.1–ii.2 96
XLVII:i.1–2 97
LXXVIII:i.1 100
LXXXIV:iv.1 100
CXII:iv.2 100
CXII:iv.3 100
CLXI:iii.2 99

Song of Songs Rabbah

I:i.1   26
I:i.3–9   26
I:iv.8   150
I:v.1   150
I:v.9   150
II:ii.1   150
II:ii.13   150
IV:ii.1   151
IV:ii.2   151
IV:ii.5   151
V:i.1–12   154
V:ii.5   155
V:iv.1   152
V:iv.3   152
VI:iii.7   151
IX:i.10   150
X:i.1–2   150
X:ii.1–2   150
X:ii.1–4   150
XI:i.1–8   150
XV:i.1   153
XVIII:iii.1–3   152
XIX:i.5   147
XIX:i.8   149
XIX:i.9   149
XIX:i.11   148
XX:i.1   149
XXII:i.1–8   151
XXIII:i.1–4   156
XXIV:i.1–4   147
XXIV:ii.1   154
XXIV:ii.4   154
XXIV:iii.2   154
XXV:i.1–4   154
XXVI:ii.1   150
XXIX:i.1–2   148
XXX:i.1   151
XXXI:ii   148
XXXII:ii.1   149
XXXII:ii.4–6   149
XXXIII:i.1–8   147
XXXV:i.3–4   151
XXXVI:i   151
XXXVII:i   151
XXXVIII:ii.1   151
XLIII:i–v   150
XLIV:i.1–4   153
XLIV:ii.1   147
XLV:i   153
XLVII:i.1–3   153
XLVIII:i.8   151
XLVIII:ii   149
XLVIII:v   149
XLVIII:vi–ix   149
XLVIII:ix.6–10   152
LII:ii.1   154
LII:ii.5   154
LII:ii.7   154
LXIII:i.1–2   150
LXV:i.1   150
LXV:i.3   150
LXV:i.4   150
LXV:i.10   150
LXIX:i.1   149
LXXI:i.1–8   151
LXXI:i.21–22   151
LXXII:i.1   151
LXXII:i.3   151
LXXIV:i.1–9   151
LXXV:i.1   151
LXXVII:i.1   149
LXXX:i.1–2   147
LXXXVII:i.7   152
LXXXVII:i.9   151
LXXXVIII:i.1–5   152
LXXXIX:i.1–11   150
XCIV:i.4–7   147
XCV:i.1   153
XCVII:i.1   146
XCVII:i.4   146
XCVIII:i.1   146
XCVIII:i.2   147
XCIX:i.1–2   148
CI:i.1   147
CII:i.1–2   147
CII:i.6–7   147
CIX:i.1–3   149
CXII:i–iii   152
CXIII:i.1   152
CXV:i.1–5   153
CXV:ii.1–3   153

j621.8   MRL

Ford, Barbara.

The elevator

APR 26 1994
WITHDRAWN

DATE DUE

C S NOV 1983	5-51 1/22/98				
R H X AUG 1984	5-57 3/18/99				
L S FEB 1985					
V S DEC. 1986					
1988					

VERMONT DEPT. OF LIBRARIES
0 0 0 0 1 0 4 5 4 7 2 5 2

DEMCO 38-301

ACKNOWLEDGEMENTS

A number of people helped make this book possible. My special thanks to Robert L. Leiner of the Otis Elevator Company for reviewing the manuscript and clarifying some technical points. Thanks also to the following:

John Mayo, Peter C. Thompson, William J. Mount, and Alex Kelemen, Otis Elevator Company
Kathy Rucki and Andrew Popp, Westinghouse Elevator Company
Edward A. Donoghue, National Elevator Industry, Inc.
William C. Sturgeon, *Elevator World*
Robert D. Millar, Park Plaza Services

PHOTOCREDITS
The Metropolitan Museum of Art   p. 16
Barbara Ford   pp. 18, 19, 21, 22
David Wool   pp. 26, 39
J. W. Taylor, Chicago Historical Society   p. 36
Matthew Mauro, Publicity Department, The Waldorf-Astoria Hotel   p. 45
Sears, Roebuck and Company   p. 57
Westinghouse Elevator Company   p. 47
All others courtesy of Otis Elevator Company

Pulleys, 18–19, 24, 30, 37, 58
Pumps: steam, 27; electric, 40

Radio City Music Hall stage, 40
Rail-making machine, 9
Ratchet bars, 25
RCA Building, 45
"Real time," 56
Rockefeller Center, 45–46, 49
Ropes, 8, 20, 24, 25, 30

Safety codes, 41
Safety devices, 10, 24, 25, 27, 41
St. Paul Building, 36
Sears, Roebuck and Company, 56
Sears, Tower, 56–57
Selector, 49
Semiconductor, 50
Shaduf, 17–18
Siemens, Werner von, 32
Signal Control, 43, 45, 46
Silicon, 54
"Sky Lobby," 57
Skyscrapers, 35–37, 43
Solid state device, 49–50, 54
Speech recognition devices, 58
Speech synthesizer, 55
Steam engine, 24, 25, 32

Steam power, 12, 13, 24, 25, 29, 32
Swiss Building, 46
Syracuse, siege of, 21

Tingely Company, 9
Treadmill, 23
Trinity Church, New York, 12
Tubes, 25, 27. *See also* Vacuum tubes

United Technologies, 58

Vacuum tubes, 46, 50
Von Siemens, Werner. *See* Siemens, Werner von

Waldorf Astoria Hotel, 46
Water power, 25, 27, 40
Watt, James, 24
Wells, 20
Westinghouse Electric Corporation, 45
Westinghouse Elevator Company, 45, 48, 54, 56, 58
Wheels, 18, 20, 23,
Windlass, 20, 23
Wires, 50
Woolworth Building, 37, 39–40
World Trade Center, 50–51

63

"observation," 58; oldest extant, 23; roped hydraulic, 30, 32, 35, 37, 40–41; safety, 7; space saving, 56–57; speed of, 45, 57; steam-powered, 12, 13, 29, 32; talking, 52–55
Elisha Graves Otis Research and Development Center, 58
Empire State Building, 43, 45
Escalator, 56

"Flying chair," 24

Gears, 37, 40
Gold Rush, 10
Governor, 41
Grease rack, 27
Guide rails, 9, 24, 25, 41

Hale Elevator Company, 30
Haughwout, E. V., & Company, 12–13
Hoists, 24–27; first passenger, 12; hydraulic, 25, 27; safety, 8, 10, 12, 13; steam, 12, 24–25, 27
Home Insurance Building, 35
Hotels, 12, 46, 58
Hydraulics, 25–27, 29–32, 35, 37, 40

Integrated circuits, 54

Leiner, Robert L., 64
Leonard, Harry Ward, 32
Leveling, 43, 48
Lifting devices, early, 17–27
Lord and Taylor Department Store, 33

Machine room, 37, 48, 58
Magnetism, 59
Maize, Josia, 9
Masonry frame buildings, 35–36
Master controller, 48–49
Metal frame buildings, 35–36
Microprocessors, 54-56, 58
Monasteries, 23–24

Net, 23–24
Newhouse, Benjamin, 9, 10, 11, 12

Oil, 40
Otis, Charles R., 11, 15, 29, 30, 50
Otis, Elisha Graves, 8, 9, 10, 11, 12, 14, 15, 25, 27, 29, 41, 50
Otis, Norton, 29, 30
Otis Brothers and Company, 29, 30, 34
Otis Elevator Company, 37, 39, 43, 48, 50, 54, 56, 58, 60, 64; Transportation Technology Divison, 58
Otis Steam Elevator Works, 13, 29

Paul, Saint, 22–23
Pencil sharpener, as windlass model, 20
"People Mover," 58–60
Platforms, 7–8, 25, 27; enclosed, 12
Plunger, 25, 30, 37, 40
Power sources, 24–25, 32, 37, 40
Printed circuits, 50, 54
Public Service Electric & Gas Building, 56

INDEX

Abbey of Mont St. Michel, 23
Aircraft carriers, 40
American Society of Mechanical Engineers (ASME), 41
Archimedes, 20
Architecture, elevator's effect on, 27, 29–41
Art Deco style, 46
Assyria, 18
Automatic controls, 42–51
Axle, 20

Baldwin, Cyrus W., 30
Bank, of cars, 48–49
Baskets, 22–25
Beaver Building, 39
"Brain transplants," 49
Brakes, 25, 41

Cab, 12
Cables, 37, 38, 39, 58; safety, 41
Cars, 12, 38, 46–47, 48, 49; scheduling of, 48; with a view, 58
China, 20
Chip, 54
Chrysler Building, 46
Computers, 48, 50, 54, 56
Controllers, 48–49
Convent of St. Catherine, 23
Counterweight, 17, 18, 24, 25, 38–39, 58

Crank, 20
Crystal Palace Exhibition, New York, 7–8, 12, 25
Cylinder, 37

Demerest Building, 32
Diptheria epidemic, 13–14
Display panels, 53–55
Double Deckers, 56
Drive sheave, 37–39, 40, 41
Drum, 20, 25, 37

Edison, Thomas, 15
Egypt, 16–18; tomb paintings, 17
Eiffel Tower, 34–35
Electric call buttons, introduced, 34
Electric motor, 32, 37, 39, 40
Electromagnets, 59
Electronics, 46, 48, 49, 54
Elevator mechanics, 50
Elevator operators, 11, 42–43, 45, 46
Elevator starters, 42–43, 46
Elevators: automatic, 40, 42–51; beauty of early, 29, 30; with "brains," 42–51; electric, 32, 34, 37–40; fastest, 57; geared traction, 40; gearless traction, 37, 39–40, 42, 43, 48; name used, 12–13;

61

Someday elevators may run on a cushion of air like Otis's People Mover.

The People Mover runs horizontally, but Otis engineers say there is no technical reason why the same type of motor could not be used for elevators, too. Someday, you may be able to take a vehicle that will move you horizontally to your destination and then vertically to your floor—all without your ever getting out of the vehicle.

Glass-walled elevators give passengers a view. Hyatt Regency Hotel, Atlanta, Georgia.

there is a row of electromagnets on the bottom of the vehicle and a strip of non-magnetic metal in the center of the vehicle's track. The electromagnets create a moving wave of magnetism that results in another wave of magnetism in the track. The waves push against each other and move the vehicle along. It actually glides on a cushion of air.

Another new feature in elevators is the car with a view. Ever since the turn of the century, elevator cars have been enclosed boxes traveling in enclosed shafts. Most of them still are, but Otis recently introduced the glass-walled "observation elevator." There wouldn't be much to see in a glass-walled elevator if it ran up an enclosed shaft, so Otis put the shaft outside the building, where people could see the surroundings. These elevators have proved very popular, especially for hotels, and now Westinghouse and some smaller firms offer them, too.

What's ahead for elevators? Increased use of microprocessors, for one thing. At the new Elisha Graves Otis Research and Development Center in Farmington, Connecticut (Otis became part of United Technologies, a Connecticut-based corporation, in 1976), engineers are looking at microprocessor-based speech recognition devices. These devices understand human speech. Today they are very primitive but someday you will be able simply to tell the elevator your floor. Elevators like this would also recognize your voice. If someone gets on an elevator and asks to be taken to a certain floor, the elevator could be programmed so as not to move unless it recognized the voice as that of someone who belongs on the floor.

Elevators may not even have cables, pulleys, and counterweights in the future. Engineers in Otis's Transportation Technology Division, which is located in Denver, Colorado, have developed a new vehicle called the "People Mover." In these vehicles,

both offer another space-saving design, the "Sky Lobby." Instead of elevator cars running from the first floor to the top, there are lobbies at two in-between points where you change for cars to higher floors. Fewer elevators are needed for the upper floors because some of the people have gotten off at lower floors. The space saved on elevator shafts on the upper floors can be used for offices. In this design the shafts are stacked one on top of the other, like a layer cake, with a machine room on top of each layer.

These two 110-story buildings do have several large express cars that run all the way from the first floor to floors near the top. The ones in the Sears Tower make the trip to the 103rd floor observation deck in just 55 seconds, traveling at 2000 feet per minute. It's the fastest elevator ride in the world.

The Westinghouse express elevators in the Sears Tower in Chicago make the world's fastest elevator trip.

Public Service Electric & Gas Building in Newark, New Jersey, to see microprocessor elevators in action. The Otis elevators in this glass-walled building don't look much different from other modern elevators, but they answer 90 percent of the calls within ten seconds. This fast response is possible because the microprocessors that control them work in what is called "real time" in computer terminology. This means they respond to what is happening while it is happening.

The PSE&G elevators have some unusual features made possible by microprocessors. I watched an Otis serviceman put a special card into the elevator wall. The card communicates with a microprocessor that directs the car to stop on a floor open only to people with the card.

Elevators are changing in other ways, too. To save space in very tall buildings, elevator engineers have figured out how to make one car do the work of two. They call them "Double Deckers" because one car is mounted on top of the other and they move together, like a double decker bus. If you want to go to an even-numbered floor, you take the Double Decker on one floor, but if you want to go to an odd-numbered floor, you take an escalator to the next level and catch the elevator there. The 110-story Sears Tower in Chicago, the highest building in the world (1454 feet), has over 100 Westinghouse elevators, 18 of which are Double Deckers. It is the headquarters of Sears, Roebuck and Company.

The Sears Tower and the World Trade Center

Technician working on Otis's Elevonic panel.

man is used because the voice is easier to reproduce) by computer and store the information in a special microprocessor called a *speech synthesizer.* A speech synthesizer combines sounds to reproduce speech. Then the synthesizer is connected to another microprocessor. When a signal is sent to this microprocessor that a passenger is aboard the elevator, the microprocessor picks the right message and tells the synthesizer to reproduce it.

The first elevators to use microprocessors appeared in the mid-1970s. They do not talk or display information, but they work more efficiently than any elevators before them. I visited the new 26-story

it. As you are riding down, you read the news. There is a stock market report on the display panel, too, for anyone who wants to read it. At the lobby level, the voice says: "First floor lobby level, getting off. Enjoy your weekend."

There is a disturbance in the first floor lobby one day as you are riding down. The elevator stops at the nearest floor and the voice says: "The elevator is needed for an emergency. Please exit when doors open."

An elevator like this isn't a dream. Both Otis and Westinghouse have talking elevators with display panels that will be installed in buildings as early as 1983. Otis's model has a standard vocabulary of 111 words, but special messages can be added to the vocabulary. Tiny computers called *microprocessors* are the secret of the talking elevator. After the development of solid state devices and printed circuits, electronic engineers went a step further and developed the *integrated circuit*. An integrated circuit is a very small chip of a material called silicon that is divided into regions. Each region does a different kind of electrical job.

The integrated circuit is the heart of the microprocessor. These tiny computers can do most of the work of large computers and do it just as fast and accurately. Microprocessors are inexpensive, too, so they have found a wide variety of applications, including elevators.

To make an elevator talk, engineers first analyze the spoken message of a male announcer (a

5

Elevators Today and Tomorrow

"GOOD MORNING. First floor lobby level, going up."

The male voice coming from the elevator sounds like that of an operator, but there is no operator in the car. You get on, push a button for your floor, and ride up. During the ride, you look at a blue-green display panel that flashes the news. When you reach your floor, the voice announces: "Floor ten, getting off." As you leave, the voice says: "Have a good day."

Later that day, when you get on the elevator to go down, the voice says: "Good afternoon. It's raining outside and the temperature is 52 degrees." You aren't wearing your raincoat, so you go back to get

This elevator is talking to a passenger.

ment for the vacuum tube. In the solid state device, electric signals flow through a solid material called a semiconductor, instead of through a tube. To wire the new devices, engineers made another breakthrough. Rather than lead a tangle of wires into them, they printed the wires chemically on a piece of plastic or other material. The printed wires are called printed circuits.

Solid state devices and printed circuits are smaller, cheaper, and more reliable than tubes and wires, so before long they were being used in many applications, including elevators. The 110-story World Trade Center, in New York City, the world's second highest building, was completed in 1969, just when solid state technology was becoming widely available. Computers based on solid state devices and printed circuits direct the movements of the WTC's 208 Otis elevators. To keep all these elevators in good running condition, Otis has 20 mechanics working out of an office right in the Center. Today all very large buildings have elevator mechanics on the premises to maintain the machines.

The period when the elevator was acquiring "brains" was a period of big changes in the elevator industry, too. Elisha Otis's last surviving son, Charles, died in 1927 at the age of 92. By this time, Otis had become the largest elevator manufacturing firm not only in the United States but in the world. It's still No. 1 today.

The World Trade Center

A modern controller high atop Detroit's Plaza Hotel.

chines what to do. Meanwhile, the master controller coordinates the movements of all the cars in a bank. Another machine, the *selector*, tells the controllers where the car is in the shaft.

Every large new building erected after 1950 put in completely automatic elevators and most older buildings began converting to them, too. These conversions were "brain transplants," as one elevator expert describes it. The biggest brain transplant took place in Rockfeller Center.

Could elevators get any brainier than they were in the early 1950s? The answer was yes.

During the 1950s and 1960s, electronics engineers perfected the solid state device as a replace-

will know when to start, they stop the car on the right floors, level it, and open and close the doors. The car will not start unless the doors are closed. If someone enters the opening as the doors are closing, they immediately slide back.

In the first automatic system, the cars took off one after another. But after completely automatic elevators were in service a short time, engineers at Otis and Westinghouse developed better systems for scheduling the cars in a building. Instead of taking off one after the other, automatic elevators now respond to the changing needs of individual buildings. For passengers, this means they have to wait less time for an elevator after they push a button in the lobby. The new system also saves energy because the cars do not keep running back and forth on a fixed schedule all day long.

The electronic "brains" are located in the machine room at the top of the elevator shaft. If you could look inside the machine room of an automatic elevator system, you would see a number of tall electronic control panels called *controllers*. There is one for each car, plus a *master controller* for a whole bank of cars (normally there are six to eight cars in a bank).

The controllers are really computers that control the movements of the cars. When a passenger pushes a button in the lobby or in the car itself, messages flash to the master controller, which in turn communicates with the car controllers. The car controllers tell the individual gearless traction ma-

the Center, Westinghouse uses an automatic system much like Signal Control.

Some of the automatic elevators installed during this period were elegant as well as efficient. The Chrysler Building in midtown New York City has elevator doors and interiors of fine wood and metal in abstract designs. The Waldorf-Astoria Hotel in the same area has figures of goddesses on its elevator doors. The Swiss Building near Rockefeller Center has elevator doors of silver, bronze, brass and nickel in an intricate design. All these handsome elevators are in the artistic style called Art Deco, which was popular in the 1920s and 1930s.

The automatic elevators of the 1920s and 1930s were very efficient for their time but they still needed people to do jobs like closing doors and scheduling cars. It took electronics to make the elevator with "brains" possible. Beginning in the 1920s, engineers working for a number of different organizations developed small, speedy devices to pass electrical signals. The first of these devices were vacuum tubes—glass tubes from which most of the air had been removed. Elevator engineers adapted them for automatic elevators.

By the late 1940s, both Otis and Westinghouse came out with completely automatic elevator systems based on electronics. These systems do everything the operator and starter did and a few things they couldn't do. They weigh the car load so the car

The RCA Building, tallest of the skyscrapers in Rockefeller Center, has had all its elevators converted to fully automatic systems by Westinghouse Elevator Company.

move 1200 feet per minute and take passengers from the first floor lobby to the 80th floor in less than a minute (two tower elevators take them the rest of the way). Operators could never have controlled these fast-moving elevators, but Signal Control handles it easily.

During the early days of elevator automation, a new elevator company with an old name was formed. It is Westinghouse Elevator Company, a division of Westinghouse Electric Corporation. Westinghouse had been making parts for elevators for years, and in 1926 it bought out some small elevator companies and began making its own machines. Westinghouse has made important contributions to the automatic elevator.

Westinghouse's biggest installation is the 388 elevators in the 19 skyscrapers in New York City's Rockefeller Center. The elevators in the RCA Building in the Center travel at 1454 feet per minute. When Rockefeller Center was completed in 1933, these elevators were the fastest ones in the world and the record stood for many years afterwards. To run the RCA elevators and the others throughout

An elegant elevator door in the Waldorf-Astoria Hotel.

45

The 102-story Empire State Building was the tallest building in the world for many years.

nounced floors. The operator's trickiest job was leveling—bringing the car level with the floor. Sometimes the car had to be jockeyed back and forth to level the car.

Since cars often weren't level, the operator usually called out "Watch your step!" when people got off.

Elevator operators and starters did a good job for many years but as elevators became faster and buildings became taller and busier, it was impossible for them to keep up with the traffic. Elevators needed automatic controls that would work faster than people.

Some automatic controls appeared early. By the 1920s, for instance, some small buildings with light traffic had elevator cars that could answer one call at a time and take a passenger to a floor. The passenger had to open the car door, but the elevator did everything else. Then, in 1924, Otis Elevator Company developed an automatic system called *Signal Control* for busy commercial buildings. The elevator operator pushed the floor buttons, closed the door, and started the car. Then the elevator took over. It controlled speed, stopped at the right floors, and leveled itself, all automatically.

Signal Control came along just in time for the new generation of tall skyscrapers. In 1931, the Empire State Building, the tallest building in the world for many years, was completed. It has 102 stories. The 59 gearless traction machines Otis installed

4

Elevators with Brains

BY THE TIME THE GEARLESS traction machine had been perfected, it must have seemed as if the elevator had gone as far as it could go. And in a sense it had. No better elevator for tall buildings has yet been invented. But modern elevators are automatic. They do all the work that used to be done by the elevator starter and operator. Today's elevators are elevators with "brains."

Elevator starters and operators were very busy in the early days of the elevator. The starter, who worked in the lobby of busy buildings, told the operators when to leave and where to bring the car at the end of a run. If it was a busy period, the starter tried to move the cars around to give the best service. The operator pressed buttons for floors, opened and closed doors, started and stopped the car, and an-are roped hydraulics.

The modern traction elevator is even safer than the old elevator because it has two different safety systems. If an elevator starts going too fast, a mechanism called a *governor* senses it and opens a safety switch that cuts off the power and activates the brake. The brake works like a car brake to stop the sheave. If the speed continues to increase, the governor pinches the safety cable, a special cable that runs from the governor to the car. This activates two powerful clamps beneath the car that wedge themselves between the guide rails, stopping the car. The second, or backup, system is really a modern version of Elisha Otis's safety device.

In 1920, the first elevator safety code was developed by the American Society of Mechanical Engineers (ASME). All elevator manufacturers in this country consult the code and build their elevators to its specifications. ASME completely revises its code every three years. Some cities with many elevators also have their own elevator safety codes. New York City, for instance, now has a regulation requiring elevators to return automatically to the first floor in the event of a fire. After that the elevators can only be operated by firemen using a special key.

As a result of the various elevator safety devices and the codes, the elevator is the safest form of modern transportation. There is only one serious accident for every 65 million miles traveled.

building. It performed so well that it became the standard elevator for all very tall buildings. Gearless machines last a long time. All of the gearless machines that have been put into service are still running, unless the building has been torn down. The Woolworth Building's original elevators are in good condition, although they have been converted to automatic operation.

Another traction-type elevator, the geared traction, was developed about the same time as the gearless traction design and was for buildings that range from 8 to 20 stories. It works much like the gearless traction, but the electric motor that drives it is connected to gears instead of to the drive sheave. The gears slow the motor's speed and make the sheave turn slowly. The geared traction machine moves only at a rate of 350 feet per minute, while the gearless goes up to 2000 feet per minute.

Most buildings lower than six stories are served by hydraulic plunger machines. The present-day hydraulic works on oil, not water, and uses electric pumps. It is slow, but it can lift heavy weights safely over short distances. The stage at Radio City Music Hall in New York City is really a hydraulic elevator or, rather, three hydraulic elevators. They have lifted more than 500 people plus stage equipment during some performances.

There are only a few roped hydraulics now left in service. The only new ones being manufactured are made solely for aircraft carriers. The elevators that raise and lower airplanes on these huge ships

bottom of the counterweight—thus forming a sort of endless loop.

When the electric motor is running, it turns the sheave, the cables move, and the counterweight slides down as the car goes up.

The gearless traction design proved to be safe, fast, and sturdy in the Beaver Building in New York City, the first building in which it was used. Otis received contracts to put the new machine in three tall New York skyscrapers including the Woolworth

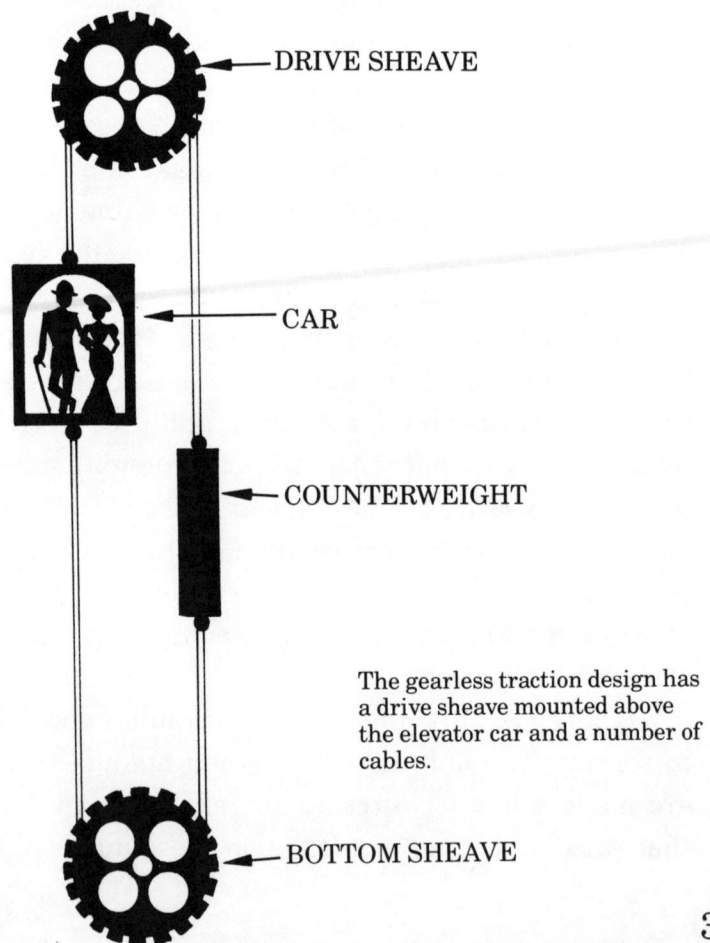

The gearless traction design has a drive sheave mounted above the elevator car and a number of cables.

The 51-story Woolworth Building still has the Otis gearless traction machinery installed in 1912.

the elevator shaft. Six to eight cables are attached at one end to the top of the elevator car and then wrapped around the drive sheave. The other end of the cables is attached to a counterweight. Another set of cables goes from the bottom of the car to the

remain the world leader in skyscrapers until very recently. Between 1906 and 1912, three buildings of between 40 and 51 stories arose in the city. The 51-story Woolworth Building has five times the number of stories as the first skyscraper built just 27 years before.

All these skyscrapers, of course, needed elevators. But not just any elevator would do. Roped hydraulics were not really safe for buildings over 30 stories. The standard hydraulic (the one using plungers) was slow and it was too expensive to dig a hole deep enough for the cylinder for a very tall building. That left the electric elevator. But the old-style electric elevator had problems, too. It was slow and the bigger the building, the bigger the drum needed in the basement to wind cable. Huge drums took up too much room and made winding cable difficult.

What was needed was an electric elevator designed specifically for skyscrapers. Engineers all over the world worked on the problem and in 1903 the Otis Company—a new firm created when Otis Brothers merged with 14 other firms—came up with the solution. It was the *gearless traction elevator.*

The gearless traction elevator has no winding drum, so any amount of cable can be used. The heart of the machine is a *drive sheave,* a large pulley with grooves cut into it, that is run by an electric motor. It is called "gearless" because it is powered directly by the motor instead of through gears. The sheave is mounted in a machine room at the top of

not rise very high because of the tremendous bulk of masonry needed on the lower floors to support many stories above. With metal frames, buildings can rise to 100 stories or more.

By 1891, Chicago had a 22-story metal frame building, the highest in the world. But New York took back the tall building title in 1898 with the 26-story St. Paul Building. After that, New York was to

Home Insurance Building in Chicago—the world's first skyscraper.

In 1889 an Otis roped hydraulic elevator was installed in the 1000-foot tall Eiffel Tower in Paris. The elevator ran up the curved part of the Tower's leg.

than the roped hydraulic.

Between 1883 and 1885, Chicago had put up the first real skyscraper, the ten-story Home Insurance Building. A skyscraper is a tall building with a metal frame. The masonry frame—the type of construction used with tall buildings up to 1883—can-

Otis Brothers & Co.

<u>STANDARD</u>
<u>HYDRAULIC</u>

Passenger and Freight
ELEVATORS.

Steam
Passenger and Freight
Elevators.

SPUR AND SCREW-GEARED

Factory Elevators.

HOISTING ENGINES
FOR
Blast Furnaces, Inclines,
Coal and Iron Mines.

HYDRAULIC DUMB WAITERS.

SEND FOR CIRCULARS.
OTIS BROTHERS & CO.,
36 & 38 Park Row, New York, U. S. A.

BALDWIN GAS ENGINE

MANUFACTURED BY

Otis Brothers & Co.

36 & 38 Park Row.

NEW YORK,
U. S. A.

Most Efficient and Steadily Running
Gas Engine ever built.

ADAPTED FOR

ELECTRIC LIGHTING,

<u>AND ALL PURPOSES</u>
<u>WHERE POWER IS REQUIRED.</u>

ALSO FOR RUNNING

Passenger and Freight

ELEVATORS.

An early advertisement for Otis Brothers and Company.

out their own roped hydraulic design in 1878.

Three roped hydraulic elevators from this era are still operating in a nine-story cooperative apartment building in New York City. Installed by Otis in 1883, they are probably the oldest elevators in the world. Many years ago, the open cab was covered with wood paneling, but the machinery that runs the elevators was never changed. I visited the building in 1981 and rode on the passenger elevator. The doorman operated the car by pulling on a rope that runs from the floor to the ceiling. The car moves rather slowly by today's standards but it is a surprisingly smooth ride.

The biggest step forward for the young elevator industry followed the development of the electric motor in 1860. A German inventor, Werner von Siemens, built the first electric elevator in 1880. Nine years later, Otis Brothers had another first—the first electric elevator in a commercial building, the Demerest Building in New York City. These first electrics weren't very impressive. They were slow—much slower than roped hydraulics—and they worked just like the steam elevator, except that they were driven by an electric motor instead of by a steam engine.

But Otis and other elevator companies quickly realized that electricity made many elevator improvements possible. In 1892, Harry Ward Leonard invented a method of controlling the power in electric elevators that gave passengers the smoothest ride they had yet experienced and brought the car to

The Lord and Taylor Department Store in New York City installed an Otis steam elevator in 1870. The operator pulled on a rope to run the car.

a gentle stop. The invention is still used today. Two years later, Otis Brothers introduced electric call buttons. Now you could just push a button to call the elevator instead of yelling or ringing a hand bell.

But the biggest advantage of electric elevators was that they could serve even higher buildings

cabs of open ironwork in intricate patterns and looked like giant birdcages. Later the birdcage was covered with fine wood paneling. Inside, there were mirrors on the walls and chandeliers hanging from the ceiling. A comfortable upholstered bench gave passengers a place to sit down. A trip on an early elevator may have been slow but it must have been a very pleasant experience.

Buildings were getting taller and taller, however, and a new type of elevator was needed to serve them.

In 1873, New York City had approved plans for two tall buildings, one nine stories and the other ten stories. When they were completed in 1880, they were the tallest buildings in the world. Without elevators, neither of them would have been designed. Elevators not only made it possible to get to the top stories without a lot of huffing and puffing, but they also made the top floors more desirable. From then on, top floors would rent for more than bottom floors.

The year before the plans for these two buildings were approved, Cyrus W. Baldwin of the Hale Elevator Company in Chicago invented an elevator that could rise higher and travel faster than the steam elevator. Called the *roped hydraulic*, it had ropes, pulleys, and a short horizontal plunger instead of the long vertical plunger of the water hydraulic. It was the most popular elevator in the country by 1880. Charles and Norton Otis brought

3

The Elevator and the Skyscraper

AFTER ELISHA GRAVES OTIS died in 1861, his sons Charles and Norton took over the Otis Steam Elevator Works and renamed it Otis Brothers and Company. The young brothers were good businessmen. By 1870, 17 years after Elisha had begun making elevators in the Yonkers bedstead factory, Otis Brothers had passed the million-dollar mark in total sales. There were thousands of Otis elevators in factories, department stores, offices, and even private residences. The first Otis elevators ran on steam but later the firm began making hydraulics, too.

The elevators of this period were probably the most beautiful ones ever made. The earlier ones had

Charles and Norton Otis in later life.

CHARLES OTIS

NORTON OTIS

ratus is attached below a platform. When a steam pump forces water into the bottom of the tube, the plunger and the platform are pushed up. When water flows out, the plunger and platform go down by means of gravity. The grease rack in your local gas station is a simple form of hydraulic hoist.

The hydraulic hoist is safer than the standard steam hoist because it doesn't use ropes. But it does have one drawback: to use it, you have to dig a hole below ground as deep as the building is tall. Otis's steam hoist, with its safety feature, did not have this drawback, and it changed the architecture of our cities.

An early hydraulic hoist being used in a factory. The piston holding the platform goes into a hole in the ground when the elevator comes down.

undoubtedly in use at one of the factories where Elisha Otis was working during the early 1850s. When he studied it, his inventive mind quickly came up with an idea for making it safe for people to ride on.

In most ways the invention Otis exhibited at the Crystal Palace was a standard steam hoist. It had ropes, a drum on which the rope was wound, pulleys, guide rails along the sides, and a counterweight. When a steam engine supplied power, the rope was wound up on the drum, pulling the platform upward. The heavy counterweight made the lifting job easier by dropping as the platform rose. The guide rails kept the platform from moving sideways.

All steam hoists worked much the same way, but Otis's hoist had a special safety feature. Along the guide rails were ratchet bars, bars with toothlike projections. A pair of devices attached to springs was mounted on the metal structure above the platform. When the rope broke or was cut, the release of tension activated the spring devices, which flashed sideways and caught the ratchet bars. The safety mechanism really worked like a kind of automatic brake. The operator of the hoist didn't have to do anything to make it work.

During this same period a completely new kind of hoist, the *hydraulic hoist,* also came on the scene. The word hydraulic comes from the Greek word for water, and water is what makes it run. A rod called a plunger is placed inside a tube and the whole appa-

people or animals walking inside it. The motion of the wheel pulls up a basket. Both materials and people came up by basket at Mont St. Michel.

It must have been a bumpy ride for passengers on these early lifting devices and not very safe, either. If the rope broke, down came basket, net, and everything in them.

During the 18th century, another simple kind of elevator appeared in France. Called the "flying chair," it went up and down by means of a rope passed over a pulley and a counterweight. The first guide rails—two vertical rails—kept the chair from bumping around. Several European rulers installed flying chairs in their palaces, but the device became unpopular after a member of the French royal family had a serious accident in one. There were no safety devices on flying chairs.

Up until the 18th century, almost all lifting devices were run by human or animal muscle power. Then, in the late 18th century, a new source of power became available: steam. The steam engine is built around the principle that steam takes up more room than water. A steam engine burns fuel to heat water and change it into steam, then uses the steam to push or spin the parts of machines. An improved steam engine invented by James Watt, an Englishman, made steam practical for many different kinds of machines, including hoists and elevators.

By 1850 there was at least one steam hoist in operation in a New York City factory. It ran only from the first to the second floor. A similar hoist was

of the elevator? Possibly. The Romans, who were in control of Damascus at the time, had many lifting devices, some with baskets. Paul might have used one to make his escape.

Records do tell us that in the sixth century, A.D., monks at the Convent of St. Catherine on Mt. Sinai in the Holy Land used a net and a windlass to reach their establishment. So did monks at some monasteries in Greece that were built on high, pointed rocks. The oldest known "elevator" still in existence is at the Abbey of Mont St. Michel on the French coast. Installed in 1203, it has a windlass attached to a treadmill—a large wheel turned by

The elevator in the convent of St. Catherine had a windlass (right, top) turned by manpower and a pulley (left, top).

An old-fashioned well. To raise the bucket, you turn the crank on the windlass arm.

But ancient lifting devices were used for people on occasion. St. Paul in the New Testament of the Bible may have used an "elevator" to descend from the walls of Damascus. The Bible passage reads: "Then the disciples took him by night and let him down by the wall in a basket." Was this an early use

large ships during the seige of the Greek city of Syracuse about 212 B.C.

As far as we know, the early lifting machines usually lifted materials such as water, stone, or anchors. They rarely carried people. People walked up stairs and since it is hard work to walk up many flights, buildings had few stories.

The ancient Chinese may have invented the *windlass,* a device with a wheel or drum, a crank, and a rope. A load is attached to the rope, which is wound up on the drum with the crank. The bucket on the old-fashioned well is raised with a windlass.

TWO WHEELS MAKE A WINDLASS

Basically, the windlass is two wheels, one big and one small. The smaller one is called the *axle.* They are connected in such a way that as you turn one, the other turns too. By turning the big wheel, you can bring up a load attached to the small wheel with less effort.

To see this in action, look at a pencil sharpener. The axle is inside the sharpener, and the big wheel is the crank. Take off the pencil sharpener cover, being careful not to spill the shavings. Then tie a weight such as a small rock to a string and attach the end of the string to the axle. Turn the crank. You have made a windlass.

All these devices allow the user to lift objects with less effort than would be needed if there were no device. The pulley also allows the user to change the direction of the effort. When these devices are used together, they work even better. The ancient Greeks and Romans combined pulleys and windlasses, as well as other devices, to lift heavy loads high up in the air. Archimedes, the Greek mathematician, designed lifting machines that raised

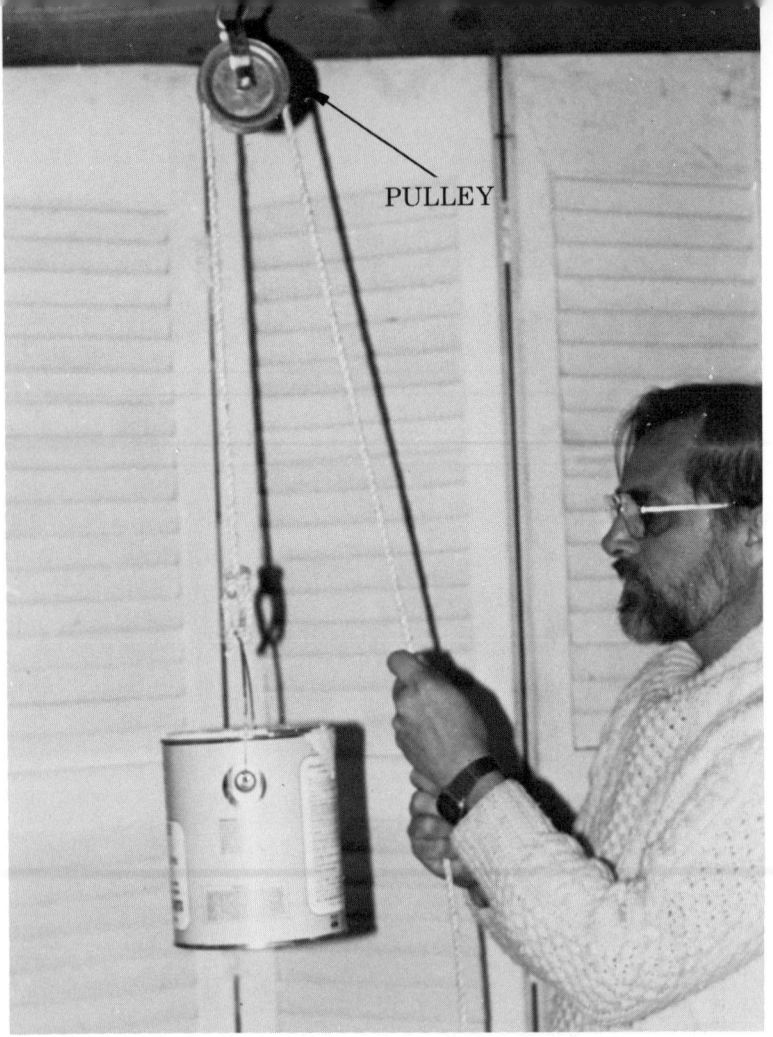

HOW A PULLEY WORKS

Ask your mother or father for a clothesline pulley to try this experiment.

Attach the pulley to a hook overhead. Then run a rope over the pulley and tie one end to a weight. Pull down on the other end. A simple pulley is useful because it is easier to pull *down* a rope than to pull *up* a load.

19

LIFTING—THE EGYPTIAN WAY

This diagram shows how the shaduf is operated. A long stick is placed in a notch at the top of an upright stick. At one end of the long stick is a string attached to a bucket or small pail. At the other end is a counterweight. When the bucket is filled with water and the hold on the string is released, the counterweight will help to lift the bucket.

The Egyptians' neighbors, the Assyrians, used wooden pulley wheels. The *pulley* is a wheel with a rim in which a rope can run. In the simplest kind of pulley, the lifter pulls down on one end of the rope to raise a load attached to the other end.

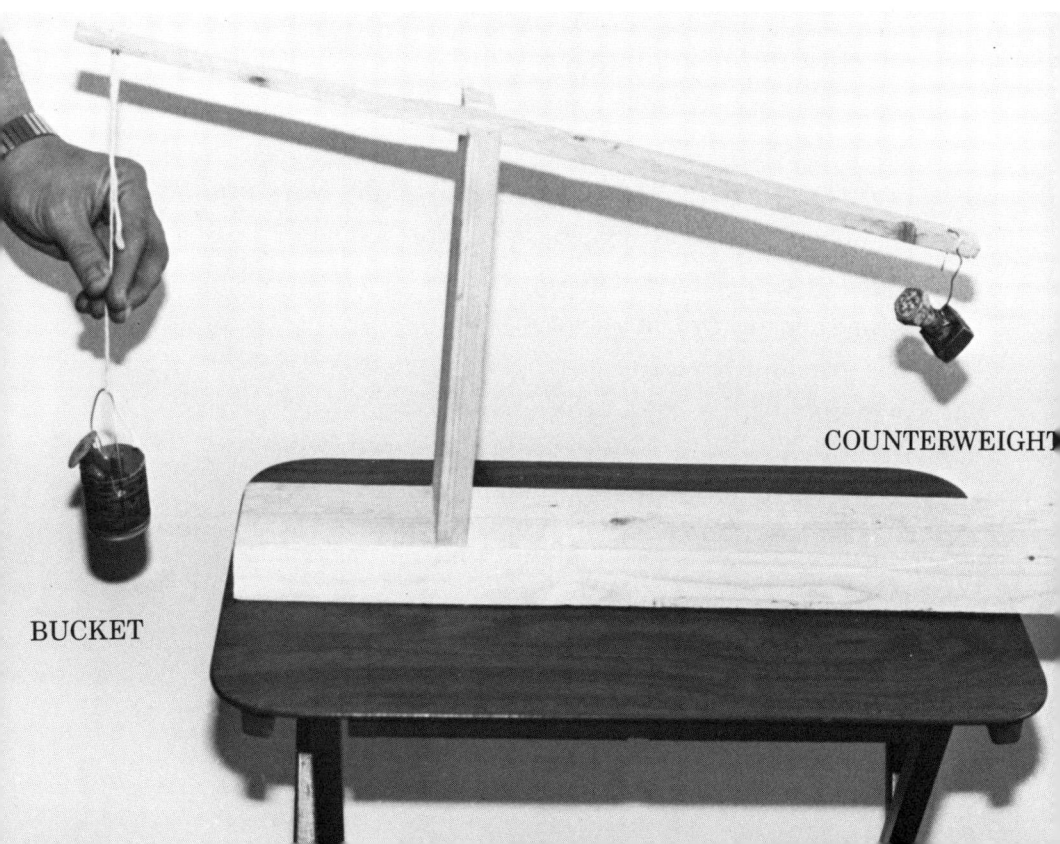

COUNTERWEIGHT

BUCKET

2

Making Lifting Easier

LONG BEFORE there were hoists or elevators, people raised heavy objects by means of devices that made lifting easier. Some of these devices would later turn up in the elevator.

Ancient Egyptian tomb paintings illustrate the principle of the *counterweight*. A heavy object was tied to one end of a pole, pulling it down, while the other end raised a container of water. This device was called a *shaduf.*

This detail of a painting from a tomb in Thebes, Egypt, shows a man watering plants with a shaduf. The counterweight—probably a lump of clay—is on the end of the pole.

An Otis elevator with its own steam engine (lower right) came out in 1861.

In 1911, on the centennial of his father's birth, Charles Otis reminisced about the inventor's method of designing machines:

> He could invent, design and construct a perfect working machine or improve anything to which he gave his mind, without recourse to any of the modern drafting room methods. He needed no assistance, asked no advice, consulted with no one and never made much use of pen or pencil in designing the various machines . . . of which he was the inventor. In short, he exemplified the reverse of a remark attributed to Edison, who defined American genius as "Two percent inspiration and ninety-eight percent perspiration."

for diphtheria and the disease killed many people. Elisha Otis caught the disease and died on April 8, 1861. That same month, the bombardment of Fort Sumter began the Civil War. At the time of his death, Otis had become a modest success, although not a rich man. His plant employed only eight to ten people and was worth perhaps $5000.

The Otis Steam Elevator Works in 1860. The gun and carriage shown were part of the payment made for the firm's first two elevators.

Otis installed the first passenger elevators in the E.V. Haughwout & Co. Building in New York City in 1857.

referred to as elevators. A sign on the front of the Otis factory in 1860 reads:

OTIS STEAM ELEVATOR WORKS

In the spring of 1861, an epidemic of a contagious disease called diphtheria swept the United States. There was no vaccine available at that time

Luckily, another order came in almost at once from a picture frame factory near the Newhouse factory. Business, however, was slow at first. The Crystal Palace Exhibition gave the new enterprise a boost. In 1855, 15 hoists were sold; in 1856, 27.

All of these early hoists were used not for passengers but for freight. There were no safety hoists in department stores, in office buildings, in hotels, or in apartment buildings. One reason for this was that before the late 19th century, buildings were not very high, making it fairly easy to climb to the top floor. A five-story building was considered tall, a six-story building very tall. The tallest building in New York City in the 1850s was Trinity Church, with its 286-foot steeple.

Still, walking up even five or six flights was something many people preferred to avoid. In 1857, Otis installed the first passenger hoist in a building. Called the elevator, it went into the five-story E. V. Haughwout & Company building at Broadway and Broome Street in New York City. The firm sold china and glassware. The steam-powered elevator traveled 40 feet per minute and could carry 1000 pounds. Unlike the hoists, the elevator had an enclosed platform, so that a number of people could ride on it without any danger of falling off. The enclosed platform was called the *car* or *cab*.

After this time more and more hoists were used for people, and both hoists and elevators began to be

enough to throw a safety lever. The machine plummeted to the basement of the building and two men were killed.

Otis's invention, Newhouse remembered, required no action on the part of the operator. Newhouse contacted Otis. Could he make two of his safety hoists for the Newhouse factory?

Otis quickly decided to pin his future hopes not on gold, but on the safety hoist. He opened a hoist manufacturing business in part of the bankrupt Yonkers bed factory, with Newhouse as his first customer. Newhouse paid for the hoists partly with cash and partly with a gun and carriage, which were worth $58.60. Charles R. Otis, Elisha Otis's older son, was working with his father by this time and he later remembered that the new business started with a small three-horsepower engine, a boiler, a couple of lathes, a drill press, a forge, and two or three vises. Otis had to struggle to pay for all the new equipment.

Elisha Otis's shop in Yonkers, 1853

Elisha Graves Otis

he invented the safety hoist. It was used to move beds and other materials from one floor of the two-story factory to another. But hardly had the new factory opened when it went bankrupt. Otis was out of a job again. At this point he was so discouraged that he considered joining the Gold Rush. Gold had been discovered in California in 1849 and many Easterners were going west in hopes of making their fortunes. A fatal accident at a furniture factory in New York City changed Otis's mind about the trip west.

The factory was owned by Benjamin Newhouse. It had a hoist equipped with a safety device but the device was not automatic, like Otis's invention. When the rope on the Newhouse hoist broke one day in 1852, the operator was not able to act quickly

and made carriages. None of the work was very profitable.

It wasn't until the 1840s that Elisha Otis had a chance to show where his real talents lay—in the design of machinery. He had moved to Albany, New York, where he took a job as a mechanic with the Tingley Company. It made four-poster wooden beds, the parts of which were connected with wooden rails. A trained woodworker could turn out about 50 rails a day on a small machine. After watching this operation for a while, Otis designed a machine in his head that could do the job better. Otis Tingley and his partner, Josia Maize, offered him $500 if he could produce the machine.

Although he had no plans on paper, Otis set to work and soon finished his machine. Operating it, an untrained laborer could turn out 200 rails a day. Otis got his $500.

In spite of the success of this invention and several others Otis made for the Tingley Company, it went out of business in a few years. Otis started his own little machinery business but it soon failed, too. Josia Maize, meanwhile, had opened a furniture factory in Bergen, New Jersey, and he gave Otis a job as a mechanic. In 1852, Maize went into partnership with Benjamin Newhouse, who owned a tract of land in Yonkers, New York. The two partners built a factory there to manufacture beds.

Elisha Otis was sent to Yonkers to install the machinery and it was there, sometime in 1852, that

and cut through the rope. There was a gasp from the crowd and a woman screamed. The platform jerked a little, then remained stationary.

The bearded man aboard the platform took off his top hat and bowed. "All safe, ladies and gentlemen, all safe," he called out.

Elisha Graves Otis had just concluded the first public demonstration of his new invention, *the safety hoist*. He was to perform the same demonstration again and again during the exhibition, always with the same result. After the rope holding the machine had been cut, the platform remained fastened securely to the guide rails—the two vertical rails that prevented sideways motion. When a new rope was put on the machine, it descended to the floor and landed without a barrel or box out of place. The *New York Tribune* newspaper called Otis's demonstration "daring."

Actually, the demonstration wasn't really daring. Otis's machine was perfectly stable even without a rope.

For Elisha Otis, the safety hoist was the beginning of a business that would make his name known all over the world. For most of his life, however, he was anything but successful. He was born on a Vermont farm in 1811, the youngest of six children. Young Elisha never liked farming and after his marriage in 1834, he tried a number of different careers. He worked as a builder, drove a team of horses, operated several different kinds of mills,

1

A Safe Elevator

THE CRYSTAL PALACE EXHIBITION was one of the biggest events in New York City during 1853 and 1854. It was a kind of indoor fair and it featured industry from many nations. Several new inventions were introduced at the exhibition. One day in 1854, a demonstration of one of these inventions was held in a prominent place in the huge exhibition hall. People stopped to watch as a bearded man in a top hat climbed onto a platform full of boxes and barrels. The platform began to rise, pulled by a rope.

It had gone up about 40 feet when another man, who was on a scaffold below the roof, leaned over

"All safe, ladies and gentlemen, all safe," called out Elisha Graves Otis as he demonstrated his safety elevator.

CONTENTS

Chapter 1   A SAFE ELEVATOR   7

Chapter 2   MAKING LIFTING EASIER   17

Chapter 3   THE ELEVATOR AND THE SKYSCRAPER   29

Chapter 4   ELEVATORS WITH BRAINS   42

Chapter 5   ELEVATORS TODAY AND TOMORROW   53

                 INDEX   61

Library of Congress Cataloging in Publication Data

Ford, Barbara.
   The elevator.

   (Inventions that changed our lives)
   Includes index.
   Summary: Discusses the basic principles of the elevator, the relationship between the skyscraper and the elevator, how heavy weights were lifted in ancient times, and the computerized elevators with "brains".
   1. Elevators—Juvenile literature. [1. Elevators]
I. Title. II. Series.
TJ1370.F668   621.8'77   82-70440
ISBN 0-8027-6450-9   AACR2
ISBN 0-8027-6451-7 (lib. bdg.)

Copyright © 1982 by BARBARA FORD

All rights reserved. No part of this book may be reproduced or transmitted in any form or by any means, electric or mechanical, including photocopying, recording, or by any information storage and retrieval system, without permission in writing from the Publisher.

First published in the United States of America in 1982 by the Walker Publishing Company, Inc.

Published simultaneously in Canada by John Wiley & Sons Canada, Limited, Rexdale, Ontario.

Trade ISBN: 0-8027-6450-9
Reinf. ISBN: 0-8027-6451-7

Library of Congress Catalog Card Number: 82-70440

Book designed by Lena Fong Hor

Printed in the United States of America

10 9 8 7 6 5 4 3 2 1

THE ELEVATOR

INVENTIONS THAT CHANGED OUR LIVES

by Barbara Ford

WALKER AND COMPANY New York

THE ELEVATOR

State of Vermont
Department of Library
Midstate Regional Library
RFD #4
Montpelier, Vt. 05602

WITHDRAWN